CONTENTS

Targeting Homework
Year 5 New Edition

Copyright © 2024 Blake Education
Reprint 2024

ISBN: 978 1 92572 647 3

Published by Pascal Press
PO Box 250
Glebe NSW 2037
www.pascalpress.com.au
contact@pascalpress.com.au

Author: Frances Mackay
Publisher: Lynn Dickinson
Editors: Marie Theodore & Ruth Schultz
Cover and Text Designer: Leanne Nobilio
Typesetters: Ruth Schultz
Proofreader: Tim Learner
Images & Illustrations: Dreamstime (unless otherwise indicated)
Printed by Wai Man Book Binding (China) Ltd

Acknowledgements
p.19: The Sea © James Reeves from COMPLETE POEMS FOR
CHILDREN
(Faber Finds)

Thank you to the publishers, authors and illustrators
who generously granted permission for their work
to be reproduced in this book.

Introduction

Targeting Homework aims to build and reinforce English and Maths skills. This book supports the ACARA Australian Curriculum for Year 5 and helps children to revise and consolidate what has been taught in the classroom. ACARA codes are shown on each unit and a chart explaining their content descriptions is on pages v and vi. The inside back cover (Maths) and front cover (English) show the topics in each unit.

The structure of this book

This book has 32 carefully graded double-page units on English and Maths. The English units are divided into three sections:

★ Grammar and Punctuation

★ Spelling and Phonic Knowledge

★ Reading and Comprehension — includes a wide variety of literary and cross-curriculum texts.

This also includes a Reading Review segment for children to record and rate their home reading books.

The Maths units are divided between:

★ Number and Algebra

★ Measurement and Space

★ Statistics and Probability

★ Problem Solving.

My Book Review

Title _____

Author _____

Rating ☆☆☆☆☆

Comment _____
_____

Assessment

Term Reviews follow Units 1–8, 9–16, 17–24 and 25–32 to test work covered during the term, and allow parents and carers to monitor their child's progress. Children are encouraged to mark each unit as it is completed and to colour in the traffic lights at the end of each segment. These results are then transferred to the Marking Grid. Parents and carers can see at a glance if their child is excelling or struggling!

● **Green** = Excellent — 2 or fewer questions incorrect

● **Orange** = Passing — 50% or more questions answered correctly

● **Red** = Struggling — fewer than 50% correct and needs help

SCORE **/18** (0-6) (8-14) (16-18) *Score 2 points for each correct answer!*

How to Use This Book

The activities in this book are specifically designed to be used at home with minimal resources and support. Helpful explanations of key concepts and skills are provided throughout the book to help understand the tasks. Useful examples of how to do the activities are provided.

Regular practice of key concepts and skills will support the work your child does in school and will enable you to monitor their progress throughout the year. It is recommended that children complete 8 units per school term (one a week) and then the Term Review. Every unit has a Traffic Light scoreboard at the end of each section.

Score 2 points for each correct answer!

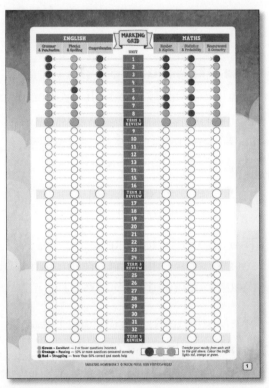

NOTE: The Maths Problem Solving questions do not appear on the Marking Grid as they often have multiple or subjective answers that cannot be easily scored.

You or your child should mark each completed unit and then colour the traffic light that corresponds to the number of correct questions. This process will enable you to see at a glance how your child is progressing and to identify weak spots. The results should be recorded at the end of each term on the Marking Grid on page 1. The Term Review results are important for tracking progress and identifying any improvements in performance. If you find that certain questions are repeatedly causing difficulties and errors, then there is a good reason to discuss this with your child's teacher and arrange for extra instruction in that problem area.

Home Reading Journal

Each English unit provides space for your child to log, review and rate a book they have read during the week. These details can then be transferred to the handy Reading Journal Summary on page 146, which can be photocopied and shared with their teacher or kept as a record.

Answers

The answer section on pages 147–162 can be removed, stapled together and kept somewhere safe. Use it to check answers when your child has completed each unit. Encourage your child to colour in the Traffic Light boxes when the answers have been calculated.

TARGETING HOMEWORK 5 © PASCAL PRESS ISBN 9781925726473

Australian Curriculum Correlations: Year 5 English

CODE	CODE DESCRIPTION	Grammar & Punctuation UNITS	Phonic Knowledge & Spelling UNITS	Reading Comprehension UNITS
LANGUAGE				
AC9E5LA02	Understand how to move beyond making bare assertions by taking account of differing ideas or opinions and authoritative sources	24		
AC9E5LA03	Describe how spoken, written and multimodal texts use language features and are typically organised into characteristic stages and phases, depending on purposes in texts	11, 15, 16		3, 26
AC9E5LA04	Understand how texts can be made cohesive by using the starting point of a sentence or paragraph to give prominence to the message and to guide the reader through the text	30		
AC9E5LA05	Understand that the structure of a complex sentence includes a main clause and at least one dependent clause, and understand how writers can use this structure for effect	6, 7, 17, 18, 20		
AC9E5LA06	Understand how noun groups can be expanded in a variety of ways to provide a fuller description of a person, place, thing or idea	1, 2, 3, 4, 5, 10, 11, 21, 22		
AC9E5LA08	Understand how vocabulary is used to express greater precision of meaning, including through the use of specialist and technical terms, and explore the history of words	9, 12, 13, 14, 19, 23, 25		
AC9E5LA09	Use commas to indicate prepositional phrases, and apostrophes where there is multiple possession	8, 27, 28		
LITERATURE				
AC9E5LE02	Present an opinion on a literary text using specific terms about literary devices, text structures and language features, and reflect on the viewpoints of others	31		7, 22
AC9E5LE05	Create and edit literary texts, experimenting with figurative language, storylines, characters and settings from texts students have experienced	32		
LITERACY				
AC9E5LY03	Explain characteristic features used in imaginative, informative and persuasive texts to meet the purpose of the text			3
AC9E5LY04	Navigate and read texts for specific purposes, monitoring meaning using strategies such as skimming, scanning and confirming	27		ALL UNITS
AC9E5LY05	Use comprehension strategies such as visualising, predicting, connecting, summarising, monitoring and questioning to build literal and inferred meaning to evaluate information and ideas			ALL UNITS
AC9E5LY06	Plan, create, edit and publish written and multimodal texts whose purposes may be imaginative, informative and persuasive, developing ideas using visual features, text structure appropriate to the topic and purpose, text connectives, expanded noun groups, specialist and technical vocabulary, and punctuation including dialogue punctuation	5, 29		5, 10
AC9E5LY08	Use phonic, morphemic and vocabulary knowledge to read and spell words that share common letter patterns but have different pronunciations		24, 29	
AC9E5LY09	Build and spell new words from knowledge of known words, base words, prefixes and suffixes, word origins, letter patterns and spelling generalisations		ALL UNITS	ALL UNITS
AC9E5LY10	Explore less common plurals, and understand how a suffix changes the meaning or grammatical form of a word	26	1, 2, 3, 5, 10–32	
CROSS CURRICULAR COMPREHENSION TEXTS				
HEALTH & PHYSICAL EDUCATION				
AC9HP6P10	Analyse how behaviours influence the health, safety, relationships and wellbeing of individuals and communities			27
SCIENCE				
AC9S5H02	Investigate how scientific knowledge is used by individuals and communities to identify problems, consider responses and make decisions			8, 11, 25
AC9S5U01	Examine how particular structural features and behaviours of living things enable their survival in specific habitats			1
AC9S5U03	Identify sources of light, recognise that light travels in a straight path and describe how shadows are formed and light can be reflected and refracted			8, 30
AC9S5U04	Explain observable properties of solids, liquids and gases by modelling the motion and arrangement of particles			13
HISTORY				
AC9HS5K01	The economic, political and social causes of the establishment of British colonies in Australia after 1800			4
AC9HS5K02	The impact of the development of British colonies in Australia on the lives of First Nations Australians, the colonists and convicts, and on the natural environment			18
AC9HS5K03	The role of a significant individual or group, including First Nations Australians and those who migrated to Australia, in the development of events in an Australian colony			31
GEOGRAPHY				
AC9HS5K04	The influence of people, including First Nations Australians and people in other countries, on the characteristics of a place			16, 20
AC9HS5K05	The management of Australian environments, including managing severe weather events such as bushfires, floods, droughts or cyclones, and their consequences			3, 14, 16
CIVICS & CITIZENSHIP				
AC9HS5K06	The key values and features of Australia's democracy, including elections, and the roles and responsibilities of elected representatives			9
AC9HS5K07	How citizens (members of communities) with shared beliefs and values work together to achieve a civic goal			32
ECONOMICS & BUSINESS				
AC9HS5K08	Types of resources, including natural, human and capital, and how they satisfy needs and wants			12, 23

Australian CURRICULUM

Australian Curriculum Correlations: Year 5 Maths

ACARA CODE	CONTENT DESCRIPTION	Number & Algebra UNITS	Statistics & Probability UNITS	Measurement & Space UNITS	Problem Solving UNITS
NUMBER					
AC9M5N01	Interpret, compare and order numbers with more than 2 decimal places, including numbers greater than one, using place value understanding; represent these on a number line	6, 7, 10, 16, 24, 25			
AC9M5N02	Express natural numbers as products of their factors, recognise multiples and determine if one number is divisible by another	1, 26, 32			1, 15
AC9M5N03	Compare and order fractions with the same and related denominators including mixed numerals, applying knowledge of factors and multiples; represent these fractions on a number line	5, 27			
AC9M5N04	Recognise that 100% represents the complete whole and use percentages to describe, represent and compare relative size; connect familiar percentages to their decimal and fraction equivalents	11, 19			
AC9M5N05	Solve problems involving addition and subtraction of fractions with the same or related denominators, using different strategies	8, 12, 21			12
AC9M5N06	Solve problems involving multiplication of larger numbers by one- or two-digit numbers, choosing efficient calculation strategies and using digital tools where appropriate; check the reasonableness of answers	3, 4, 9, 20, 30			30
AC9M5N07	Solve problems involving division, choosing efficient strategies and using digital tools where appropriate; interpret any remainder according to the context and express results as a whole number, decimal or fraction	14, 15, 17, 18, 23			21, 23
AC9M5N08	Check and explain the reasonableness of solutions to problems including financial contexts using estimation strategies appropriate to the context	2, 17, 29			
AC9M5N09	Use mathematical modelling to solve practical problems involving additive and multiplicative situations including financial contexts; formulate the problems, choosing operations and efficient calculation strategies, using digital tools where appropriate; interpret and communicate solutions in terms of the situation	2, 13, 31			3, 9, 10, 13, 18, 24, 26, 27, 30
AC9M5N10	Create and use algorithms involving a sequence of steps and decisions and digital tools to experiment with factors, multiples and divisibility; identify, interpret and describe emerging patterns	22, 23, 28			32
ALGEBRA					
AC9M5A01	Recognise and explain the connection between multiplication and division as inverse operations and use this to develop families of number facts	23, 29			
AC9M5A02	Find unknown values in numerical equations involving multiplication and division using the properties of numbers and operations	9, 14			
MEASUREMENT					
AC9M5M01	Choose appropriate metric units when measuring the length, mass and capacity of objects; use smaller units or a combination of units to obtain a more accurate measure			1, 4, 5, 6, 7, 15, 16, 23, 26, 32	6, 7, 26
AC9M5M02	Solve practical problems involving the perimeter and area of regular and irregular shapes using appropriate metric units			3, 9, 27	3, 4, 22, 29
AC9M5M03	Compare 12- and 24-hour time systems and solve practical problems involving the conversion between them			2, 17, 22, 24	2, 5, 17
AC9M5M04	Estimate, construct and measure angles in degrees, using appropriate tools including a protractor, and relate these measures to angle names			13, 14, 18, 25	14, 25
SPACE					
AC9M5SP01	Connect objects to their nets and build objects from their nets using spatial and geometric reasoning			10, 19, 30	8, 11, 16, 31
AC9M5SP02	Construct a grid coordinate system that uses coordinates to locate positions within a space; use coordinates and directional language to describe position and movement			11, 21, 31	
AC9M5SP03	Describe and perform translations, reflections and rotations of shapes, using dynamic geometric software where appropriate; recognise what changes and what remains the same, and identify any symmetries			8, 12, 20, 28, 29	19, 20, 28
STATISTICS					
AC9M5ST01	Acquire, validate and represent data for nominal and ordinal categorical and discrete numerical variables to address a question of interest or purpose using software including spreadsheets; discuss and report on data distributions in terms of highest frequency (mode) and shape, in the context of the data		3, 7, 11, 15, 17, 23, 27, 29		
AC9M5ST02	Interpret line graphs representing change over time; discuss the relationships that are represented and conclusions that can be made		31		
AC9M5ST03	Plan and conduct statistical investigations by posing questions or identifying a problem and collecting relevant data; choose appropriate displays and interpret the data; communicate findings within the context of the investigation		7, 11, 15, 17, 23, 29		
PROBABILITY					
AC9M5P01	List the possible outcomes of chance experiments involving equally likely outcomes and compare to those which are not equally likely		1, 9, 25		
AC9M5P02	Conduct repeated chance experiments including those with and without equally likely outcomes, observe and record the results; use frequency to compare outcomes and estimate their likelihoods		1, 3, 5, 13, 19, 21, 25		

TARGETING HOMEWORK 5 © PASCAL PRESS ISBN 9781925726473

MARKING GRID

ENGLISH

Grammar & Punctuation	Phonics & Spelling	Comprehension	UNIT	Number & Algebra	Statistics & Probability	Measurement & Space
◯	◯	◯	1	◯	◯	◯
◯	◯	◯	2	◯	◯	◯
◯	◯	◯	3	◯	◯	◯
◯	◯	◯	4	◯	◯	◯
◯	◯	◯	5	◯	◯	◯
◯	◯	◯	6	◯	◯	◯
◯	◯	◯	7	◯	◯	◯
◯	◯	◯	8	◯	◯	◯
◯	◯	◯	TERM 1 REVIEW	◯	◯	◯
◯	◯	◯	9	◯	◯	◯
◯	◯	◯	10	◯	◯	◯
◯	◯	◯	11	◯	◯	◯
◯	◯	◯	12	◯	◯	◯
◯	◯	◯	13	◯	◯	◯
◯	◯	◯	14	◯	◯	◯
◯	◯	◯	15	◯	◯	◯
◯	◯	◯	16	◯	◯	◯
◯	◯	◯	TERM 2 REVIEW	◯	◯	◯
◯	◯	◯	17	◯	◯	◯
◯	◯	◯	18	◯	◯	◯
◯	◯	◯	19	◯	◯	◯
◯	◯	◯	20	◯	◯	◯
◯	◯	◯	21	◯	◯	◯
◯	◯	◯	22	◯	◯	◯
◯	◯	◯	23	◯	◯	◯
◯	◯	◯	24	◯	◯	◯
◯	◯	◯	TERM 3 REVIEW	◯	◯	◯
◯	◯	◯	25	◯	◯	◯
◯	◯	◯	26	◯	◯	◯
◯	◯	◯	27	◯	◯	◯
◯	◯	◯	28	◯	◯	◯
◯	◯	◯	29	◯	◯	◯
◯	◯	◯	30	◯	◯	◯
◯	◯	◯	31	◯	◯	◯
◯	◯	◯	32	◯	◯	◯
◯	◯	◯	TERM 4 REVIEW	◯	◯	◯

MATHS

● **Green** = Excellent — 2 or fewer questions incorrect
● **Orange** = Passing — 50% or more questions answered correctly
● **Red** = Struggling — fewer than 50% correct and needs help

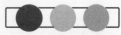

Transfer your results from each unit to the grid above. Colour the traffic lights red, orange or green.

Grammar & Punctuation

AC9E5LA06

Nouns

> **Common nouns** are the names of people, places, animals and things.
>
> *Examples:* doctor, teacher, husband, river, mountain, tiger, tractor
>
> **Proper nouns** are the special names given to people, places and things. They always begin with a **capital letter**.
>
> *Examples:* Michael, London, Mount Everest, September, Derwent River

Add capital letters to all the proper nouns in the text below. Hint: There are 16 in total!

① – ⑯ The continent of north america is made up of 23 countries and 9 dependent territories. The largest country is canada and the second largest is the united states of america (USA). Other countries in north america include: mexico, cuba, panama and barbados. The atlantic ocean is on the east side of the continent and the pacific ocean is on the west side.

Write if the underlined noun is a common noun or proper noun. Write C or P.

⑰ The capital <u>city</u> of the USA is Washington DC. ___

⑱ The capital city of Canada is <u>Ottawa</u>. ___

⑲ Mexico has beaches, <u>mountains</u>, deserts and jungles. ___

⑳ <u>Barbados</u> is a Caribbean island. ___

㉑ Cuba is an <u>island</u> to the south of Florida.

___

㉒ Panama is a <u>country</u> that joins Central America to South America. ___

Phonic Knowledge & Spelling

AC9E5LY09, AC9E5LY10

Short vowel sounds – a, e, i, o, u

Say each word. They all contain short vowel sounds — the sound is short and snappy!

Word Bank

admit	address	affect	effect
promise	picnic	subject	signal
collect	correct	collapse	model
mimic	muffin	travel	pumpkin

Choose words from the word bank to complete these sentences.

① I have an uncle who likes to collect _____ trains.

② My aunt has grown the largest _____ I have ever seen!

Circle the words in each line that have short vowels.

③ commit   connect   float   wheel

④ wipe   climb   object   inject

The doubling rule

> When a word ends in a short vowel, followed by a **single consonant**, double the last consonant before adding **–ed** or **–ing**.
>
> Remember! Consonants are all the letters that are not vowels.
>
> *Example:* model, mode**ll**ed, mode**ll**ing
>
> If a word has more than one consonant after the short vowel, you do not double the last consonant.
>
> *Example:* affect, affect**ed**, affect**ing**
>
> **NOTE:** Words that end in **c** such as picnic and mimic are exceptions. You add a **k** before adding an ending.
>
> *Example:* picni**c**, picni**ck**ed, picni**ck**ing

Add –ed and –ing to these words. Decide if you need to double the last consonant.

	–ed	–ing
⑤ admit	_____	_____
⑥ collect	_____	_____
⑦ permit	_____	_____
⑧ commit	_____	_____
⑨ relent	_____	_____
⑩ signal	_____	_____

Score 2 points for each correct answer! **SCORE** /44  0-20 22-38 40-44

Score 2 points for each correct answer! **SCORE** /20 0-8 10-14 16-20

TARGETING HOMEWORK 5 © PASCAL PRESS ISBN 9781925726473

TERM 1 ENGLISH

Desert plants

Informative text – Report
Author – Frances Mackay

How do plants survive in hot deserts? Here are some of the ways desert plants adapt to their dry environment:

Some plants, called succulents, store water in their stems or leaves.

Some plants have no leaves at all or small leaves that only grow after it rains. The lack of leaves helps reduce water loss during photosynthesis (the process by which plants make their own food). Leafless plants carry out photosynthesis in their green stems.

Some plants have long root systems that spread out wide or go deep into the ground to absorb water.

Some plants have a short life cycle and produce seeds only after it has rained — they grow, flower and die within one year. These plants can avoid drought altogether. Some seeds can remain dormant for years.

Many desert plants have leaves with hairs on them. This helps shade the plant, reducing water loss.

Some plants have leaves that turn throughout the day to expose a minimum surface area to the sun.

Many desert plants have spines and spikes. This stops animals from eating the plants for the water they contain.

Some plants have a waxy coating on their stems and leaves to help reduce water loss.

The flowers on some plants only open at night to attract insects and other pollinators who are more likely to be active during the cooler evening.

Many desert plants are very slow growers. Slower growth uses less energy. The plants do not have to make as much food and therefore do not lose as much water.

Source: *Science Comprehension and Writing Response Centres*, Upper Primary, Blake Education.

Write or circle the correct answers.

① **What type of text is this?**

  a narrative **b** informative **c** persuasive

Scan the text to find words that have these meanings.

② to make smaller: r_____

③ the process by which green plants make their own food: p_____

④ not active, alive but resting: d_____

⑤ a long period of little or no rainfall: d_____

⑥ plants that store water in their stems or leaves: s_____

⑦ to make: p_____

⑧ **Pollinators are:**

  a animals or insects that transfer pollen from one plant to another.

  b a type of desert plant.

  c flowers that open at night.

⑨ **Write down THREE different ways the leaves on desert plants can help them survive the desert environment.**

_____

_____

⑩ **Where do leafless plants carry out photosynthesis?**

  a in their green stem

  b in their flowers

  c We are not told.

⑪ **How does slow growth help a desert plant to survive a dry environment?**

_____

_____

_____

Score 2 points for each correct answer!

SCORE **/22**   0-8   10-16   18-22

My Book Review

Title _____

Author _____

Rating ☆ ☆ ☆ ☆ ☆

Comment _____

_____

Number & Algebra

AC9M5N02

Factors

Factors are numbers you can multiply together to get another number. They can be divided into another number with no remainder.

Example:

4 × 9 = 36   36 ÷ 9 = 4

4 and **9** are factors of 36

All numbers (except for 1) have at least two factors – 1 and the number itself.

Some numbers have many factors. The factors of 36 are: 1, 2, 3, 4, 6, 9, 12, 18 and 36.

1 × 36 = 36
2 × 18 = 36
3 × 12 = 36
4 × 9 = 36
6 × 6 = 36

Circle the correct answers.

① Which number is a factor of 10?

   a 4   **b** 8   **c** 2   **d** 6

② Which number is a factor of 12?

   a 9   **b** 10   **c** 4   **d** 11

③ Which number is **not** a factor of 20?

   a 2   **b** 10   **c** 8   **d** 5

④ Which number is **not** a factor of 24?

   a 10   **b** 6   **c** 4   **d** 24

⑤ Which number is a factor of 30?

   a 8   **b** 7   **c** 5   **d** 4

⑥ Which number is a factor of 18?

   a 4   **b** 1   **c** 12   **d** 7

⑦ List all the factors of 12.

_____

⑧ List all the factors of 24.

_____

Multiples

The **multiple** of a number is a **skip counting number**. A multiple of a whole number is the answer (product) of the whole number and any number.

Multiples of **4**: 4, 8, 12, 16, 24, 28, 32, 36, and so on

Multiples of **9**: 9, 18, 27, 36, 45, 54, 63, and so on

Use skip counting to complete the multiples of these numbers.

⑨ Multiples of 5:

5, 10, 15, ____, ____, ____, ____, 40

⑩ Multiples of 6:

6, 12, 18, ____, ____, ____, ____, 48

⑪ Multiples of 100:

100, 200, _____, _____, _____, _____, 700

⑫ Multiples of 3:

____, ____, ____, 12, ____, ____

⑬ Multiples of 1000:

1000, _____, _____, 4000, _____,

_____

Score 2 points for each correct answer! | **SCORE** | **/26** (0-10) (12-20) (22-26)

Statistics & Probability

AC9M5P01, AC9M5P02

Chance events and probability

Use the spinner to answer the questions. Circle the correct answers.

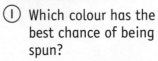

① Which colour has the best chance of being spun?

   a red   **c** green

   b blue   **d** orange

   e All colours have an equal chance.

② What is the chance of red being spun?

   a 4 out of 1   **b** 1 out of 4

   c 1 out of 3   **d** 1 out of 1

③ If the spinner is spun 12 times, how many times is orange likely to come up?

   a 12   **b** 6   **c** 4   **d** 3

④ If the spinner is spun 12 times, how many times are blue **or** green likely to come up?

   a 12   **b** 6   **c** 4   **d** 3

Probability as fractions

We can use **fractions** to represent probability chances.

- If the chance of spinning red on a spinner is 1 out of 4, it has a probability of $\frac{1}{4}$
- If the chance of rolling a die and getting a six is 1 in 6, it has a probability of $\frac{1}{6}$
- If the chance of spinning red or blue on a spinner is 2 out of 4, it has a probability of $\frac{2}{4}$

TARGETING HOMEWORK 5 © PASCAL PRESS ISBN 9781925726473

What are the probabilities of these things happening? Write your answers as fractions.

⑤ The chance of getting a correct answer in a quiz is 1 out of 3. It has a probability of

____

⑥ The chance of pulling a red marble out of a bag is 2 out of 5. It has a probability of

____

⑦ The chance of spinning yellow on a spinner is 4 out of 8. It has a probability of

____

⑧ The chance of winning the raffle is 1 in 1000. It has a probability of

_____

What is the probability of each colour on this spinner being spun? Circle the correct answer.

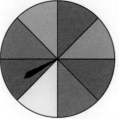

⑨ green   a $\frac{1}{4}$ b $\frac{1}{8}$ c $\frac{8}{1}$ d $\frac{5}{8}$

⑩ blue   a $\frac{2}{8}$ b $\frac{8}{2}$ c $\frac{4}{8}$ d $\frac{3}{8}$

⑪ red   a $\frac{1}{8}$ b $\frac{8}{3}$ c $\frac{3}{8}$ d $\frac{2}{8}$

⑫ yellow   a $\frac{1}{8}$ b $\frac{1}{4}$ c $\frac{8}{1}$ d $\frac{1}{2}$

⑬ orange   a $\frac{8}{1}$ b $\frac{2}{4}$ c $\frac{1}{8}$ d $\frac{3}{8}$

Score 2 points for each correct answer!   **SCORE** /26   (0-10)   (12-20)   (22-26)

Measurement & Space

AC9M5M01

Length

We measure length in **millimetres (mm)**, **centimetres (cm)**, **metres (m)** and **kilometres (km)**.

Would you use millimetres, centimetres, metres or kilometres to measure the length of these things?

① a school desk   _____

② a flea   _____

③ a netball court   _____

④ a country   _____

⑤ the head of a nail   _____

⑥ a book   _____

Circle the measuring tool you would use to measure these lengths.

⑦ the width of a classroom

   a ruler   **b** measuring tape

⑧ the distance a car has travelled

   a odometer   **b** ruler

⑨ the distance around a netball court

   a trundle wheel   **b** ruler

Measure these lines in millimetres.

⑩ _____

⑪ _____

⑫ _____

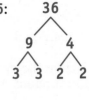

Score 2 points for each correct answer!   **SCORE** /24   (0-10)   (12-18)   (20-24)

Problem Solving

AC9M5N02

Factor trees

Factor trees are a fun way to work out the factors of numbers.

Here are some of the factors of **36**:

To make this tree, you write 36 at the top. Then make branches of factors – numbers that multiply to give you the original number: **9 × 4 = 36**.

Next, take each of those numbers and break them down into more factors: **3 × 3 = 9**.

Continue until all the remaining numbers are prime numbers (a number with only two factors, one and itself) and cannot be factored anymore.

Make two different factor trees for 36.

Grammar & Punctuation

AC9E5LA06

Count nouns

> **Count nouns** name things we can count. They can be **singular** (one) or **plural** (more than one).
>
> To make the plural of most count nouns, you just add **s**.
>
> *Examples:* elephant, elephant**s**
> document, document**s**
>
> For nouns that end in **ch, sh, s, ss, x, z** and **zz**, you add **–es**.
>
> *Examples:* lun**ch**, lunch**es** wi**sh**, wish**es**
> ga**s**, gas**es** gla**ss**, glass**es** bo**x**, box**es**
> walt**z**, waltz**es** bu**zz**, buzz**es**
>
> There are exceptions to this rule.
> *Examples:* ox, oxen quiz, quizzes axis, axes
> fish, fish

Write the plurals of these nouns.

1. village _____
2. eyelash _____
3. princess _____
4. virus _____
5. beach _____
6. prefix _____

Plural nouns

> Some nouns are **always plural**.
> *Examples:* scissors, jeans, pyjamas, fireworks, pliers, trousers, goggles, tongs, cattle
>
> Some nouns have special plural forms.
> *Examples:* child, children man, men
> mouse, mice

Change the nouns in bold to plural. Write the plural nouns on the lines.

7. The **woman** finished the race.

_____

8. I broke my **tooth**.

_____

9. The **fisherman** fished all day long.

_____

10. I chased the **goose** away from our house.

_____

Phonic Knowledge & Spelling

AC9E5LY09, AC9E5LY10

Short vowel sounds

Say each word. These two-syllable words contain short vowel sounds. The first syllable of each word is stressed more than the second syllable.

Word Bank

shabby	shudder	shimmer	village
stirrup	stubborn	tranquil	trolley
vandal	victim	wicked	wisdom
symbol	pantry	public	terror

Choose words from the word bank to complete these sentences.

1. "Please get a litre of orange juice from the _____," said Mum.
2. The supermarket _____ was approximately one metre in height.
3. The _____ was attacked when he was on his way home.

Match the words in the box to their meanings. .

shuddering vandalise symbolise shimmering

4. to represent something with a symbol: _____
5. glistening: _____
6. shaking, vibrating: _____
7. deliberately destroy or damage property: _____

Suffix –ise

> When you add the suffix **–ise** to a noun, you change the noun to a verb.
> *Examples:* symbol, symbol**ise**
> vandal, vandal**ise**

Change these nouns into verbs by adding the suffix –ise.

8. legal _____
9. advert _____
10. terror _____
11. capital _____

The Great Race

Imaginative text – Narrative
Author – Paul McEvoy, **Illustrator** – Warren Eyre

The local council had organised a rubbish pick-up so everyone put out their old lawnmowers, scooters, prams, washing machines and other junk for the council to collect. Jah and his friends decide to use the junk to make billycarts or anything else they could ride on to have a race.

The next day at school we decided to have a race. During Art we drew a poster to announce *The Great Race* at 2 o'clock on Saturday afternoon. Jah hung the poster in the corridor and the word went out like crazy. There wasn't a prize, but that didn't matter. Just being at the starting line and ready to race was enough.

That afternoon the bell couldn't ring soon enough. Everyone rushed home to prepare. All over the neighbourhood you could see kids scouring the streets in search of something to enter the race. It didn't have to be a pram. As long as it had a driver, a passenger and wheels, it qualified.

As race time approached, kids started to come from all over. A couple of

billycarts, a lawnmower with a chair tied on top and a scooter with a cushion for a seat. Last of all, our large, freshly painted bright red, wooden pram, still dripping red paint like a trail of blood.

Jah got everyone together to explain the rules.

"This is the start and the finishing line," he shouted, pointing to a chalk line on the road. "You have to go around that pole at the top of the cul-de-sac and then back to here. There'll be no biting or gouging. We want a fair race."

People had practice runs up and down the course trying to work out the best way to run their machines. Some contraptions fell apart before the start and were hastily repaired.

As the 2 o'clock starting time approached the air was buzzing with excitement. Jah checked his watch and called everyone to the start line.

"2 minutes!" he yelled.

Source: *The Great Race*, Sparklers, Blake Education.

Write or circle the correct answers.

① **What does the phrase 'the word went out like crazy' mean?**
   a Everyone in school quickly told others about the race.
   b Everyone thought it was a crazy idea.
   c The race poster had crazy words on it.

② **Which word in the text means 'fitted the requirements'?**
   a approached b qualified c repaired

③ **What type of language is the phrase 'still dripping with red paint like a trail of blood'?**
   a alliteration   c metaphor
   b simile   d pun

④ **What is a cul-de-sac?**
   a a park   one end
   b a playground   d a race track
   c a street closed at

⑤ **What did Jah mean when he said: "We want a fair race"?**

Match the words in the box to their meanings.

| neighbourhood   scouring   gouging |
| contraptions |

⑥ machines that are badly made:
_____

⑦ the area where people live:
_____

⑧ looking: _____

⑨ scratching: _____

⑩ **Which phrase in the text tells you that everyone was really excited as the start time approached?**

_____

My Book Review

Title _____

Author _____

Rating ☆☆☆☆☆

Comment _____

Score 2 points for each correct answer!

SCORE **/20** 0-8 10-14 16-20

Number & Algebra

AC9M5N08, AC9M5N09

Rounding to the nearest 10

Sometimes it is useful to round numbers when you want an **approximate** answer.

Example: **32 + 47 = ?**

Round the numbers to the nearest 10.
If the number ends in 0, 1, 2, 3 or 4, round down.
If the number ends in 5, 6, 7, 8 or 9, round up to the next 10.

30 + 50 = 80

Round these numbers to the nearest 10.

① 14 _____
② 67 _____
③ 25 _____
④ 39 _____
⑤ 93 _____
⑥ 51 _____
⑦ 88 _____
⑧ 66 _____

To round numbers in the 100s to the nearest 10, round the tens only.

Example: 154 + 579

rounded: 150 + 580

Round these numbers to the nearest 10.

⑨ 123 _____
⑩ 659 _____
⑪ 548 _____
⑫ 812 _____
⑬ 724 _____
⑭ 456 _____
⑮ 377 _____
⑯ 265 _____

Round the numbers to the nearest 10 and quickly make an estimate of the answer.

Examples:

63 + 56 = 60 + 60 = 120

129 + 242 = 130 + 240 = 370

⑰ 62 + 29 = _____

⑱ 78 + 14 = _____

⑲ 53 + 47 = _____
⑳ 36 + 25 = _____
㉑ 132 + 55 = _____
㉒ 568 + 12 = _____
㉓ 361 + 126 = _____
㉔ 747 + 233 = _____

Rounding to the nearest 100

When you round to the nearest 100, look at the last two digits.
• If they are between 1 and 49, round down.
• If they are 50 or more, round up.

424 is rounded down to 400
(the number is closer to 400 than 500)

468 is rounded up to 500
(the number is closer to 500 than 400)

Round these numbers to the nearest 100.

㉕ 215 _____
㉖ 569 _____
㉗ 582 _____
㉘ 647 _____
㉙ 749 _____
㉚ 351 _____
㉛ 633 _____
㉜ 370 _____

You use the same method to round to the nearest 100 when using larger numbers.

Examples: 1245 rounds to 1200
32 578 rounds to 32 600

Round these numbers to the nearest 100.

㉝ 4569 _____
㉞ 5321 _____
㉟ 2349 _____
㊱ 7890 _____
㊲ 24 563 _____
㊳ 67 468 _____
㊴ 134 541 _____
㊵ 786 675 _____

Score 2 points for each correct answer!

SCORE  **/80** (0-38) (40-74) (76-80)

Statistics & Probability

There are no statistics & probability activities in this unit.

TARGETING HOMEWORK 5 © PASCAL PRESS ISBN 9781925726473

Measurement & Space

AC9M5M03

24-hour clock

There are **24 hours in a day**, so sometimes we use 24-hour times instead of 12-hour times.

Many travel timetables are in 24-hour time, such as bus timetables and flight times. This is so we do not confuse times like 4 am and 4 pm.

The 24-hour clock does not have am and pm. Up to 12 noon, you write the times the same as for the 12-hour clock.

24-hour clock

After 12 noon, keep counting up to 24. So 1 pm becomes 13:00 (add 1 to 12) in 24-hour time; 2 pm becomes 14:00 (add 2 to 12), and so on.

The last minute of the day is 23:59. When you get to midnight, start again from zero. So midnight in 24-hour time is 00:00.

The minutes do not change: 2:15 pm = 14:15.

Write these 12-hour times as 24-hour times.

① 7 am _____
② 5:30 am _____
③ 4:20 am _____
④ 6:42 am _____
⑤ 12 noon _____
⑥ 2 pm _____
⑦ 7:30 pm _____
⑧ 6:45 pm _____
⑨ 12:30 am _____
⑩ 8:59 pm _____

Write these 24-hour times in 12-hour digital time. Use am or pm.

Examples: 15:25 = 3:15 pm
06:40 = 6:40 am

⑪ 13:25 _____
⑫ 15:30 _____
⑬ 12:15 _____
⑭ 07:20 _____
⑮ 06:45 _____
⑯ 19:10 _____
⑰ 23:50 _____
⑱ 21:30 _____
⑲ 16:12 _____
⑳ 22:05 _____

How do we say 24-hour times?

23:00 is said as 'twenty-three hundred'

07:30 is said as 'oh seven thirty' or 'zero seven thirty'

18:05 is said as 'eighteen oh five'

06:00 is said as 'oh six hundred' or 'zero six hundred'

09:00
Friday, May 26

Write these 24-hour times as numbers.

㉑ fourteen hundred _____
㉒ twenty-three thirty _____
㉓ eleven thirty-eight _____
㉔ nineteen-oh-five _____
㉕ oh-five hundred _____
㉖ twenty-two forty-two _____

Write true or false.

㉗ 7:25 am is the same as 07:25. _____
㉘ Noon is the same as 12:00. _____
㉙ 14:55 is the correct way to write 5 minutes to 3. _____
㉚ 22:59 is closer to midnight than 23:40. _____
㉛ 5 past midnight is written as 12:05. _____

SCORE **/62** (0-28) (30-56) (58-62)

Problem Solving

AC9M5M03

Time puzzles

Solve these 24-hour time problems.

① Jackie started reading at 16:40. She finished reading at 18:15. How long did she read?

_____

② Tim got up at 06:45. He left home to walk to school at 08:15. How long did it take him to get ready for school?

_____

③ Dad started cooking at 17:30. The meal took him 45 minutes to make. At what time was the meal ready?

_____

④ The 75-minute football match started at 14:15. What time did it finish?

_____

Grammar & Punctuation

AC9E5LA06

Noun groups

A **noun group** is a chunk of words built around a noun. All the information in the noun group is about the key or main noun. The words in the noun group tell us more about the key noun.

key or main noun ⎯ noun group

Example: A **monster** with <u>a round, red body and eight, googly eyes</u> jumped in front of me.

Circle the key noun and then underline the noun groups in these sentences.

① The bauble had sparkly crystals and iridescent gems.

② His bright yellow jacket made him stand out.

③ The snarling, ferocious tiger rushed out of hiding.

Determiners

A **determiner** is part of a noun group. Its job is to point out (determine) which noun is being spoken about.

Examples: **those** books, **my** house, **her** garden

The articles **a (an)** and **the** are determiners. They are often used to introduce a noun group.

Determiners include: a, an, the, my, your, her, his, its, our, their, this, that, those, some, both, each, every.

Underline the determiners in these noun groups.

④ the abandoned house

⑤ every pair of red shoes

⑥ Tina's mobile

⑦ our new car

Noun groups using 'and'

There can be more than one noun group in a sentence.

Example: <u>Those rotten **apples**</u> made <u>my new **pantry**</u> smell.

A noun group may contain two or more nouns connected by **and**, which is known as a **joining word**.

Examples: <u>Tom **and** his friends</u> raced to the sandy beach.

I bought some <u>new socks **and** shoes</u>.

Underline the noun groups in these sentences.

⑧ Sam and Su played for hours in the old, haunted house.

⑨ Each new player received a warm, blue hoodie.

Score 2 points for each correct answer! SCORE **/18** (0-6) (8-14) (16-18)

Phonic Knowledge & Spelling

AC9E5LY09, AC9E5LY10

Long vowels with a final 'e'

Say each word. All the words begin with **a** and end in **e**. The **e** on the end of the word makes the vowel sound long.

Word Bank

abuse	abate	achieve	acquire
accuse	accrue	amaze	amuse
approve	appraise	arrange	arrive
assume	assure	adore	

Choose words from the word bank to complete these sentences.

① Mum tried to _____ a visit to the dentist on the fourth.

② The teacher said we had to _____ early at school tomorrow.

③ For my eighth birthday, Dad paid for a magician to _____ us.

④ I have forty toy bears and I _____ them all.

Adding a suffix to words that end in 'e'

Remember! When a word ends in **e**, you drop the **e** when you add a suffix that begins with a vowel or a **y**. Keep the **e** if the suffix begins with a consonant.

Examples: amaze + ing = amazing
amaze + ment = amazement

Build the new words by adding the suffix. Write the new word.

⑤ adore + ing = _____

⑥ arrange + ment = _____

⑦ appraise + al = _____

⑧ amuse + ed = _____

⑨ achieve + ment = _____

⑩ arrive + al = _____

⑪ assure + ance = _____

⑫ acquire + ing = _____

Score 2 points for each correct answer! SCORE **/24** (0-10) (12-18) (20-24)

TARGETING HOMEWORK 5 © PASCAL PRESS ISBN 9781925726473

TERM 1 ENGLISH

Protecting Antarctica

Persuasive text – Exposition
Author – Merryn Whitfield

Recently there has been much media publicity over plans by Exciting EcoWorld Tours to operate expeditions to Antarctica. We must be vigilant and not allow any sort of tourism in this environmentally sensitive region.

Antarctica, the last bastion of the world's natural environment, remained largely untouched by human exploration until the 1820s. Its sub-zero temperatures, dangerous crevasses and icy fjords serve to keep away all but the most ardent explorer. This is something for which we should all be grateful. But unfortunately, Antarctica's perils are also her attractions, as the current generation of risk-seeking travellers will confirm.

Sadly, we all know what has happened to Australia's natural landscape after just 200 years of European settlement. Many unique and fragile environments have been damaged and countless animal species have become extinct or critically endangered. Is this what we want to happen to Antarctica?

Exciting EcoWorld Tours make the unlikely claim that their expeditions will not affect the environment. How can they guarantee this?

And regardless of this flawed assertion, once Antarctica is opened to one tourist operator, it becomes difficult to deny access to others. The rot will have set in!

We have many places around the world that we can visit without restriction. Let Antarctica retain its mystery.

If we sanction ecotourism in Antarctica, if we allow the fragile natural environment to be disturbed further, if we put profits first, then we will be throwing away the once in a lifetime opportunity to conserve this wild yet precious environment. Exciting EcoWorld Tours might have good intentions, but Antarctica is too fragile to withstand any form of tourism.

Source: *Writing Centres: Persuasive Texts*, Upper Primary, Blake Education.

Write or circle the correct answers.

1 **What does the title tell us about the author's viewpoint?**

   a The author wants Antarctica to be exploited.

   b The author wants Antarctica to be protected.

   c You can't tell until you read the text.

2 **Which sentence in the opening paragraph tells us the author's point of view?**

   a Recently there has been much media publicity over plans by Exciting EcoWorld Tours to operate expeditions to Antarctica.

   b We must be vigilant and not allow any sort of tourism in this environmentally sensitive region.

3 **What does vigilant mean?**

   a strong   b positive

   c keeping careful watch

4 **What does 'the last bastion of the world's natural environment' mean?**

   a a place that strongly maintains its special natural environment

   b a place that encourages change to its environment

   c a place that has endured negative changes to its environment

Which words in the second paragraph have these meanings?

5 deep open cracks in a glacier: c_____

6 long, narrow deep inlets of the sea between cliffs: f_____

7 very enthusiastic or persistent: a_____

What are the three things the author lists in the conclusion that she believes will destroy the environment of Antarctica?

8 _____

9 _____

10 _____

Score 2 points for each correct answer!

SCORE /20 0-8 10-14 16-20

My Book Review

Title _____

Author _____

Rating ☆☆☆☆☆

Comment _____

_____

Number & Algebra

AC9M5N06

Multiplying larger numbers

Multiplying larger numbers can be tricky! Here's an easy way to do it, using a **lattice grid**.

Example: 16 × 54

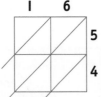

- Write the first number (**16**) across the top and the second number (**54**) down the right side.

- Do 1 × 5.   • Then do 6 × 5.

- Then do 1 × 4.   • Then do 6 × 4.

   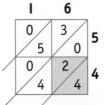

- Now add down the diagonals, starting with the bottom right triangle. This is the ones column.

$3 + 5 + 0 = 8$

$0 + 2 + 4 = 6$

- You get the answer by reading down the left side and then along the bottom (ignore the first zero).

So, 16 × 54 = **864**.

Complete these multiplications using the lattice method.

① 13 × 43 = _____   ③ 14 × 34 = _____

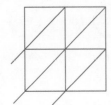   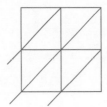

② 23 × 12 = _____   ④ 42 × 53 = _____

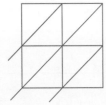   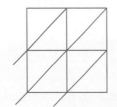

Sometimes when you add at the end, you need to **carry a ten**.

Example:

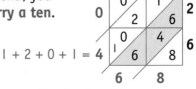

$1 + 2 + 0 + 1 = 4$

$6 + 4 + 6 = 16$

Write **6** and carry the **1** to the next column.

Complete these multiplications.

⑤ 28 × 15 = _____   ⑥ 37 × 61 = _____

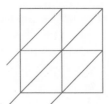   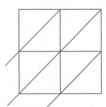

Score 2 points for each correct answer!

SCORE /12 (0-4) (6-8) (10-12)

Statistics & Probability

AC9M5P02, AC9M5ST01

Collecting data

When you are conducting a survey, you must ask the right questions to get the information you need. Learning to ask the right questions can sometimes be tricky!

Example: English is the most important subject in school. Do you agree?

A better question might be: Which subject in school do you think is the most important? The first question could influence people to think that English is the most important subject. The second question lets people give their own opinions.

Circle the question that would be better to ask than the sample question.

① **Sample: Did you go to the cinema last year?** • Yes • No

  a How often did you go to the cinema last year? • never • 1–3 times • once a month • every week

  b I went to the cinema last year. Did you? • Yes • No

② **Sample: Car racing is a dangerous sport. Do you agree?** • Yes • No

  a How dangerous is the sport of car racing? • not very dangerous • very dangerous

  b Car racing is a dangerous sport. • agree • neither agree nor disagree • disagree

TARGETING HOMEWORK 5 © PASCAL PRESS ISBN 9781925726473

TERM 1 MATHS

③ **Sample: How many languages do you speak?** • I • 2 • 3

a Which languages do you speak? List them.

_____

b Do you speak more than one language?
• Yes • No

④ **Sample: My favourite fast food is fish and chips. Do you like fish and chips?**
• Yes • No

a Do you have a favourite fast food?
• Yes • No

b Which of these is your favourite fast food?
• burgers • fish & chips • kebabs
• other _____

Score 2 points for each correct answer! SCORE **/8** (0-2) (4-6) (8)

Measurement & Space

AC9M5M02

Perimeter and area

Perimeter is the distance around the outside of a 2D shape. **Area** is the amount of space inside a 2D shape.

Look at this shape:

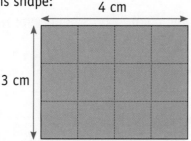

4 cm

3 cm

To find the **perimeter** of this rectangle, add the lengths of the sides:

4 cm + 3 cm + 4 cm + 3 cm = **14 cm**

Each square inside the shape represents I cm × I cm. To find the **area** of the rectangle, count all the I cm squares inside it. A quick way to do this is to multiply the length by the width: 4 cm × 3 cm = 12 cm²

The area of this shape is **12 cm²**.
We call this 12 square centimetres.

Calculate the perimeter and area.

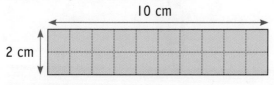

10 cm

2 cm

① Perimeter = _____ ② Area = _____

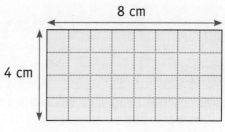

8 cm

4 cm

③ Perimeter = _____ ④ Area = _____

Calculate the perimeter and area of these shapes. Be careful — not all measurements are in centimetres!

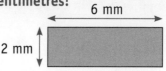

6 mm

2 mm

⑤ Perimeter = _____ ⑥ Area = _____

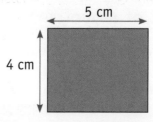

5 cm

4 cm

⑦ Perimeter = _____ ⑧ Area = _____

9 m

2 m

⑨ Perimeter = _____ ⑩ Area = _____

Score 2 points for each correct answer! SCORE **/20** (0-8) (10-14) (16-20)

Problem Solving

AC9M5M02, AC9M5N09

Carpet it!

Mr Jackson wants new carpet in his bedroom. He is going to fit it himself.

Carpet gripper has to be laid all around the edge of the room to hold the carpet in place.

The carpet costs $40 per square metre.

The carpet gripper costs $2 per metre.

Calculate the area and perimeter of the room to work out how much carpet and carpet gripper he needs.

① Perimeter = _____

② Area = _____

③ Cost of gripper
= _____

④ Cost of carpet
= _____

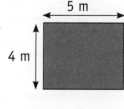

5 m

4 m

Grammar & Punctuation

AC9E5LA06

Adjectives

> **Adjectives** describe people, places and things. They work with the noun to create a particular picture in the mind of the reader.
> *Examples:* **cold**, **misty** morning
> **dilapidated**, **mysterious** house

Underline the adjectives in these noun groups.

① thick, juicy hamburgers

② three red robins

③ a delightful concert

④ a magnificent, weather-beaten house

Placement of adjectives

> Adjectives can come **before** the noun, or **after** the noun.
> *Examples:* We saw **ten**, **tiny** <u>caterpillars</u>.
> The <u>kitten</u> was **fluffy**, **funny** and **cuddly**.

Underline the adjectives that describe the nouns in bold.

⑤ The new **house** was enormous and had ten **bedrooms**.

⑥ The **players** were eager to start the game.

⑦ The frightened **rat** scurried past the watchful **cat**.

Types of adjectives

> Some adjectives **describe** nouns and some adjectives **classify** them.
> Classify means to say what type they are.
> *Examples:*
> Describing adjectives: a **busy** city, **spicy** food, **dense** rainforest
> Classifying adjectives: an **Australian** city, **Indian** food, **tropical** rainforest

Underline the adjectives that classify the nouns in bold in these sentences.

⑧ The Dalmatian **dog** was covered in black spots.

⑨ I prefer rap **music** to rock **music**.

⑩ The steam **train** pulled into the rickety, old station.

Phonic Knowledge & Spelling

AC9E5LY09

First syllables ending in a long vowel

Say each word in the word bank. All the words have two syllables. The first syllable of each word ends in a long vowel sound.

Word Bank

major	minor	motive	fatal
fluent	sofa	solo	social
cable	canine	mobile	motor
moment	trifle	trophy	truant

Choose words from the word bank to complete these sentences.

① We had to position the _____ away from the cupboard so we could open the doors.

② My cousin won a _____ for winning a cycling race.

③ My nephew is _____ in two languages — English and French.

④ We have a relation who owns a _____ food van.

Make compound words beginning with motor.

⑤ _____home

⑥ _____boat

⑦ _____cycle

⑧ _____cyclist

Circle how many syllables are in these words.

⑨ motivation   1   2   3   4

⑩ majority   1   2   3   4

⑪ soloist   1   2   3   4

⑫ momentous   1   2   3   4

⑬ mobility   1   2   3   4

Growth of Australian Colonies: 1800s

Informative text – Explanation
Authors – Frances Mackay and
Catherine Gordon

Why did Britain want more people to migrate to Australia in the 1800s?

Food was in very short supply in the early days of the New South Wales colony. Very few convicts had farming experience and people did not know how to grow crops in the hot and dry Australian climate, as it was very different to the one back in England. The authorities wanted the British Government to send out farmers in exchange for land grants and free convict labour. This meant the British Government could colonise more areas of Australia and make money from agricultural exports.

Why did British people want to migrate to Australia at that time?

People wanted to come to Australia in order to find better lives for themselves. Life in Britain in the 1800s was difficult for many people. The Industrial Revolution put thousands out of work, as machines had been invented that meant fewer people were needed in factories. In Scotland, the Highland Clearances saw many farmers (crofters) evicted from their land so landowners could make large-scale sheep farms instead. Thousands of farmers lost their homes and needed to find new places to live. From 1845 to 1849, Ireland suffered from a Potato Famine where potato crops failed several years in a row. Many people relied on potatoes for their diet and livelihood. About a million people died as a result of the famine, and as many as two million may have migrated elsewhere.

How did the government encourage free settlers to migrate?

In the 1830s, the British Government began introducing assisted passage schemes for migrants, where the Government paid some or all of their fares. This gave poor labourers the opportunity to come to Australia.

Source: *Australian History Centres*, Upper Primary, Blake Education.

Write or circle the correct answers.

① **What is the purpose of the text?**

 a to tell us what it was like to live in Australia in the 1800s

 b to explain why Australia needed more migrants in the 1800s and how the British Government encouraged people to move to Australia

Which words in the first paragraph have these meanings?

② a country or area under the control of another country: c_____

③ prisoners: c_____

④ the weather in an area over a long period of time: c_____

⑤ **What disaster caused millions of Irish people to leave Ireland and migrate to other countries from 1845 to 1849?**

 a the Highland Clearances

 b the Industrial Revolution

 c the Potato Famine

⑥ **What is a migrant?**

 a a farmer

 b a person who moves from one place to another to find work or better living conditions

 c a labourer

⑦ **How did the British Government help free settlers to migrate to Australia?**

 _____

 _____

Score 2 points for each correct answer!

SCORE /14 (0-4) (6-10) (12-14)

My Book Review

Title _____

Author _____

Rating ☆ ☆ ☆ ☆ ☆

Comment _____

_____

Number & Algebra

AC9M5N06

Division

There are many different ways to solve a division problem. Here are some of the ways.

- Use multiplication facts. *Example:* $36 \div 6$ can be read as, '36, how many sixes?'

- Skip count. *Example:* Skip count by 6 to find out how many 6s are in 36. There are 6 sixes in 36, so $36 \div 6 = 6$. The multiplication fact you have used is 6×6.

Write the multiplication fact you use to solve these division questions.

① $30 \div 3$ _____

② $42 \div 6$ _____

③ $56 \div 7$ _____

④ $45 \div 9$ _____

⑤ $64 \div 8$ _____

⑥ $27 \div 3$ _____

⑦ $35 \div 5$ _____

⑧ $72 \div 8$ _____

⑨ $32 \div 8$ _____

⑩ $81 \div 9$ _____

Use halving

Sometimes, you can halve both numbers to find the answer.

Example: $208 \div 8$

Halve both numbers: $104 \div 4$

Keep halving: $52 \div 2$, $26 \div 1$

Answer: $208 \div 8 = 26$

Use the halving method to calculate these.

⑪ $180 \div 4$

_____

_____

_____

⑫ $288 \div 8$

_____

_____

_____

⑬ $384 \div 16$

_____

_____

_____

⑭ $328 \div 4$

_____

_____

_____

⑮ $424 \div 8$

_____

_____

_____

⑯ $656 \div 16$

_____

_____

_____

Use the split method

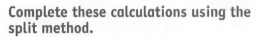

You can split the number you are dividing to make it easier to calculate.

Example: $270 \div 5$

Split 270 into two numbers that can be divided by 5, such as $250 + 20$

$$270 \div 5 = (250 + 20) \div 5$$
$$= (250 \div 5) + (20 \div 5)$$
$$= 50 + 4$$
$$= 54$$

Complete these calculations using the split method.

⑰ $336 \div 6 = (300 + 36) \div 6$

= _____

= _____

= _____

⑱ $434 \div 7 = (420 + 14) \div 7$

= _____

= _____

= _____

⑲ $425 \div 5 = (400 + 25) \div 5$

= _____

= _____

= _____

⑳ $496 \div 8 = (_____ + 16) \div 8$

= _____

= _____

= _____

㉑ $378 \div 7 = (350 + \_\_\_\_) \div 7$

= _____

= _____

= _____

㉒ $657 \div 9 = (_____ + \_\_\_\_) \div 9$

= _____

= _____

= _____

Score 2 points for each correct answer!

SCORE **/44** 0-20 22-38 40-44

Statistics & Probability

There are no statistics & probability activities in this unit.

TARGETING HOMEWORK 5 © PASCAL PRESS ISBN 9781925726473

Measurement & Space

AC9M5M01

Choosing measurement units

In practical measurement situations, it is important to select the **best measurement unit** to use.

For example, millilitres would not be a good measurement unit to use for measuring the amount of water in a swimming pool.

Litres or even kilolitres would be more suitable.

Write the measurement unit best suited to measure each quantity.

① flour for a cake

_____

② water for a glass of cordial

_____

③ elastic for a hat

_____

④ wood for a shelf

_____

⑤ temperature of water in a pool

_____

⑥ mass of a person

_____

⑦ angle of a bend

_____

⑧ distance around a tree trunk

_____

⑨ the time it takes to write your name

_____

⑩ water in a bucket

_____

Write three different things you could measure with each unit.

⑪ metres

_____

_____

_____

⑫ minutes

_____

_____

_____

⑬ millilitres

_____

_____

_____

Are these quantities equal?
Write true or false.

⑭ $\frac{1}{2}$ kg = 50 g

_____

⑮ 200 mL = 0.2 L

_____

⑯ $\frac{1}{2}$ metre = 500 cm

_____

⑰ 300 minutes = 3 hours

_____

⑱ 120 seconds = 2 minutes

_____

Score 2 points for each correct answer!

SCORE /36 0-16 18-30 32-36

Problem Solving

AC9M5M02

Area and perimeter

The area of a rectangle is 24 square centimetres and each side is a whole number of centimetres.

What different lengths could the perimeter be? Write the side lengths too.

Area = 24 cm²

① _____
② _____
③ _____
④ _____

Grammar & Punctuation

AC9E5LA06, AC9E5LY06

Similes

Adjectives are often used in **similes**. A simile is used in poetry or descriptive writing to add richness to the text. Similes say how one thing is **like** another. They are usually phrases and often begin with the words **like** or **as**.

Examples:
The twins were <u>like two peas in a pod</u>.
Those two fight <u>like cats and dogs</u>.
Mum was <u>as busy as a bee</u>.
The boy was <u>as bright as a button</u>.

Underline the simile in each sentence.

① The baby was as good as gold when I looked after her.

② The thief was as bold as brass when he broke into the house.

③ My teacher has eyes like a hawk.

④ It was as clear as crystal what the man was trying to do.

⑤ I felt as wise as an owl when I got my test marks back.

⑥ I could sleep like a log after my long journey.

⑦ That girl can sing like an angel.

Choose the most suitable word/phrase from the box to complete the simile in each sentence.

toast	house	toddler's toy box
lion	firecracker	

⑧ My hair was as messy as a _____.

⑨ The angry woman exploded like a _____.

⑩ My dad is as tall as a _____.

⑪ I was as brave as a _____ at the dentist.

⑫ We were as warm as _____ in our beds.

Phonic Knowledge & Spelling

AC9E5LY09, AC9E5LY10

Suffix –ic

Say each word in the word bank. The words all end in the suffix **–ic**.

Word Bank

topic	tropic	toxic	music
panic	relic	fabric	garlic
attic	comic	classic	clinic
critic	scenic	historic	terrific

Choose words from the word bank to complete these sentences.

① During our _____ tour, we saw an ancient monument.

② I panicked when I tore the _____ of the expensive shirt.

③ Dad sometimes puts too much _____ in the Bolognese!

④ It's a healthy pastime to dance to _____.

Add the suffix –al to these words to make adjectives.

⑤ critic _____

⑥ tropic _____

⑦ historic _____

⑧ music _____

–ic or –ick?

Some words that make the 'ick' sound end in **–ic** and others end in **–ick**.

How do you know which suffix to use?

If the word only has one syllable, it usually ends in **–ick**. *Examples:* st**ick**, br**ick**, t**ick**

If it has two or more syllables, it usually ends in **–ic**. *Examples:* pan**ic**, trop**ic**, elast**ic**

Exceptions – Compound words can end in **–ick**. *Examples:* candlest**ick**, homes**ick**

More exceptions: gimm**ick**, roll**ick**, foss**ick**

Sort these words into –ick or –ic endings. Write the words in the correct column.

traffic automatic thick flick fantastic
wick ethnic chick

⑨ –ick   ⑩ –ic

_____   _____

_____   _____

_____   _____

_____   _____

TARGETING HOMEWORK 5 © PASCAL PRESS ISBN 9781925726473

AC9E5LY04, AC9E5LY05, AC9E5LY06

Imaginative text – Poems
Authors – Stewart Mackay and James Reeves

The Sea

The sea is a hungry dog,
Giant and grey.
He rolls on the beach all day.
With his clashing teeth and shaggy jaws
Hour upon hour he gnaws
The rumbling, tumbling stones,
And 'Bones, bones, bones, bones!'
The giant sea-dog moans,
Licking his greasy paws.

And when the night wind roars
And the moon rocks in the stormy cloud,
He bounds to his feet and snuffs and sniffs,
Shaking his wet sides over the cliffs,
And howls and hollos long and loud.

But on quiet days in May or June,
When even the grasses on the dune
Play no more their reedy tune,
With his head between his paws
He lies on the sandy shores,
So quiet, so quiet, he scarcely snores.

James Reeves

My puppy

We have a new puppy, as fat as butter,
He moves about like a clockwork toy.
As he walks, the legs just stutter,
Tripping around like an unfettered buoy.

Inside his mouth is a bundle of pins,
His tongue, like a sponge, just drips on the mat.
When he hears my voice the madness begins,
And he runs in circles like a scalded cat.

With eyes like coal and a nose to match,
His corner flag ears and semaphore tail.
His coat resembles a cottage thatch,
And three of his feet are the colour of ale.

This is my puppy and I love him to bits,
And I would not swap him for all the world.
As I write this, he quietly sits,
Waiting for mayhem to again unfurl.

Stewart Mackay

Source: The Sea © James Reeves from COMPLETE POEMS
FOR CHILDREN (Faber Finds), *My Puppy* by Stewart Mackay

Write or circle the correct answers.

① **What is the poem *The Sea* about?**

   a a dog   b the sea   c a storm

② **A metaphor is when you say something *is* something else. Write a sentence from one of the poems that gives an example of a metaphor.**

_____

③ **A simile says how one thing is *like* something else. Similes are usually phrases and often begin with the words 'like' or 'as'.**

Write two examples of similes from either poem.

_____

_____

④ **Onomatopoeia are words that sound like their meaning. Circle the words that are onomatopoeic.**

   a beach   d cloud   g tail
   b clashing   e flop   h howls
   c rumbling   f snuffs

Choose words from the poems that have these meanings.

⑤ long and untidy: sh_____

⑥ hardly: s_____

⑦ loose, free: un_____

⑧ injured with a hot liquid: sc_____

⑨ a roof covering of reeds or straw:
th_____

⑩ chaos: m_____

⑪ **How does James Reeves describe the behaviour of the sea on stormy days as that of a dog?**

_____

_____

My Book Review

Title _____

Author _____

Rating ☆☆☆☆☆

Comment _____

_____

Score 2 points for
each correct answer!

SCORE **/22** (0-8) (10-16) (18-22)

TERM 1 MATHS

Number & Algebra

AC9M5N03

Fractions

Look at the fraction bars below. Colour the following fractional parts of each bar.

① $\frac{1}{2}$

② $\frac{2}{3}$

③ $\frac{1}{4}$

④ $\frac{4}{5}$

⑤ $\frac{6}{6}$

⑥ $\frac{3}{7}$

⑦ $\frac{1}{2}$

⑧ 1

⑨ $\frac{1}{10}$

Use the fraction bars above to help you answer these questions.

⑩ Circle the largest fraction.

    a $\frac{1}{2}$ b $\frac{1}{5}$ c $\frac{1}{10}$

⑪ Circle the smallest fraction.

    a $\frac{1}{2}$ b $\frac{1}{5}$ c $\frac{1}{10}$

⑫ Write these fractions in order from smallest to largest.

$$\frac{1}{9}, \frac{1}{5}, \frac{1}{3}, \frac{1}{6}, \frac{1}{8}, \frac{1}{7}, \frac{1}{10}, \frac{1}{4}, \frac{1}{1}, \frac{1}{2}$$

_____

Write true or false.

⑬ $\frac{2}{3}$ is larger than $\frac{1}{2}$ _____

⑭ $\frac{2}{4}$ is equal to $\frac{1}{2}$ _____

⑮ $\frac{1}{7}$ is smaller than $\frac{1}{10}$ _____

⑯ $\frac{10}{10}$ is equal to $\frac{5}{5}$ _____

⑰ $\frac{3}{6}$ is smaller than $\frac{3}{7}$ _____

Write these fractions on the number lines.

⑱ $\frac{1}{8}$ ⑲ $\frac{4}{8}$ ⑳ $\frac{7}{8}$ ㉑ $\frac{9}{8}$ ㉒ $1\frac{1}{2}$

0                               $\frac{8}{8}$

1                            $1\frac{7}{8}$ 2

Statistics & Probability

AC9M5P02

What are the chances?

We can use **fractions** to represent **probability chances**.

- If the chance of spinning green on a spinner is 1 out of 4, we say it has a probability of $\frac{1}{4}$.
- If the chance of rolling a die and getting a three is 1 in 6, we say it has a probability of $\frac{1}{6}$.
- If the chance of picking a red marble out of a bag is 3 out of 12, we say it has a probability of $\frac{3}{12}$.

Write the probability fractions in the box beside the correct events.

$$\frac{1}{1000} \quad \frac{1}{1} \quad \frac{1}{3} \quad \frac{1}{20} \quad \frac{1}{6} \quad \frac{1}{2}$$

① I will pull out the only red marble from a bag of 20 marbles. ____

② Jack will throw a 5 with a regular die. ____

③ Su will flip a coin and it will land on heads. ____

④ You will spin blue on a spinner evenly divided into red, blue and green. ____

⑤ Ada will win first prize in a raffle that has one thousand tickets. ____

⑥ The sun will rise tomorrow. ____

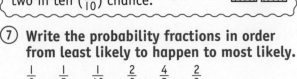

A one in ten chance ($\frac{1}{10}$) has less chance of happening than a one in five ($\frac{1}{5}$) chance.

A two in three chance ($\frac{2}{3}$) is more likely to happen than a two in ten ($\frac{2}{10}$) chance.

⑦ **Write the probability fractions in order from least likely to happen to most likely.**

$$\frac{1}{2} \quad \frac{1}{5} \quad \frac{1}{10} \quad \frac{2}{2} \quad \frac{4}{5} \quad \frac{2}{3}$$

_____

Write true or false.

⑧ When you roll a die, there is a $\frac{1}{6}$ chance that you will roll a 2. _____

⑨ When you toss a coin, there is a $\frac{1}{1}$ chance it will land on a tail. _____

⑩ When choosing a day, there is a $\frac{2}{7}$ chance that the day begins with a T. _____

⑪ When putting on your socks there is a $\frac{1}{4}$ chance of putting the right sock on first.
_____

⑫ When a baby is born, there is a $\frac{1}{2}$ chance that it will be a girl. _____

⑬ When choosing a name, there is a $\frac{1}{26}$ chance that the name will begin with K.
_____

SCORE **/26** (0-10) (12-20) (22-26)

Measurement & Space

AC9M5M01

Capacity

Capacity is the amount a container can hold. The capacity of smaller amounts is measured in **millilitres** (mL). The capacity of larger amounts is measured in **litres** (L).

Write the correct capacity above each item. Choose from the amounts in the box.

5 mL	50 L	1.7 mL	1.7 L
4 mL	4 L	200 mL	200 L
2 mL	2 L	10 mL	10 L

① _____

② _____

③ _____

④ _____

⑤ _____

⑥ _____

Calculate the capacity.

Remember: 1000 mL = 1 litre

500 mL = $\frac{1}{2}$ litre

⑦

capacity of each
= _____ mL

⑧

capacity of each
= _____ mL

SCORE **/16** (0-6) (8-12) (14-16)

Problem Solving

AC9M5M03

Time puzzles

Sometimes it helps to work backwards in order to work out the answer to a problem.

Example:

Ben was walking home from his gran's house. It took him $1\frac{1}{2}$ hours to walk from his gran's to the park. He stopped at the park for 25 minutes then he walked for another 50 minutes. Ben arrived home at 3:30 pm. What time did he leave his gran's house?

Solution:

Start at 3:30 pm and work backwards. From 3:30, take away 50 minutes to get 2:40 pm. From 2:40 pm, take away 25 minutes to get 2:15 pm as the time he arrived at the park. Then take away 1 hour 30 minutes, which makes it 12:45 pm when Ben left his gran's house.

Hint: Check that your answer is correct by starting at 12:45 pm and adding on the times.

Solve this time puzzle in the same way.

Jade's family went for a Sunday walk.

It took them 30 minutes to walk to the beach. They had some lunch and played on the beach for an hour before taking the walking track to the lookout. It took them 40 minutes to reach the lookout. They stayed there for 10 minutes then walked home the short way, along the footpath. This took them 45 minutes. They arrived home at 4:15 pm.

What time did they leave home?

_____

TERM 1 ENGLISH

Grammar & Punctuation

AC9E5LA05

Simple sentences and statements

A **simple sentence** has a subject and a verb and (usually) other information.

Examples: Trad **played** hockey in the park.
subject   verb

Thousands of people **watched** the eclipse.

A **statement** is a sentence that tells us about everyday things, facts and ideas. Statements begin with a capital letter and end with a **full stop**.

Underline the subjects and circle the verbs in these statements.

① Jasmine cycled all the way to her cousin's house.

② Tracy and Tamsin play netball every Saturday.

③ The eastern pygmy possum of Australia can hibernate for a long time.

④ Lee's father owns the local bakery.

Simple sentences and objects

Many sentences also contain an **object**. An object is someone or something that receives the action of the subject.

Examples:
The caterpillar **ate** several cabbage leaves.
subject   verb   object

Underline the objects in these statements.

⑤ The race horses crossed the finish line together.

⑥ The policeman rescued the elderly lady from her crashed car.

⑦ We found fifteen broken bottles and five empty cans in the park.

⑧ The cheetah tried to capture a young wildebeest.

Phonic Knowledge & Spelling

AC9E5LY09

Words that begin with a soft `c` and a soft `g` sound

Say each word in the word bank. The words begin with a soft **c** or a soft **g** sound.

Word Bank

citizen	citrus	circus	circle
cycle	cyclone	cement	centre
giant	ginger	gymnast	genius
general	generous	germs	gesture

Choose words from the word bank to complete these sentences.

① "Would you like some _____ fruit instead of an apple?" she asked.

② The _____ waved to her parents sitting in the stadium as she passed by.

③ All homes in a _____ region need to be built strong enough to withstand the strong winds and rain.

Add these prefixes to the word cycle to make new words. Write the words.

④ bi + cycle = _____

⑤ tri + cycle = _____

⑥ uni + cycle = _____

⑦ re + cycle = _____

⑧ mono + cycle = _____

⑨ hemi + cycle = _____

Match the words from the box to their meanings.

circle circuit circular circulate circulation

⑩ movement to and fro, or around something: _____

⑪ a round, 2D shape: _____

⑫ to move continuously in an area: _____

⑬ having the shape of a circle: _____

⑭ a circular route: _____

Score 2 points for each correct answer! **SCORE** **/16** (0-6) (8-12) (14-16)

Score 2 points for each correct answer! **SCORE** **/28** (0-12) (14-22) (24-28)

TARGETING HOMEWORK 5 © PASCAL PRESS ISBN 9781925726473

Box Night News

"Get a move on, Kevin, or by the time you deliver those papers they'll be old news."

"Just leaving now, Mr Bates."

I throw the last of the morning newspapers in my satchel and scurry out the back of Bates's General Store. Elvis is waiting for me in the lane. He races to the end of the street and woofs at me to hurry along.

My dad named him Elvis after his favourite singer, Elvis Presley. Whenever dad and I visit the milk bar we always play Elvis songs on the jukebox.

I haul my bicycle away from the shop and begin my paper run. I've only just taken up delivering the morning papers. Elvis really likes it. He gets to sniff his way around the neighbourhood.

My suburb, Wattle Grove, is fairly new. Most of the houses look the same apart from different plants in the garden or the letterbox. The fibro houses sit neatly in rows on big flat blocks. Wattle Grove is a really friendly place to live and almost everyone knows each other.

Elvis races ahead sniffing every letterbox and the occasional plant. I practise my javelin throw by hurling the morning newspaper into front yards.

Imaginative text – Narrative
Author – Lisa Thompson
Illustrator – Serena Geddes

I'd never heard of javelin until I saw it on the television when the Melbourne Olympics were on. Mum and Dad took my older brother Robert and me into the city and we saw a television in the shop window. That was the first time Robert and I ever saw one. The picture was black and white and a bit grainy, sometimes it even rolled around a bit, but we couldn't take our eyes off that magic box.

We begged Dad to buy one. He just laughed and told us to keep dreaming, they were so expensive.

I wave to Mr Corvini as he waters his tomato plants. Mr Corvini moved here from Italy. He makes the best pasta sauce. Whenever he makes a new batch he always gives Mum a few jars.

"You no use any other sauce once you try mine," he likes to say proudly, and he's right.

There are lots of people in my suburb from different countries — Poland, Germany, Hungary, England and Italy.

Most moved to Australia after the war. My neighbour, Mrs Dodunski, is from Poland. Whenever I complain about the cold in winter she laughs at me and says I don't know what cold really is.

Source: *Box Night News*, Sparklers, Blake Education.

Write or circle the correct answers.

① **What type of text is this?**

   a discussion   b explanation   c narrative

② **Write three words or phrases from the 3rd or 4th paragraphs that tell you that this story is set in the past.**

_____

_____

③ **What is a jukebox?**

   a a type of music

   b a machine that plays music after a coin has been inserted

   c a record

④ **Which is the odd word?**

   a occasional   c frequent

   b regular   d constant

⑤ **What is a fibro house?**

   a a house made from fibrous cement sheeting

   b a new house

   c an old house

Score 2 points for each correct answer! **SCORE** /10   0-2   4-8   10

My Book Review

Title _____

Author _____

Rating ☆☆☆☆☆

Comment _____

_____

UNIT 6

Number & Algebra

AC9M5N01

Place value

Digits have different values depending on their place in the number. We can expand a number to show the value of each digit.

32 486

ten thousands hundreds tens ones
thousands

Examples:

32 486 = 30 000 + 2000 + 400 + 80 + 6

5674 = 5000 + 600 + 70 + 4

Expand these numbers.

① 8439 = _____

_____

② 6215 = _____

_____

③ 14 636 = _____

_____

④ 38 051 = _____

_____

Example: 5 632 821

We read this number as: five million, six hundred and thirty-two thousand, eight hundred and twenty-one.

Here is **5 632 821** in a place value grid:

	M	H Th	T Th	Th	H	T	O
	5	6	3	2	8	2	1
⑤							
⑥							
⑦							
⑧							
⑨							
⑩							

Write these numbers in the place value grid above.

⑪ sixteen thousand four hundred and eighty-three

⑫ 568 349

⑬ three million, nine hundred and forty thousand, seven hundred and thirty-five

⑭ twenty-seven thousand and ninety-nine

⑮ one hundred and sixty-two thousand, four hundred and eighty

⑯ 7 804 293

Write the value of the 7 in each number.

⑰ 247 805 _____

⑱ 7 234 651 _____

⑲ 700 453 _____

⑳ 608 741 _____

Write the number 1000 smaller and 1000 larger than the given number.

	1000 smaller	1000 larger
54 678	53 678	55 678
㉑ 28 401	_____	_____
㉒ 45 900	_____	_____
㉓ 39 439	_____	_____
㉔ 135 688	_____	_____
㉕ 899 651	_____	_____
㉖ 5 675 449	_____	_____

Score 2 points for each correct answer!

SCORE **/52** (0-24) (26-46) (48-52)

Statistics & Probability

There are no statistics & probability activities in this unit.

Measurement & Space

AC9M5M01

Mass

Mass or weight is measured in **milligrams (mg), grams (g), kilograms (kg)** and **tonnes (t).**

Examples:

• The ingredients in a vitamin pill are measured in milligrams.

• A paperclip has a mass of approximately 1 gram.

• A 1 litre bottle of water has a mass of approximately 1 kilogram.

• A small car has a mass of approximately 1 tonne.

1000 mg = 1 g
1000 g = 1 kg
1000 kg = 1 tonne

TARGETING HOMEWORK 5 © PASCAL PRESS ISBN 9781925726473

Match each object to a suitable unit for measuring its mass.

| milligrams | grams | kilograms | tonnes |

①  _____

②  _____

③  _____

④  _____

Example: 1 kg 400 g can be written as 1.4 kg or 1400 g.

Circle the three masses that are equal in each set.

⑤ 5500 g
5.5 kg
55 kg
5 kg 500 g
550 mg

⑥ 1.02 kg
1 kg 200 g
1.2 kg
1200 g
220 g

⑦ 2 kg 300 g
230 kg
2300 g
2.3 kg
2.03 kg

To convert kilograms to grams, you multiply by 1000.
Examples:
2 kg × 1000 = 2000 g
3.5 kg × 1000 = 3500 g

Convert these masses from kilograms to grams.

⑧ 5 kg = _____ g

⑨ 7 kg = _____ g

⑩ 12 kg = _____ g

⑪ 25 kg = _____ g

⑫ 2.5 kg = _____ g

⑬ 6.4 kg = _____ g

To convert grams to kilograms, you divide by 1000.
Examples:
5000 g ÷ 1000 = 5 kg
1400 g ÷ 1000 = 1.4 kg
1250 g ÷ 1000 = 1.25 kg

Convert these masses from grams to kilograms.

⑭ 4000 g = _____ kg

⑮ 7000 g = _____ kg

⑯ 15 000 g = _____ kg

⑰ 32 000 g = _____ kg

⑱ 4500 g = _____ kg

⑲ 1450 g = _____ kg

Score 2 points for each correct answer! | SCORE | /38 | 0-16 | 18-32 | 34-38 |

Problem Solving

AC9M5M01

Fairground puzzles

Solve these problems.

① A fairground ride has a maximum weight of 75 kg per carriage. There are three carriages on the ride. Only two people are allowed in each carriage. Work out who could sit in each carriage.

• Mignonne 40 kg

• Su 48 kg

• Kate 35 kg

• Tamsin 25 kg

• Max 50 kg

• Tim 26 kg

Carriage 1 could hold:

_____

Carriage 2 could hold:

_____

Carriage 3 could hold:

_____

② Max bought a bag of chocolates. The bag had a mass of 150 g. He shared the chocolates evenly with his 5 friends. How many grams of chocolates did each person get?

_____

TERM 1 ENGLISH

Grammar & Punctuation

AC9E5LA05

Verb groups

> A **verb group** has more than one verb. The last verb in the group is the main verb, the other words are 'helping' or **auxiliary verbs**. Auxiliary verbs can tell us when something happened — now, past, ongoing or future.
>
> *Examples:*   Beccy **is writing**. (now)
> auxiliary verb ⟨ ⟩ main verb
>
>   We **have eaten** our lunch. (past)

Underline the verb groups in these sentences.

① My dad has been to Switzerland.

② The kittens were sleeping in the sun.

③ Jackie is building a model aeroplane.

Prepositions in verb groups

> A verb group can be made up of a verb + **preposition**. Prepositions can tell us where and when people or things are positioned. Some examples are: on, away, down, off, up.
>
> *Examples:*   I <u>hung **out**</u> all the washing.
>   verb ⟨ ⟩ preposition
>   The runners <u>filled **up**</u> their water bottles.

Underline the verb groups in these sentences. Circle the prepositions.

④ I turned off the television in the living room.

⑤ Riley tripped over a rocky outcrop.

⑥ Harry will give away all of his unused toys!

Write a suitable preposition to complete the verb groups.

⑦ I took _____ all my wet clothes and put _____ my robe.

⑧ We will look _____ our neighbour's dog while he is away.

⑨ The students are putting _____ all their books.

Phonic Knowledge & Spelling

AC9E5LY09

Words ending in 'a' or 'ar'

Say each word in the word bank. The words make the same sound at the end, but some words end in **a** and some end in **ar**.

Word Bank

area	extra	pasta	panda
camera	cinema	vanilla	umbrella
dollar	cellar	solar	polar
hangar	vinegar	regular	angular

Choose words from the word bank to complete these sentences.

① Last month we went to the _____ to see my favourite movie.

② I seldom put _____ on my chips, I prefer to just have salt.

③ We regularly eat _____ on a Friday night.

Homophones

> **Homophones** are words that sound the same but have different spellings and meanings.

Choose the correct homophone to complete the sentences.

④ I hung my jacket up on the (hangar   hanger).

⑤ At the winery, the wine barrels were kept in the (seller   cellar).

⑥ The ice-cream (seller   cellar) parked his van near our street.

⑦ The plane was kept in a (hangar   hanger) near the airport.

Match the words from the box to their meanings.

beggar   peculiar   lunar   spectacular   familiar

⑧ amazing in a dramatic way: _____

⑨ well known to you: _____

⑩ person who begs for food or money: _____

⑪ different to what is normal: _____

⑫ relating to the moon: _____

TERM 1 ENGLISH

The New Supermarket

Persuasive text – Argument
Author – Frances Mackay

Say NO!

Do we really need another supermarket in our community? Any intelligent person would say no! Why? Well firstly, we already have a supermarket in the area so there is no need for another one.

Secondly, we need all the green spaces we can get! Some of our precious green spaces have already been swallowed up by a new housing scheme, so we don't want to lose any more for the sake of a supermarket.

The real truth is — we don't need another supermarket — and that's a fact!

Therefore, fight with us against the planned supermarket — for all our sakes!

Say YES!

The nation's favourite supermarket chain is planning to open near you soon. Yes, that's right, you will no longer have to travel to get the best quality food and household wares because the very best will be right on your doorstep.

We aim to build a brand new shopping complex with free parking, an adventure playground and free crèche facilities. We will also provide a free hourly bus service to our store! What more could you ask for?

The current supermarket is outdated and tired. There are insufficient parking spaces and limited facilities. In contrast, our state-of-the-art complex will be bigger, brighter and more convenient. Surely you can't afford to miss out on all these advantages — so make sure you support us!

Write or circle the correct answer.

① **What type of texts are these?**
 a narrative   c recount
 b advertisement   d argument

② **What is the aim of the two texts?**
_____
_____

Write fact or opinion next to each phrase or sentence.

③ Any intelligent person would say no!
_____

④ ... we already have a supermarket in the area ... _____

⑤ The nation's favourite supermarket chain ...
_____

⑥ ... we need all the green spaces we can get!
_____

⑦ **Who has written the text for the 'Yes' campaign?**
 a a builder
 b someone representing the new supermarket
 c someone representing the current supermarket

⑧ **List two reasons the 'no' campaigners provide for rejecting the new supermarket.**
_____
_____

⑨ **List two reasons the 'yes' campaigners provide for accepting the new supermarket.**
_____
_____

Score 2 points for each correct answer!

SCORE **/18**   (0-6) (8-14) (16-18)

My Book Review

Title _____

Author _____

Rating ☆☆☆☆☆

Comment _____
_____

TERM 1 MATHS

Number & Algebra

AC9M5N01

Decimal place value

A **decimal number** is another way of expressing a **fraction**.

This diagram shows you the place value names for a large decimal number:

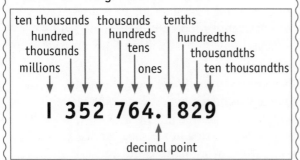

ten thousands · thousands · tenths
hundred thousands · hundreds · hundredths
tens · thousandths
millions · ones · ten thousandths

1 352 764.1829

decimal point

Here are the values of the digits after the decimal number:

- 0.1 or one **tenth** or $\frac{1}{10}$
- 0.08 or eight **hundredths** or $\frac{8}{100}$.
- 0.002 or two **thousandths** or $\frac{2}{1000}$.
- 0.0009 or nine **ten-thousandths** or $\frac{9}{10000}$.

This is a smaller number. Look at the value of each digit.

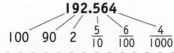

192.564

100 · 90 · 2 · $\frac{5}{10}$ · $\frac{6}{100}$ · $\frac{4}{1000}$

Circle the correct answer.

① How many tenths in 1.24?
   a 1   b 2   c 4

② How many hundredths in 24.56?
   a 4   b 5   c 6

③ How many thousandths in 0.159?
   a 1   b 5   c 9

④ How many ones in 5.678?
   a 5   b 6   c 7

⑤ How many hundredths in 536.982?
   a 3   b 9   c 8

Circle the correct value of the digit in bold in these numbers.

⑥ 56.**2**4
   a 2   b 20   c $\frac{2}{10}$ d $\frac{2}{100}$

⑦ 2**5**4.18
   a 5   b 50   c $\frac{5}{10}$ d $\frac{5}{1000}$

⑧ 187.**7**
   a 7   b 70   c $\frac{7}{10}$ d $\frac{7}{100}$

⑨ 4562.**8**94
   a $\frac{4}{10}$ b 4   c 40   d $\frac{4}{1000}$

⑩ 5603.296**5**
   a 5 000   b 50   c $\frac{5}{1000}$ d $\frac{5}{10000}$

Writing fractions as decimals

Complete the table.

Fraction	Decimal
$\frac{2}{10}$	0.2
⑪ $\frac{3}{10}$	
$\frac{5}{100}$	0.05
⑫ $\frac{54}{100}$	
$\frac{3}{1000}$	0.003
⑬ $\frac{8}{1000}$	
⑭ $\frac{458}{1000}$	
$\frac{5}{10000}$	0.0005
⑮ $\frac{3457}{10000}$	

Score 2 points for each correct answer!

SCORE **/30**   0–12   14–24   26–30

Statistics & Probability

AC9M5ST01, AC9M5ST03

Column graphs

Lee did a survey of the students in her class on how often they walk to school. Lee recorded the results in a frequency table.

Walk to school	Tally	Frequency
Always	卌 卌	10
Often	卌 II	7
Sometimes	III	3
Never	卌 卌 卌	15
	Total	35

① **Use the data in the table to complete this column graph.**

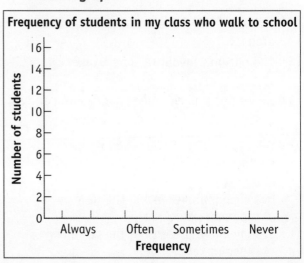

Frequency of students in my class who walk to school

Number of students
16
14
12
10
8
6
4
2
0
Always   Often   Sometimes   Never
Frequency

② Lee also surveyed her class on favourite hobbies. Complete her frequency table.

Hobbies	Tally	Frequency
Sport	╫╫ ╫╫ ╫╫	15
Computer games	╫╫ IIII	
Reading		2
Bike riding	III	
Collecting		1
Cooking/making	╫╫	
	Total	

If you drew a column graph for Lee's data, what would be:

③ the title?

_____

④ the label on the vertical axis?

_____

⑤ the label on the horizontal axis?

_____

⑥ the hobby with the shortest column?

_____

⑦ the hobby with the tallest column?

_____

Score 2 points for each correct answer! SCORE  /14 (0-4) (6-10) (12-14)

Measurement & Space

AC9M5M01

Temperature

Thermometers are used to measure temperature in **degrees Celsius** (°C). Different types of thermometers are used for different purposes.

This is a **medical thermometer**:

It is used to measure the temperature of human bodies. The human body normally has a temperature of 37 °C, so a medical thermometer only has a range of 35 °C to 42 °C.

① The red line on the medical thermometer shows the temperature. What temperature does it show? _____

② If the temperature on the medical thermometer fell by 4 degrees, what would the new temperature be? _____

This is a **weather thermometer**. It measures the temperature of the air. The numbers below zero are negative or minus numbers. They show when the temperature is below zero degrees Celsius.

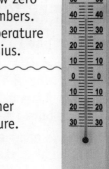

③ Circle the range of temperatures the weather thermometer can measure.
  a 0 °C to 50 °C
  b −30 °C to 50 °C
  c 30 °C to 50 °C

④ What temperature does the weather thermometer show? _____

⑤ How many degrees Celsius does each mark on the thermometer represent? _____

⑥ If the temperature on this thermometer rose by 6 degrees, what would the new temperature be? _____

⑦ If the temperature on this thermometer fell by 50 degrees, what would the new temperature be? _____

Score 2 points for each correct answer! SCORE  /14 (0-4) (6-10) (12-14)

Problem Solving

AC9M5M01

Temperature puzzles

Answer the questions. Show your working out.

① When Jackson left home this morning, the temperature was 14 °C. By 3 pm, the temperature had risen to 25 °C. By how much had the temperature risen?

_____

② The weather for Saturday was predicted to be 31 °C. The actual temperature was 8 degrees lower than predicted. What was the temperature reached on Saturday?

_____

③ The recipe said to set the oven at 180 °C. Sam set it 18 degrees lower. What temperature did Sam set the oven at?

_____

④ The temperature at 6 pm was 25 degrees Celsius. During the night, the temperature dropped by 13 degrees. What was the lowest temperature recorded that night?

_____

Grammar & Punctuation

AC9E5LA09

Apostrophe for ownership

An **apostrophe (')** is used to show ownership.

For a single owner, add **'s**.

Examples: the bird**'s** nest (the nest belonging to the bird)

Tom**'s** book (the book belonging to Tom)

If a person's name ends in **s**, add the apostrophe after the **s**. *Example:* Chris' book

NOTE: Chris**'s** book is also correct.

For more than one owner (plural nouns that already end in **s**), put the apostrophe after the **s**.

Examples: the birds' nests (the nests belonging to the birds)

my parents' house (the house belonging to both of my parents)

Add the apostrophes to these sentences.

① The dogs tail was wagging happily.

② The girls coats were hanging up in the hallway.

③ I put the books back in Tinas room.

④ Mum picked up Tims bag and Helens suitcase.

Apostrophes with plural subjects

Look at these examples:

Judy and Michael**'s** children (the children belonging to Judy and Michael)

Su**'s** and Tracy**'s** bikes (they both have their own bike)

Add the apostrophes to these sentences.

⑤ Tony and Saras cat is a blue Persian.

⑥ Riley and Jacks mother came to collect them after school.

⑦ Mandys and Cams toys were sold at the fair.

⑧ Johnno loaned me his dads camera.

⑨ Lisa and Tanya copied Annas dance steps.

⑩ Galen played a game on his brothers phone.

Phonic Knowledge & Spelling

AC9E5LY09

Words that end in 'y'

Say each word in the word bank. All the words end in **y**.

Word Bank

army	fussy	diary	dairy
poetry	beauty	wallaby	every
entry	sentry	enemy	energy
empty	duty	jury	juicy

Choose words from the word bank to complete these sentences.

① My sister is allergic to all types of _____ food.

② My cousin is very _____ about the style of clothes she wears.

③ The word 'entry' rhymes with _____.

The 'y' rule

If a word ends in **y**, we usually change the **y** to **i** before adding an ending.

Examples: bus**y**, bus**iest** empt**y**, empt**ied**

Exceptions to the rule:

You do **not** change the **y** to **i** when adding **–ing**.

Example: hurr**y**, hurr**ied**, hurr**ying**

You do **not** change the **y** to **i** before adding an ending if the letter before the **y** is a vowel.

Example: obe**y**, obe**ys**, obe**yed**, obe**ying**

Add the endings **–ed**, **–ing** and **–est** to these words. Write the new words.

④ steady

_____

_____

_____

⑤ dirty

_____

_____

_____

⑥ tidy

_____

_____

_____

 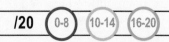

TERM 1 ENGLISH

How does a bicycle reflector work?

Informative text – Explanation
Author – Frances Mackay

Most bicycles have reflectors on the back, front and wheels of the bicycle as a safety measure for cyclists riding at night. Their purpose is to warn other road users that the cyclist is there. But how do they work?

When light hits an object, it can go through it (transmit), bounce off (reflect) or be stopped (absorbed). A bicycle reflector is made to reflect light straight back with a minimum scattering of light.

The reflector itself is usually made from transparent plastic. The outside surface is very smooth. This allows light (such as from a car's headlights or from a torch) to enter the reflector. The back of the reflector is made up of lots of angled prisms. The light enters the reflector, hits the prisms and is directed back out the front of the reflector in the direction it came from. This alerts the person close to the light source, such as the driver of a vehicle, that the cyclist is there.

These types of reflectors can also be used on road surfaces, road signs, vehicles and clothing. A pedestrian can see these reflectors in the dark only if there is a light source directly between them and the reflector (such as via a torch they are carrying) or directly behind them (such as via a car approaching from behind).

Do you also need lights on your bicycle?

In many countries bicycles are required by law to have a front and rear light — so you may be breaking the law if you do not have them. Reflectors do not always work. Sometimes the reflector may be outside the beam of the car's headlights and the cyclist's reflector will not be seen. Reflectors do not work in fog and if they are dirty, they will not reflect back light. So it is much safer to ride at night with lights.

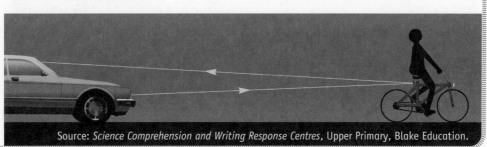

Source: *Science Comprehension and Writing Response Centres*, Upper Primary, Blake Education.

Write or circle the correct answers.

1. **What type of text is this?**

   a narrative   b explanation   c procedure

Which words in the text have these meanings?

2. to bounce off: r_____

3. the smallest amount: m_____

4. see-through: t_____

5. a person walking: p_____

6. **Name the three things that light can do when it hits an object.**

   _____
   _____
   _____

7. **Explain what happens when the light from a car headlight hits a reflector.**

   _____
   _____

8. **What does via mean?**

   a behind   b next to   c by means of

9. **Another word for alerts is:**

   a lights.   b reflects.   c warns.

10. **Give two reasons why a reflector on a bicycle may not work.**

    _____
    _____

Score 2 points for each correct answer!

SCORE **/20** (0-8) (10-14) (16-20)

My Book Review

Title _____

Author _____

Rating ☆☆☆☆☆

Comment _____

_____

TERM 1 MATHS

Number & Algebra

AC9M5N05

Adding and subtracting fractions

Look at this fraction:

$\frac{3}{4}$ ← The digit on the top is called the **numerator**.

← The digit on the bottom is called the **denominator**.

When we add or subtract fractions, we have to use the same denominator.

Examples:

$\frac{1}{6} + \frac{3}{6} = \frac{4}{6}$ one sixth plus three sixths = four sixths

$\frac{8}{10} - \frac{4}{10} = \frac{4}{10}$ eight tenths take away four tenths = four tenths

The things we add or subtract need to be **the same**. Think of it in the same way as one apple plus three apples equals four apples. Or eight pies take away four pies = four pies.

We can use diagrams to help us add and subtract fractions with the same denominator:

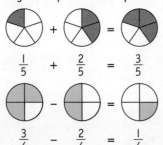

$\frac{1}{5} + \frac{2}{5} = \frac{3}{5}$

$\frac{3}{4} - \frac{2}{4} = \frac{1}{4}$

Colour the diagram and write the answer.

①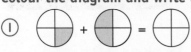

$\frac{1}{4} + \frac{2}{4} = $ ____

②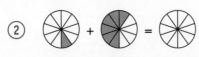

$\frac{1}{10} + \frac{6}{10} = $ ____

③

$\frac{3}{8} - \frac{2}{8} = $ ____

④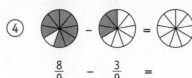

$\frac{8}{9} - \frac{3}{9} = $ ____

Complete these additions without a diagram.

⑤ $\frac{2}{4} + \frac{1}{4} = $ ____

⑥ $\frac{1}{6} + \frac{3}{6} = $ ____

⑦ $\frac{3}{8} + \frac{4}{8} = $ ____

⑧ $\frac{5}{10} + \frac{4}{10} = $ ____

⑨ $\frac{1}{4} + \frac{3}{4} = $ ____

⑩ $\frac{2}{5} + \frac{2}{5} = $ ____

Complete these subtractions without a diagram.

⑪ $\frac{6}{10} - \frac{2}{10} = $ ____

⑫ $\frac{7}{8} - \frac{1}{8} = $ ____

⑬ $\frac{5}{6} - \frac{3}{6} = $ ____

⑭ $\frac{9}{10} - \frac{8}{10} = $ ____

⑮ $\frac{4}{7} - \frac{2}{7} = $ ____

⑯ $\frac{8}{8} - \frac{2}{8} = $ ____

Score 2 points for each correct answer! SCORE **/32** 0-14 16-26 28-32

Measurement & Space

AC9M5SP03

2-D shapes

Here are the names of some 2D shapes.

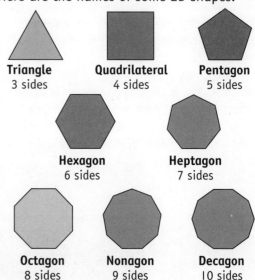

Triangle — 3 sides Quadrilateral — 4 sides Pentagon — 5 sides

Hexagon — 6 sides Heptagon — 7 sides

Octagon — 8 sides Nonagon — 9 sides Decagon — 10 sides

There are different types of **quadrilaterals**:

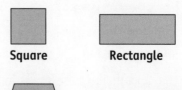

Square Rectangle Rhombus

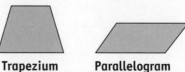

Trapezium Parallelogram Kite

NOTE: Parallel lines are lines that are the same distance apart.

Write the shape names below the correct meanings.

| square | triangle | pentagon |
| nonagon | trapezium | rectangle |

① a shape with nine sides

_____

② a shape with four sides and four right angles where the opposite sides are parallel and equal

_____

TARGETING HOMEWORK 5 © PASCAL PRESS ISBN 9781925726473

③ a shape with four equal sides and four right angles

_____

④ a shape with three sides and three angles

_____

⑤ a shape with five sides

_____

⑥ a four-sided shape with one pair of parallel sides

_____

Translation, reflection and rotation

When we slide a shape to move it to a different position, it is called a **translation**. The shape is not turned or flipped, it just slides.

- A **horizontal translation** is when the shape slides on a horizontal line.

- A **vertical translation** is when the shape slides on a vertical line.

When a shape is flipped over, it is called a **reflection** or mirror image.

- A **horizontal reflection** is when the shape flips over horizontally.

- A **vertical reflection** is when the shape flips vertically.

When a shape is turned, it is called a **rotation**.

How has the first shape been transformed to get the second shape? Circle the correct answer.

⑦
     a slide
     b reflection
     c rotation

⑧
     a slide
     b reflection
     c rotation

⑨
     a slide
     b reflection
     c rotation

⑩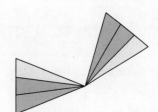
     a slide
     b reflection
     c rotation

⑪
     a slide
     b reflection
     c rotation

Score 2 points for each correct answer! **SCORE** **/22** (0-8) (10-16) (18-22)

Problem Solving

AC9M5SP01

Tangram puzzles

Tangrams are ancient Chinese puzzles. Trace this puzzle onto card. Cut out the pieces.

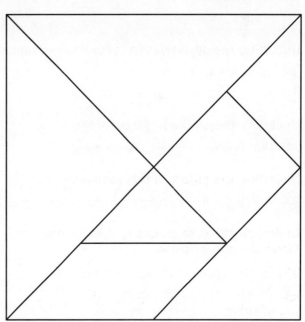

Make the shapes of these animals using all the pieces.

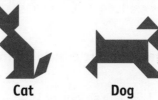

Cat   **Dog**   **Swan**

Rabbit   **Fish**   **Horse**

Grammar & Punctuation

Give all the proper nouns a capital letter.

① melanie lives in adelaide and her sister, jackie, lives in london.

② *the sea* is a well-known poem written by james reeves.

Write the plurals of these nouns.

③ village _____

④ eyelash _____

⑤ virus _____

⑥ trolley _____

Circle the key noun and underline the noun group in this sentence.

⑦ The clown wore a funny hat and enormous shoes.

Underline the determiners in these noun groups.

⑧ his bright hat

⑨ those old shoes

Underline the adjectives in these noun groups.

⑩ thick, woolly jumpers

⑪ an exciting new movie

Underline the simile in this sentence.

⑫ That boy can chatter like a monkey.

Underline the object in this statement.

⑬ The firefighter rescued the cat from the tree.

Underline the verb groups in these sentences. Circle the prepositions.

⑭ Emma tripped over her own shoelaces.

⑮ We will get up really early tomorrow morning.

Add the apostrophes to these sentences.

⑯ The horses rein was hanging loose.

⑰ The boys bikes were leaning up against the wall.

Underline the subject and circle the verb in this sentence.

⑱ The Tasmanian Tiger once roamed the bushland of Tasmania.

Score 2 points for each correct answer!   SCORE **/36** (0-16) (18-30) (32-36)

Phonic Knowledge & Spelling

Add –ed and –ing to these words. Decide if you need to double the last consonant.

	–ed	–ing
① picnic	_____	_____
② collect	_____	_____

Change these nouns into verbs by adding the suffix –ise. Write the new word.

③ vandal _____

④ terror _____

Build the new words by adding the suffix. Write the new word. Remember your rules!

⑤ adore + ing = _____

⑥ arrange + ment = _____

Circle the number of syllables in these words.

⑦ motivation   1   2   3   4

⑧ soloist   1   2   3   4

Add the suffix –al to make adjectives.

⑨ critic _____

⑩ historic _____

Choose the correct homophone to complete the sentences.

⑪ Frank keeps his plane in a (hanger   hangar) at the airport.

⑫ The hat (seller   cellar) sold me a baseball cap.

Write the plurals of these words.

⑬ wallaby _____

⑭ city _____

Add –er and –est to these words. Write the new words.

	–er	–est
⑮ lazy	_____	_____
⑯ empty	_____	_____

Make compound words by adding the prefix to the word cycle. Write the new words.

⑰ bi _____

⑱ mono _____

Score 2 points for each correct answer!   SCORE **/36** (0-16) (18-30) (32-36)

TARGETING HOMEWORK 5 © PASCAL PRESS ISBN 9781925726473

Forests

Informative text – Report
Author – Ian Rohr

A forest is an **ecosystem** dominated by trees. Forests cover about 30 per cent of the Earth's land surface.

Types of forests

There are three main types of forest: tropical forests (including rainforests), temperate forests and boreal forests.

Tropical forests grow in areas of high rainfall. They consist of tall trees, which form a **canopy**, and layers of shorter trees between the tallest trees and the ground. The Amazon rainforest in South America contains one-third of the world's trees.

Temperate forests contain mostly broad-leafed, **deciduous** trees with some **conifers**. They occur in warm, rainy climates.

Boreal forests consist of needle-leafed, **evergreen** conifers, such as pine trees. They grow in areas with short summers and long winters. Whereas rainforests contain many animal species, boreal forests have mainly birds and mammals, such as deer, wolves and rodents, and very few reptiles.

Forests and the planet

Forests play an important role in helping stabilise the Earth's climate. Forest trees absorb carbon dioxide and produce oxygen through a process known as **photosynthesis**.

Forests also help stabilise soil and prevent soil **erosion** by controlling the run-off of water after it rains. Without forests, a lot of soil, valuable for farming, can wash into waterways.

Source: *Conservation*, Go Facts, Blake Education.

Write or circle the correct answers.

1. **What do you think an ecosystem is?**

   a a type of forest

   b all the living things in an area

   c small trees

2. **What percentage of the Earth's surface is covered by forests?**

   _____

3. **Name the three types of forests.**

   _____

   _____

   _____

4. **Which continent contains one-third of the world's trees?**

   _____

5. **Which is the odd one out?**

   a soak up   c take in

   b absorb   d emit

Which words in the text have these meanings?

6. needle-leafed trees:
   c_____

7. make it unlikely to change:
   s_____

8. the process by which plants produce oxygen:
   p_____

9. the wearing away of soil:
   e_____

10. **Which type of forest would you find in Norway, which has short summers and long winters?**

    _____

11. **How do trees prevent soil erosion?**

    a by absorbing carbon dioxide

    b by attracting animals

    c by controlling water run-off after rain

Score 2 points for each correct answer!

SCORE  /22 (0-8) (10-16) (18-22)

TERM 1 MATHS

Number & Algebra

① List all the factors of 30.

_____

② Use skip counting to complete the multiples of 6: ____, ____, ____, 24, ____, ____.

Round these numbers to the nearest 10.

③ 53 _____

④ 239 _____

⑤ 1487 _____

Round these numbers to the nearest 100.

⑥ 382 _____

⑦ 1239 _____

⑧ 13 765 _____

⑨ Use the **lattice method to work out 15 × 23.**

15 × 23 = _____

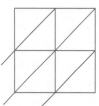

⑩ Complete the calculation using the **split method.**

$525 ÷ 5 = (500 + 25) ÷ 5$

= _____

= _____

= _____

Expand these numbers.

⑪ 5482 = _____

_____

⑫ 24 591 = _____

_____

⑬ 756 248 = _____

_____

Circle the correct value of the digit in bold.

⑭ 76.**3**3   a 3   b 30   c $\frac{3}{10}$ d $\frac{3}{100}$

⑮ 8**5**1.24   a 5   b 50   c $\frac{5}{10}$ d $\frac{5}{1000}$

⑯ 382.**7**   a 7   b 70   c $\frac{7}{10}$ d $\frac{7}{100}$

⑰ 4562.8**9**4   a $\frac{4}{10}$ b 4   c 40   d $\frac{4}{1000}$

⑱ **9**896.32   a $\frac{9}{1000}$ b 9   c 9000   d 900

Write these fractions as decimals.

⑲ $\frac{4}{10}$ = _____   ㉑ $\frac{15}{100}$ = _____

⑳ $\frac{5}{100}$ = _____   ㉒ $\frac{367}{1000}$ = _____

Complete these additions.

㉓ $\frac{2}{5} + \frac{1}{5}$ = _____   ㉕ $\frac{4}{10} + \frac{3}{10}$ = _____

㉔ $\frac{3}{7} + \frac{4}{7}$ = _____   ㉖ $1\frac{1}{5} + 1\frac{2}{5}$ = _____

Score 2 points for each correct answer! **SCORE** | **/52** | 0-24 | 26-46 | 48-52

Statistics & Probability

What is the probability of each colour on this spinner being spun? Circle the correct answer.

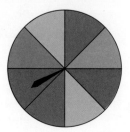

① purple   a $\frac{2}{4}$ b $\frac{1}{8}$ c $\frac{4}{1}$ d $\frac{2}{8}$

② orange   a $\frac{1}{4}$ b $\frac{3}{8}$ c $\frac{1}{8}$ d $\frac{8}{1}$

③ red   a $\frac{2}{8}$ b $\frac{2}{4}$ c $\frac{8}{2}$ d $\frac{1}{2}$

④ **Circle the question that would be better to ask than the sample question.**

Sample: Did you go to a restaurant last month? • Yes   • No

a How often did you go to a restaurant last month?   • never   • 1–2 times   • 3–4 times   • more than 4 times

b I went to a restaurant last month. Did you?   • Yes   • No

Write the probability fractions beside the correct events.

| $\frac{1}{2}$ | $\frac{1}{3}$ | $\frac{1}{6}$ | $\frac{1}{20}$ |

⑤ I will pull out the only green marble in a bag of 20 marbles.

_____

⑥ Jack will throw a 1 with a regular die.

_____

⑦ Sue will flip a coin and it will land on tails.

_____

⑧ He will spin blue on a spinner that is evenly divided into red, blue and green.

_____

TARGETING HOMEWORK 5 © PASCAL PRESS ISBN 9781925726473

Jayne did a survey of the students in her class on their favourite animal. Complete her table of results.

	Animals	Tally	Frequency
	Dog	ⅢⅠⅢ	9
⑨	Dolphin		6
⑩	Cat	ⅢⅠ	
⑪	Elephant	ⅢⅠ	
	Snake	ⅠⅠ	2
⑫	Tiger		4
	Whale	ⅢⅠ	5
⑬		**Total**	

If you drew a column graph for Jayne's data, what would be:

⑭ the title?

_____

⑮ the label on the vertical axis?

_____

⑯ the label on the horizontal axis?

_____

⑰ the animal with the shortest column?

_____

⑱ the animal with the tallest column?

_____

Score 2 points for each correct answer! SCORE **/36** (0-16) (18-30) (32-36)

Measurement & Space

Measure these lines in millimetres.

①

②

Write these 12-hour times as 24-hour times.

③ 6 am _____ ⑤ 4:20 pm _____
④ 2:30 am _____ ⑥ 10:42 pm _____

Write these 24-hour times in 12-hour digital time. Use **am** or **pm**.

⑦ 13:35 _____ ⑨ 12:30 _____
⑧ 20:50 _____ ⑩ 06:20 _____

Calculate the perimeter and area.

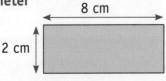
8 cm
2 cm

⑪ Perimeter = _____ ⑫ Area = _____

Calculate the perimeter of this rectangle.

⑬ _____
_____
_____
_____

75 cm
125 cm

⑭ Calculate the capacity.

5 L =
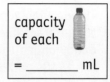
capacity of each
= _____ mL

Convert these masses from kilograms to grams.

⑮ 6 kg = _____ g
⑯ 14 kg = _____ g
⑰ 3.5 kg = _____ g
⑱ 17.8 kg = _____ g

Convert these masses from grams to kilograms.

⑲ 4000 g = _____ kg
⑳ 7500 g = _____ kg
㉑ 15 000 g = _____ kg
㉒ 32 500 g = _____ kg

Use the dial thermometer to answer the questions.

㉓ What is the highest temperature this thermometer can measure? _____

㉔ How many degrees Celsius does each mark on the dial represent? _____

㉕ What temperature is shown on this thermometer? _____

㉖ If the temperature fell by 100 degrees, what would the new temperature be? _____

How has the first shape been transformed to get the second shape? Circle the correct answer.

㉗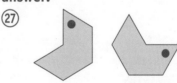

a slide
b reflection
c rotation

㉘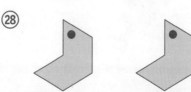

a slide
b reflection
c rotation

Score 2 points for each correct answer! SCORE **/56** (0-26) (28-50) (52-56)

Grammar & Punctuation

AC9E5LA08

Word meanings

The English language is changing all the time. The English spoken 100 years ago is very different to the English spoken today.

The development of the computer and the internet has introduced new words and changed the meanings of others. In the 1940s and 50s, for example, the word 'wireless' meant a radio, but today it refers to transmitting signals without the use of wires or cables. The term 'google it' has evolved as a verb that means using an internet search engine to find information.

Write a definition to show a modern-day technology-based meaning for the word in bold.

Example: We went to the **hardware** store to buy some nails.

    hardware: the physical parts of a computer system

① The cat chased the **mouse** across the kitchen floor.

    mouse: _____

    _____

② The cat made a **swipe** at the mouse but missed it.

    swipe: _____

    _____

③ My brothers like to go **surfing** at the beach on the weekend.

    surfing: _____

    _____

④ The type of **texts** I like to read are humorous stories.

    texts: _____

    _____

⑤ My mum has a vitamin **tablet** every morning.

    tablet: _____

    _____

Score 2 points for each correct answer! SCORE **/10** (0-2) (4-8) (10)

Phonic Knowledge & Spelling

AC9E5LY09

Hard and soft 'ch'

Say each word in the word bank. Listen to the sound that each word begins with. The letters **ch** can make three different sounds.

Word Bank

tch sound:	chore	champion	chapter
k sound:	choir	chemist	chronicle
sh sound:	chic	chateau	chauffeur

Choose words from the word bank to complete these sentences.

① Usain Bolt is a world _____ runner.

② A _____ has to study chemistry at the university.

③ The _____ drove the wealthy lady everywhere.

Here are some other words that begin with ch. Sort them into the correct beginning sound.

cheetah	chrome	chef
cholera	chance	champagne
cherish	chaos	chateau

④ **tch** sound: _____ _____

⑤ **k** sound: _____ _____

⑥ **sh** sound: _____ _____ _____

Write these words in the plural. Remember your rules!

⑦ cherry _____

⑧ child _____

⑨ chimney _____

⑩ chateau _____

NOTE: Words that end in **u**, add **x** for the plural. *Example:* plateau, plateau**x**

Match the words from the box to their meanings.

chaos	champagne	chateau

⑪ complete confusion: _____

⑫ large French mansion or castle: _____

⑬ white sparkling wine: _____

Score 2 points for each correct answer! SCORE **/26** (0-10) (12-20) (22-26)

TARGETING HOMEWORK 5 © PASCAL PRESS ISBN 9781925726473

On the Election Trail

Informative text – Report
Author – Ian Rohr

Australia has a Federal election every three years, and the Prime Minister chooses the election date. Parliament then closes down so the election **campaigns** can start.

Australia has two main political parties and several minor parties. Most **candidates** belong to one of these parties. Some people run for office as independent candidates.

The major parties usually have a candidate in each **constituency**. Each constituency's citizens elect one representative. 'Safe seat' constituencies nearly always vote in the same party or candidate. Elections are often decided in 'marginal seats', where both main parties have a strong chance of winning.

Most elections around the world focus on big issues such as education, health, defence and security and the economy. Taking **opinion polls** helps politicians identify areas of community concern.

Politicians try to attract support from their constituency by using a wide range of techniques, including meeting voters face-to-face and using adverts to get their message across.

Candidates use flyers in letterboxes and door-to-door calling to sell themselves and their message. Rallies and meetings help strengthen support from the party's followers.

We can change our representatives, and the parties and policies they support, by who we vote for in elections.

Source: *Government*, Go Facts, Blake Education.

TERM 2 ENGLISH

Write or circle the correct answers.

1. What type of text is this?
   a discussion   c procedure
   b report   d exposition

2. What is a Federal election?
   a electing politicians to govern the whole of Australia
   b electing politicians to govern each State and Territory of Australia
   c electing councillors to govern local councils in Australia

Which words in the text have these meanings?

3. a person who is nominated to stand in an election
   c_____

4. the residents in an electoral district
   c_____

5. not belonging to any political party
   i_____

6. a series of activities such as meetings and advertisements
   c_____

7. What type of seat is it when both main parties have a strong chance of winning?
   _____

8. List four big issues that most elections focus on.
   _____
   _____

9. Which is the odd word?
   a hinder   c assist
   b support   d endorse

10. Name two methods candidates use to get their message across to voters.
    _____
    _____

11. What is an **opinion poll**?
    a a meeting with voters
    b a survey to find out what voters think
    c an electoral rally

My Book Review

Title _____

Author _____

Rating ☆☆☆☆☆

Comment _____

_____

Score 2 points for each correct answer!

SCORE /22   0-8   10-16   18-22

Number & Algebra

AC9M5N06, AC9M5A02

Using the lattice method to multiply large numbers

In unit 3, you used the **lattice method** to multiply. You can also use this method to multiply larger numbers.

Example: **322 × 34**

- Multiply: 2 × 3, 2 × 3 and 3 × 3.
- Then multiply: 2 × 4, 2 × 4 and 3 × 4.
- Then add diagonally. Begin in the bottom right hand corner.

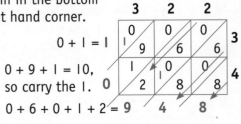

0 + 1 = 1

0 + 9 + 1 = 10, so carry the 1.

0 + 6 + 0 + 1 + 2 = 9

6 + 0 + 8 = 14, so carry the 1.

322 × 34 = 10 948

Use the lattice method to calculate these. Don't forget to carry when you add.

① 424 × 32 = _____

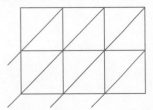

② 534 × 56 = _____

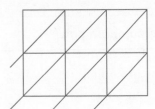

③ 206 × 46 = _____

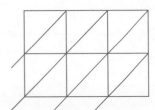

④ 540 × 83 = _____

Statistics & Probability

AC9M5P01

Chance events

We can use **numbers** to show the chance of something happening.

- Something that has **no chance** of happening has a **probability of 0**.
- Something that is **certain** to happen has a **probability of 1**.

Do these events have a probability of 0 or 1? Write the correct answers.

① You will fly to the moon tomorrow. ___

② You will grow older each day. ___

③ You will have a drink today. ___

④ Your family will turn into frogs tonight. ___

We can use a **number line** to show the chances of events happening.

- The line begins at 0 (no chance) and ends at 1 (certain).
- If there is a fifty-fifty chance that something will happen, we write this halfway along the line at 0.5.

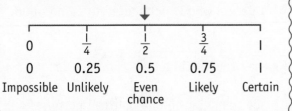

Decide where these events should go on the probability line. Write 0, 0.25, 0.5, 0.75 or 1.

⑤ You roll a regular die and get a 9. _____

⑥ You will eat an apple tomorrow. _____

⑦ Everyone in your class will eat an apple tomorrow. _____

⑧ You will blink your eyes this week. _____

TARGETING HOMEWORK 5 © PASCAL PRESS ISBN 9781925726473

⑨ A baby born will be a boy. _____

⑩ Your lottery ticket will win a prize this week. _____

⑪ A lottery ticket will win a prize this week. _____

⑫ Your feet will be twice as big tomorrow as they are today. _____

Score 2 points for each correct answer! SCORE **/24** (0–10) (12–18) (20–24)

Measurement & Space

AC9M5M02

Perimeter

Perimeter is the distance around the outside of a two-dimensional (2D) shape.

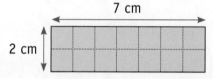

To find the perimeter of this rectangle, we add up the measurements of each side:

7 cm + 2 cm + 7 cm + 2 cm = 18 cm

We can work out the perimeter in a different way. The opposite sides of a rectangle are equal in length. Instead of adding all four sides, we can add the length and the width together and double the answer.

Perimeter = 2 × (7 + 2) cm
$\qquad$ = 2 × 9 cm
$\qquad$ = 18 cm

We can do the same calculation like this:

Perimeter = (2 × 7) + (2 × 2) cm
$\qquad$ (double 7 plus double 2)
$\qquad$ = 14 + 4 cm
$\qquad$ = 18 cm

Use two different methods to work out the perimeter of these rectangles.

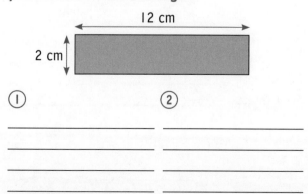

① _____
_____
_____

② _____
_____
_____

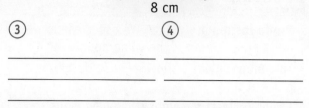

③ _____
_____
_____

④ _____
_____
_____

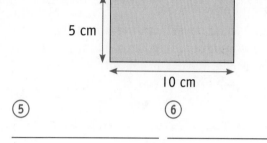

⑤ _____
_____
_____

⑥ _____
_____
_____

Score 2 points for each correct answer! SCORE **/12** (0–4) (6–8) (10–12)

Problem Solving

AC9M5N09

Multiplication triangles

This multiplication triangle has the numbers 1–6.

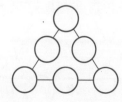

2 × 1 × 3 = 6 $\qquad$ 2 × 6 × 4 = 48

3 × 5 × 4 = 60

Total = 6 + 60 + 48 = 114

The numbers along each side have been multiplied. Then the side totals were added to make a total of 114.

Your challenge

Write the numbers 1–6 in the multiplication triangle below in a different order.

What is the highest total you can make?

You may need a calculator to help you.

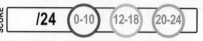

TARGETING HOMEWORK 5 © PASCAL PRESS ISBN 9781925726473

TERM 2 MATHS

Grammar & Punctuation

AC9E5LA06

Pronouns

> **Pronouns** replace nouns. We use them so we don't have to repeat the same noun over.
>
> This allows ideas to flow more smoothly in our writing.
>
> *Example:* Jasmin bought some new jeans so Jasmin put the jeans in Jasmin's wardrobe.
>
> Jasmin bought some new jeans so **she** put **them** in **her** wardrobe.
>
> Pronouns must **agree** with the nouns they replace in **number** (singular or plural) and **gender** (male, female or neutral).
>
> Singular pronouns – I, she, he, it, him, her, me, you
>
> Plural pronouns – we, us, you, they, them
>
> Some pronouns come **before** the verb: I, he, she, we, they, you, it.
>
> Some pronouns come **after** the verb: me, him, her, us, them, you, it.

Add the missing pronouns. Choose from the examples above.

(1) Alex gave Jackie a computer game for _____ birthday.

(2) Eric took his dog to the vet because _____ wasn't well.

(3) When my parents were first married, _____ lived in the city.

Circle the correct pronoun in the brackets.

(4) (She / Her) is in the school choir.

(5) Luke and (me / I) like to go fishing.

(6) "Wait for (me / I)," said Tilly.

Possessive pronouns

> Possessive pronouns show **ownership**.
>
> Singular pronouns – mine, yours, hers, his
>
> Plural pronouns – ours, yours, theirs

Circle the possessive pronouns. Write what the pronouns 'own'.

(7) That book is hers, but she gave it to me.

_____

(8) This house is ours and that one is yours.

_____

Phonic Knowledge & Spelling

AC9E5LY09, AC9E5LY10

Words that end in –ss

Say each word in the word bank. They all end in double s: –ss.

Word Bank

chess	press	compress	access
excess	express	process	progress
assess	impress	recess	success
mattress	harness	harass	embarrass

Choose words from the word bank to complete these sentences.

(1) You are certain to achieve _____ if you practise every day.

(2) "Are you sure you need a new _____ on your bed?" asked Mum.

(3) It is difficult to beat my sister in a game of _____.

(4) We had to _____ a button to gain _____ to our possessions.

Plurals

> Remember! To make the plural of words, you usually just add –s, but words that end in s, ss, sh, ch, x, z and zz, you add –es.
>
> *Examples:* waltz, waltz**es**   fox, fox**es**
> cutla**ss**, cutlass**es**
>
> NOTE: ox, ox**en**   quiz, qui**zzes**

Write the plurals of these words.

(5) class _____

(6) chalet _____

(7) canvas _____

(8) church _____

Add the suffix to each word. Write the new words.

	–ion	–ive
(9) compress	_____	_____
(10) impress	_____	_____
(11) success	_____	_____
(12) express	_____	_____

TERM 2 ENGLISH

The Big Squeeze

Imaginative text – Humorous narrative
Author – Helen Evans, **Illustrator** – John Yahyeh

Tom's mum asked him to look after Mrs Lucas' baby, Little Cyril, while the mothers played cards. Tom took Little Cyril up to his bedroom and then Tom's Uncle Andy arrived with some frogs. Uncle Andy always brings weird things to show Tom. They put the frogs in the bath to watch them jumping about. Uncle Andy then opened a bag to show Tom a python! Tom suddenly remembered he was supposed to be looking after Little Cyril and ran back to his bedroom, but Little Cyril wasn't there.

I panicked. I ran from room to room. "Cyril?" I called weakly.

My favourite uncle had brought a python home and it was loose in the house. What other monsters had escaped? My stomach lurched and my mouth was dry. I spun around in circles in confusion. Cyril was a pest. He always ruined my plans. But I didn't want him to be eaten by a python!

Then I heard a crash. The only place I hadn't looked was Dad's studio, and the crash came from there. I flung the door open.

There was Cyril, standing in a pool of purple paint. He had a brush in his hand and was dabbing at Dad's masterpiece. I swooped on him and whipped him out of that room as fast as an eagle after its prey.

I took Cyril to the bathroom and dumped him in the water with the frogs — clothes and all.

The water turned purple. That might be the end of my frogs, but at least I wouldn't be in prison all my life. That is, if I lived. Dad might kill me for the mess in his studio.

Cyril gurgled happily. He loved water. And I could tell he loved frogs too because he was pinching one.

I went to tell Uncle Andy that the baby was safe. With luck, the python would be back in the orange sleeping-bag and all would be well.

"I've found the baby, he's safe. Have you found the python?" I asked.

"No," replied Uncle Andy quietly.

Source: *The Big Squeeze*, Gigglers, Blake Education.

Write or circle the correct answers.

① **What type of text is this?**

  a explanation

  b report

  c narrative

  d discussion

② **What did Tom do wrong when his Uncle Andy arrived?**

_____

③ **What type of figurative language has the author used in this sentence?**

I swooped on him and whipped him out of that room as fast as an eagle after its prey.

  a metaphor

  b simile

  c personification

④ **Onomatopoeia are words that sound like their meaning. Give one example from the sentence in question 3.**

_____

⑤ **Why did the water turn purple when Tom put Little Cyril in the bath?**

_____

⑥ **Tom left the baby in the bath to find Uncle Andy. Did Tom do the correct thing?**

  a Yes, because he needed his Uncle to find the python.

  b No, because he shouldn't have left the baby alone in the bath.

Score 2 points for each correct answer! **SCORE** **/12** (0-4) (6-8) (10-12)

My Book Review

Title _____

Author _____

Rating ☆☆☆☆☆

Comment _____

_____

Number & Algebra

AC9M5N01

Comparing decimals

A **decimal** is another way of writing a fraction.

Example: Which decimal is largest?

     a 1.5   **b** 1.238   **c** 1.45

To work it out, we can use a place value table. We can add zeros as place holders after the decimal point because it will not alter the value of the number.

Decimal Point ▼

Ones	.	Tenths	Hundredths	Thousandths
1	.	5	0	0
1	.	2	3	8
1	.	4	5	0

Which is the largest number?
Remember – tenths are larger than hundredths and hundredths are larger than thousandths.

The ones are all the same value, so look at the tenths column next. There are 5 tenths in 1.5, which is larger than the 2 tenths in 1.238 and 4 tenths in 1.45. So **1.5** is the largest.

Circle the largest number in each row. Write the numbers in the place value table below to help you work it out.

① **a** 1.234   **b** 1.34   **c** 1.4

② **a** 1.7   **b** 0.7   **c** 1.568

③ **a** 2.3   **b** 1.359 **c** 2.24

Ones		Tenths	Hundredths	Thousandths
	.			
	.			
	.			
	.			
	.			
	.			
	.			
	.			
	.			
	.			

Write these decimals in order from **smallest** to **largest**.

④ 0.2   1.2   0.002   1.02

_____

⑤ 1.03   1.3   1.003   1.32

_____

⑥ 2.001   3.2   1.589   1.5

_____

⑦ 0.5   5.0   1.5   0.516

_____

Write >, < or = to make these statements true.

Remember, > means **greater than** and < means **less than**. The point of the arrow always points to the smaller number.

⑧ 0.50 ____ 0.5

⑨ 1.20 ____ 1.30

⑩ $\frac{5}{10}$ ____ 0.5

⑪ 3.367 ____ 3.6

⑫ $\frac{15}{100}$ ____ 0.12

⑬ 0.018 ____ 0.009

⑭ 2.2 ____ 2.02

⑮ 1.003 ____ 1.03

⑯ $\frac{134}{1000}$ ____ 0.135

Complete the sequences.

⑰ 1.2, 1.3, 1.4, ____, ____, ____

⑱ 0.3, 0.5, 0.7, ____, ____, ____

⑲ 9.8, 9.7, 9.6, ____, ____, ____

⑳ 2.2, 3.2, 4.2, ____, ____, ____

㉑ 13.6, 12.6, 11.6, ____, ____, ____

㉒ 2.0, 4.0, 6.0, ____, ____, ____

Score 2 points for each correct answer! | SCORE **/44** | 0-20 | 22-38 | 40-44

Statistics & Probability

There are no statistics & probability activities in this unit.

TARGETING HOMEWORK 5 © PASCAL PRESS ISBN 9781925726473

3D objects

A **three-dimensional object (3D)** has three dimensions: **length**, **height** and **depth**.

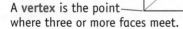

height
depth
length

3D objects are solid shapes.

The parts of a 3D object are **edges**, **faces** and **vertices**.

A **face** is the flat surface of a 3D object.

An **edge** is the line where two faces meet.

A **vertex** is the point where three or more faces meet.

A 3D object with many flat sides is called a **polyhedron** (**poly** means 'many' and **hedron** means 'face').

Write the numbers of **faces**, **edges** and **vertices** in these 3D objects.

pentagonal prism

① ____ faces
② ____ edges
③ ____ vertices

hexagonal prism

④ ____ faces
⑤ ____ edges
⑥ ____ vertices

square-based pyramid

⑦ ____ faces
⑧ ____ edges
⑨ ____ vertices

triangular prism

⑩ ____ faces
⑪ ____ edges
⑫ ____ vertices

A **net** is a flat shape that can be folded to make a 3D object. This is the net for a cube:

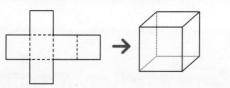

Colour each net, using the same colour for identical faces. Then write the name of the 3D object each net could fold to make.

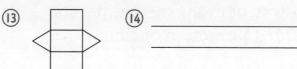

⑬　　　　　　⑭ _____

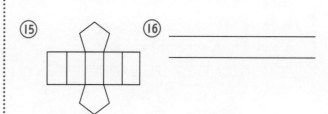

⑮　　　　　　⑯ _____

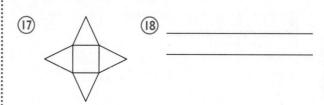

⑰　　　　　　⑱ _____

Score 2 points for each correct answer!   SCORE   **/36**   ⓪-16   18-30   32-36

Problem Solving

AC9M5N09

Decimal problems

Work out the answers to these problems. Show your working out.

① Mr Bond is 185.4 cm tall. Mrs Bond is 165.2 cm tall. What is the difference in their heights?

_____

_____

② I have 20 chocolate bars. My brother eats 7.5 of them. How many do I have left?

_____

_____

③ A tiny bug measures 0.53 cm in length. Another bug measures 1.589 cm. What is the difference in their lengths?

_____

_____

④ At the birthday party, Ian ate 0.4 of the cake, Sal ate 0.3 and Tim ate 0.2. How much of the cake was eaten? How much of the cake was left?

_____

_____

_____

Grammar & Punctuation

AC9E5LA03, AC9E5LA06

First person, second person and third person pronouns

> **Personal pronouns** represent different persons:
>
> First person – the person speaking
>
> Second person – the person spoken to
>
> Third person – the person(s) spoken about
>
> | | 1st person | 2nd person | 3rd person |
> |---|---|---|---|
> | **Before the verb** | I   we | you | she, he, it, they |
> | **After the verb** | me   us | you | her, him, it, them |

Circle the pronouns. Write if it is 1st, 2nd or 3rd person.

① She often goes with them to the park. _____

② You need to get up early tomorrow. _____

③ Yesterday, I ran in a competitive race. _____

Points of view

> Speakers and writers create language from different **points of view**.
>
> First person – diary, personal recount, autobiography, anecdote, letters
>
> Second person – directions, instruction, commands, procedures
>
> Third person – reports, stories, historical recounts, explanations

Circle the 9 pronouns in the text.

④-⑫ When I was very young, I used to stay at my Nan's house during the school holidays. I was allowed to take all my favourite toys, including my bike. Nan was very kind to me. We used to bake lots of yummy cakes to take with us on a picnic.

⑬ **Write if the text above is written from a 1st, 2nd or 3rd person point of view.**

_____

Phonic Knowledge & Spelling

AC9E5LY09, AC9E5LY10

Words beginning with `e`

Say each word in the word bank. All the words begin with the prefix e–. Many of these words have originated from an old language called Latin. The prefix **e–** means 'out'. In Latin, 'mit' means to send, so 'emit' means to 'send out'.

Word Bank

event	evolve	evade	eject
elapse	eclipse	economy	echidna
emit	emerge	erode	erupt
enough	equal	equator	equip

Choose words from the word bank to complete these sentences.

① The vet is wary of the sharp spines when she treats the _____.

② An emergency was declared because the volcano was about to _____.

③ The annual _____ varies the number and type of exhibitors.

Adding the suffix –ion. Match the verbs in the box with their nouns.

elect	evade	emit	erode

④ emission _____

⑤ election _____

⑥ evasion _____

⑦ erosion _____

Synonyms

> **Synonyms** are words that have exactly the same or nearly the same meaning.
> *Example:*
> cold – freezing, chilly, cool, icy, wintry

Circle the synonym for each of these words.

⑧ **evade:**   confront   meet   avoid

⑨ **eject:**   expel   keep   hold

The Dino Master

Luke and his best friend, Sophie, were helping Sophie's neighbour, Mr Costa, unload his boxes of dinosaur fossils. Mr Costa showed them a picture of the first dinosaur model ever made.

Mr Costa showed Luke and Sophie a picture of a group of people eating dinner inside a dinosaur. Sophie read aloud the caption below the picture, "New Years Eve 1853".

"What an excellent idea, to throw a party inside a dinosaur!" said Luke.

"This was one of the first models of a dinosaur ever made," explained Mr Costa.

"What kind of dinosaur is it?" asked Luke.

"An iguanodon," said Mr Costa. "These people were leading scientists of the day. They were invited to see the first life-size model of a dinosaur by the two people who created it. Richard Owen was a scientist, and Waterhouse Hawkins was a sculptor."

"Before this model, people weren't sure what these creatures looked like," said Mr Costa. "In fact it was Richard Owen who came up with the name Dinosauria. It means 'fearfully great lizard' in Greek."

Imaginative – Narrative
Author – Lisa Thompson, **Illustrator** – Matt Stapleton

"How did they figure out what dinosaurs looked like?" asked Luke.

"Well, Richard Owen was a professor of anatomy. He studied the structure of different animals, compared their skeletons and saw what they had in common," said Mr Costa. "So Richard Owen took his talent and looked at groups of dinosaur fossils."

"What did he see?" asked Sophie intrigued.

"He realised dinosaurs had legs that descended directly under their bodies. They weren't sprawled like the legs we see on lizards today."

"How did this help Richard Owen make a skeleton? He didn't have all the bones," said Luke.

"Well, he compared extinct dinosaurs with animals of his time. He used his knowledge of how animals' bodies are put together to fill in the blanks. He once predicted the structure of an entire bird by studying just one bone fragment!" exclaimed Mr Costa.

"How clever!" said Sophie amazed.

"Yes, it was clever, but he also made mistakes. There was still a lot of guesswork involved. People were just starting to find fossils so they didn't have the amount of information we have today. The puzzle of what these creatures looked like and how they lived was just starting to emerge," said Mr Costa.

Source: *Bony Puzzle*, Wonder Wits, Blake Education.

TERM 2 ENGLISH

Write or circle the correct answers.

① **Who created the first life-size model of a dinosaur?**

_____

Find words in the text that have these meanings.

② the study of the bodies of humans and animals: a_____

③ the internal bone framework of an animal: s_____

④ to come out, become known: e_____

⑤ **What does intrigued mean?**
   a curious   b happy   c bored

⑥ **From which language does the word 'Dinosauria' come from?**

_____

⑦ **Which is the odd word/phrase?**
   a sprawled   b spread out   c together

⑧ **How did Richard Owen use science to build the dinosaur model?**
   a He invented a method for making models.
   b He studied anatomy.
   c He used his knowledge of how animals' bodies are put together.

My Book Review

Title _____

Author _____

Rating ☆☆☆☆☆

Comment _____

_____

Score 2 points for each correct answer!

SCORE /16 0-6 8-12 14-16

Number & Algebra

AC9M5N04

Percentages

> **Percentages** are types of **fractions**. They represent a part of **one hundred**. The symbol **%** means **percent**.
>
> *Examples:*
>
> 2% (two percent) = $\frac{2}{100}$ or 2 out of 100
>
> 40% (forty percent) = $\frac{40}{100}$ or 40 out of 100
>
> 100% (one hundred percent) = $\frac{100}{100}$ or 100 out of 100
>
> This 100-square has 50 squares coloured green. The fraction of green squares = $\frac{50}{100}$
>
> The percentage of green squares = 50%

Write the number of squares coloured green as a fraction and as a percentage.

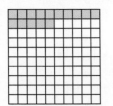

① fraction = _____

② percentage = _____

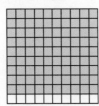

⑤ fraction = _____

⑥ percentage = _____

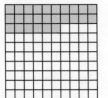

③ fraction = _____

④ percentage = _____

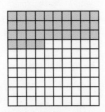

⑦ fraction = _____

⑧ percentage = _____

Look at the green colouring on the first diagram in each pair. Colour the same amount on the 100-square.

Then write the coloured amount as an equivalent fraction and as a percentage.

⑨
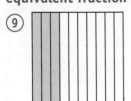 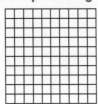

⑩ $\frac{\boxed{}}{\boxed{10}} = \frac{\boxed{}}{\boxed{100}}$ = _____ %

⑪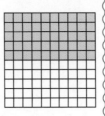

⑫ $\frac{\boxed{}}{\boxed{10}} = \frac{\boxed{}}{\boxed{100}}$ = _____ %

⑬

⑭ $\frac{\boxed{}}{\boxed{10}} = \frac{\boxed{}}{\boxed{100}}$ = _____ %

Score 2 points for each correct answer!

SCORE **/28** (0-12) (14-22) (24-28)

Statistics & Probability

AC9M5ST01, AC9M5ST03

Dot plots

> A **dot plot** is a way of representing data using dots along a number line. Each dot has a value of one.
>
> This dot plot shows the results of a survey carried out by Ria. She asked the students in her class if they had 0, 1, 2, 3 or 4 brothers and sisters.
>
>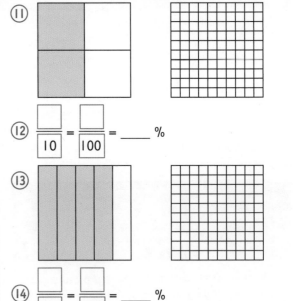
>
> **The Number of Brothers and Sisters for the Students in My Class**
>
>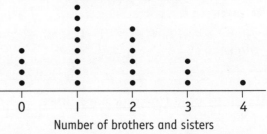
>
> Number of brothers and sisters

Use the dot plot to answer the questions.

① How many students did Ria survey? _____

② How many students have no brothers or sisters? _____

③ How many students have 1 brother or sister? _____

④ How many students have 2 or more brothers and sisters? _____

⑤ Which number of brothers and sisters was the most common? _____

⑥ Which number of brothers and sisters was the least common? _____

TARGETING HOMEWORK 5 © PASCAL PRESS ISBN 9781925726473

Ria then asked her class how many people were in their family. Here are her results.

Name	No.	Name	No.	Name	No.
Max	2	Ali	7	Ahmed	5
Tina	4	Emma	6	Peta	2
Will	3	Su	5	Tracy	4
Toni	4	Eli	4	Mike	4
Tom	6	Rosie	4	Josh	2
Jack	5	Tam	3	Ava	3
Scott	4	George	4		
Mel	4	Sally	2		

⑦ Use Ria's data to complete the dot plot.

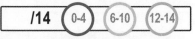

2   3   4   5   6   7

Score 2 points for each correct answer! **SCORE** /14 (0-4) (6-10) (12-14)

Use the grid map to answer these question. Write or circle the correct answers.

① Which feature is at D6?
   a house   b lake   c road

② Which feature is at G3?
   a house   b garden   c swimming pool

③ In which grid square is there a pedestrian crossing?
   a D4   b F4   c B4

④ What feature is found at G1?
   _____

⑤ What feature is found at D1?
   _____

⑥ Find the orange car. What is its grid reference? _____

⑦ Find the red car in B1. Follow these directions.

   The red car travels north for two grid squares to the intersection. It turns right, travels past the park and then turns left. It travels three grid squares north and stops outside a house. What is the colour of the house it stops outside?

   a orange   b red   c blue

Score 2 points for each correct answer! **SCORE** /14 (0-4) (6-10) (12-14)

Measurement & Space

AC9M5SP02

Grid map

This is an aerial view map of Grandtown.

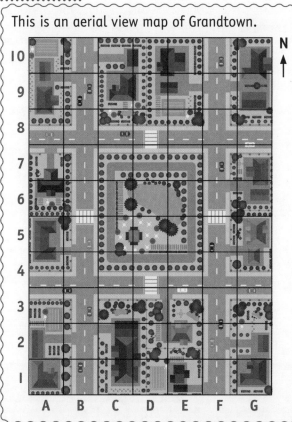

Problem Solving

AC9M5SP01

Cube puzzle

When this net is folded into a cube, which picture below can it match?

You can trace the net onto paper, cut it out and fold it into a cube to help you work it out.

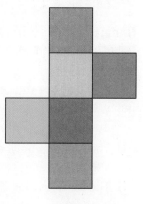

Grammar & Punctuation

AC9E5LA08

TERM 2 ENGLISH

Adverbs

Adverbs say more about <u>verbs</u>. They tell us how, how long, how often, when and where things happen.

Examples: Reece <u>ran</u> **quickly** through the park. (How did Reece run?)

Janice <u>lost</u> her watch **yesterday**. (When did Janice lose her watch?)

Underline the verbs in these sentences. Ask how, to find the adverbs. Circle the adverbs.

① The trees were swaying gently in the breeze.

② The children yelled excitedly and quickly raced out the door.

③ The man spoke angrily at the dogs who were barking loudly.

④ Ben looked anxiously at the waves that were pounding relentlessly on the boat.

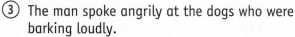

Underline the verbs in these sentences. Ask when, how often or how long to find the adverbs. Circle the adverbs.

⑤ Tomorrow Dad will play tennis. He usually wins.

⑥ We'll go now and you can join us later.

⑦ Sometimes I stay at my friend's house.

⑧ We eventually reached the beach after a long trek.

Underline the verbs. Ask where to find the adverbs. Circle the adverbs.

⑨ The bee flew here and there following the scent of the flowers.

⑩ We looked around but couldn't find him anywhere.

⑪ The cat was nowhere to be seen but we knew she was hiding somewhere.

⑫ The mother took the baby outside.

Phonic Knowledge & Spelling

AC9E5LY09, AC9E5LY10

Words that begin with 'a' and 'ad'

Say each word in the word bank. a at the beginning of words means 'on', 'in', 'of' or 'to'. ad at the beginning of words means 'to', 'towards', 'near' or 'at'.

Word Bank

apart	abrupt	abandon	alarm
adapt	afloat	alert	aware
adjacent	adjective	advise	advice
advance	adverse	adventure	advertise

Choose words from the word bank to complete these sentences.

① We heard the fire _____ so we immediately left the building.

② The yacht was attached to the buoy to keep it _____ in the harbour.

③ We had to _____ the farmer that his herd of cattle had escaped onto the road.

advice and advise

Advice and **advise** can be tricky and their meaning is often confused.

Advice is a noun. It is something you say to someone to help them. *Example:* I do not need your advice on the matter.

Advise is a verb. It means to give an opinion. *Example:* What do you advise me to do?

Write advice or advise to complete these sentences.

④ He acted on my _____ not to buy that car.

⑤ She will _____ me about which book to choose.

Find words in the word bank to match these meanings.

⑥ floating on water: _____

⑦ sudden: _____

⑧ next to: _____

⑨ an exciting event or journey: _____

What do we need?

Imaginative text – Narrative
Author – Frances Mackay

"OK, I'm off to the shops. What do you need?" asked Mum.

"I need some new sunglasses," said Ria. "These ones are scratched."

"But you only bought them a month ago," replied Mum. "You need to take better care of them."

"I need some new jeans," said Mel. "Su has some of the latest design. Mine look out-of-date compared to hers."

"But I bought them for your birthday. They were what you wanted," said Mum.

"I want a new bike!" piped up Adam.

"Well, I certainly won't be buying one today," replied Mum feeling exasperated.

"We need milk, bread and bananas," said Gran helpfully. "I'll come with you."

"I need some peace and quiet," said Grandad. "I think I'll go out for a walk."

Mum and Gran walked to the car. "They all think I'm made of money," said Mum. "Always wanting things, never happy with what they already have."

"I seem to remember you were much the same at their age," said Gran. "Always wanting the latest gizmo or gadget or the latest clothes."

"Was I?" asked Mum.

"In my day, we always had to make do with what we already had. We hardly ever had new things but we never seemed to mind. I didn't feel as if I was missing out on anything. I was happy with what I had," said Gran.

"Yes, I wish it was like that today. We all have so much stuff. The kids have so many toys they don't know what to do with them. Half the time, they've forgotten what they have until they suddenly find it again in the toy box or in the bottom of their wardrobe. They don't really need anything at the moment."

"Perhaps it's time to start giving them pocket money for doing chores. If they have to use their own money to buy things it might make them realise just how much everything costs and it will help them to choose between what they actually need and what they want," replied Gran.

"You're absolutely right! What a great idea. I'll talk to Barry and put it into action. Meanwhile, let's go and get the things we really need," laughed Mum.

TERM 2 ENGLISH

Write or circle the correct answers.

1. **Make a list of the things the family want.**

_____

2. **Make a list of the things the family need.**

_____

3. **Explain the difference between wants and needs.**

_____

_____

Find words in the text that have these meanings.

4. old-fashioned: o_____

5. irritated, annoyed: e_____

6. a gadget or device: g_____

7. **How was Gran's life different to her daughter's and grandchildren's?**

a We are not told.

b Gran didn't have many things and she didn't want anything.

c Gran was just like her grandchildren when she was young. She wanted new things.

My Book Review

Title _____

Author _____

Rating ☆☆☆☆☆

Comment _____

_____

Score 2 points for each correct answer! **SCORE** **/14** (0-4) (6-10) (12-14)

Number & Algebra

AC9M5N05

Adding and subtracting fractions

You can use a **number line** to help you add and subtract fractions with the same **denominator**.

Example: $\frac{4}{5} + \frac{3}{5}$

Begin at $\frac{4}{5}$ and make 3 jumps.
Each jump is equal to $\frac{1}{5}$.

The answer is $\frac{7}{5}$ or $1\frac{2}{5}$.

- When you add on a number line, count **up** the line, moving to the **right**.
- When you subtract, count **down**, moving to the **left**.

Use the number lines to calculate these additions and subtractions.

① $\frac{3}{4} + \frac{3}{4} =$ _____

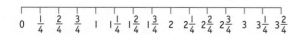

② $1\frac{4}{6} + \frac{3}{6} =$ _____

③ $\frac{8}{10} - \frac{6}{10} =$ _____

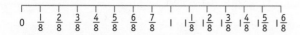

④ $1\frac{5}{8} - \frac{6}{8} =$ _____

Continue the patterns on the number lines.

⑤ The robot jumps from 0 to $1\frac{2}{4}$. It continues making jumps of the same length. Show where the robot lands each time.

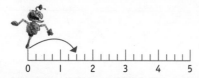

⑥ The robot jumps from 0 to $2\frac{1}{2}$. It continues making jumps of the same length. Show where the robot lands each time.

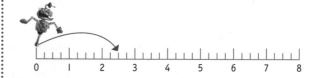

⑦ The robot jumps from 5 to $3\frac{1}{2}$. It continues making jumps of the same length. Show where the robot lands each time.

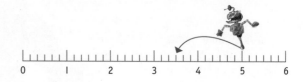

⑧ The robot jumps from 6 to $4\frac{7}{8}$. It continues making jumps of the same length. Show where the robot lands each time.

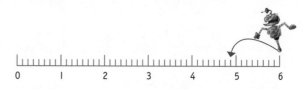

Score 2 points for each correct answer! | **SCORE** | **/16** | 0-6 | 8-12 | 14-16

Statistics & Probability

There are no statistics & probability activities in this unit.

Measurement & Space

AC9M5SP03

How to enlarge a picture

You can use a **grid** to enlarge a picture.
Example:

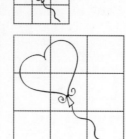

The squares on the second grid are larger than on the first grid. To enlarge the picture, you copy the lines and shapes in each square on the first grid onto the matching square on the second grid.

Use the grid method to enlarge the pictures.

①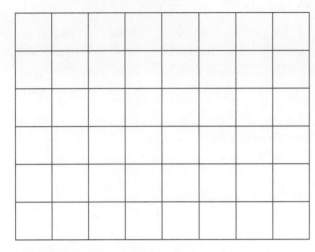

②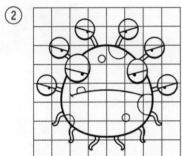

③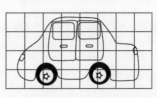

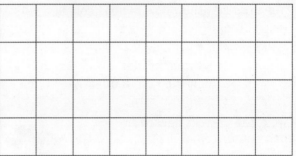

Score 2 points for each correct answer! **SCORE** | **/6** | ⓪ | ②-④ | ⑥

Problem Solving

AC9M5N05

Party puzzles

Tina's mum made lots of different pies for Tina's birthday party.

Circle the coloured fraction pies that add to make the answer for each question.

① Tina gave Rob half a strawberry pie, of which he ate one half while she ate one half of the part she kept. How much of the pie did they eat?

② Ria took three quarters of a meat pie but she only ate half of what she took. How much of the pie did she eat?

   (two more pies)

③ John ate half as much as his brother, Tim, who ate four-sixths of an apple pie. How much of the pie did they eat?

④ Su, Frankie and Venus ate one-eighth of a rhubarb pie each and Tina ate one-quarter. How much of the pie was eaten?

Grammar & Punctuation

AC9E5LA08

TERM 2 ENGLISH

Comparing adverbs

Adverbs can show how actions compare with each other.

Examples: I tried **hard**.
Su tried **harder**.
Ben tried the **hardest**.

Circle the correct adverb in each sentence.

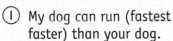
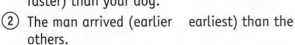

① My dog can run (fastest faster) than your dog.

② The man arrived (earlier earliest) than the others.

③ Jake jumped (higher highest) than all the contestants.

④ Dan ran the (further furthest).

⑤ I walk (shortest shorter) distances in the afternoon.

Adverbs with 'more', 'most', 'less' and 'least'

Adverbs that end in –ly and some irregular adverbs require the words **more** or **most**, or **less** or **least** to show comparison.

Examples:
Ahmed walks **more slowly** than Sinead.
Ella **most often** finishes her maths quiz first.
Tim is **less likely** to win than James.
I paint the **least carefully** in my class.

Circle the correct word in brackets to complete each sentence.

⑥ I walk our large dog (more most) often than our small dog.

⑦ Janice draws (more most) confidently than me.

⑧ Of all the dancers, she danced the (most more) gracefully.

⑨ I train (less least) often than Gina.

⑩ Tanya is the (least less) likely person to bake a cake.

Phonic Knowledge & Spelling

AC9E5LY09, AC9E5LY10

Suffixes –ful and –less

Say each word in the word bank. The suffix **–ful** means 'full of'. The suffix **–less** means 'without'.

Word Bank

awful	painful	pitiful	peaceful
resourceful	fruitful	mindful	grateful
listless	homeless	countless	cordless
flawless	faultless	pointless	reckless

Choose words from the word bank to complete these sentences.

① We tried to search for the lost watch but it was _____.

② In the wild you need to be very _____ if you want to survive.

③ The accident was caused by a careless and _____ driver.

Antonyms

Antonyms are adjectives that have the opposite meaning. We can make antonyms by adding **–ful** or **–less**.

Examples: care, care**ful**, care**less**
colour, colour**ful**, colour**less**

Write the antonyms of these words using either –ful or –less. Write the new word.

Example: powerful – powerless

④ helpless _____

⑤ harmful _____

⑥ fruitful _____

⑦ hopeless _____

Add –ly to these adjectives to form adverbs. Write the new word.

⑧ useful _____

⑨ painful _____

⑩ awful _____

⑪ fearful _____

TARGETING HOMEWORK 5 © PASCAL PRESS ISBN 9781925726473

The orange juice catastrophe

Imaginative text – Narrative
Author – Frances Mackay

Lord Bingley was sitting in his office working. It was a very warm summer's day and he was feeling hot and bothered. "I need a nice cold drink," he thought as he rang the servant's bell. The butler, Johnson, arrived immediately.

"Ah, Johnson, nice cold orange juice, please. I'm sure Cook made some fresh this morning."

"Yes, sir, straight away."

Johnson returned with a glass of orange juice.

"Perfect," said Lord Bingley as he took the glass and had a sip.

"It's warm! What on earth is Cook thinking of? Warm juice — whatever next! Go and put it in the freezer for me, Johnson, it'll soon cool off."

"Yes sir, but won't it ..."

"No buts, Johnson. And while you're there perhaps you can bring back that chocolate bar I left on a saucer on the kitchen window sill last night."

Johnson quickly returned again with the saucer.

"What on earth? What's this? I asked for the chocolate bar, not chocolate syrup. What's happened to it?"

"Well, it seems, sir, that ..." started Johnson.

"Never mind, Johnson, never mind. I've gone off chocolate! Perhaps I'll have some nice cheese instead — that should be refreshing. I asked Cook to warm it up a little in the oven after she'd cooked breakfast."

"You did, sir? But won't it ..." started Johnson.

"No buts, Johnson, just get the cheese, thanks."

"Yes sir."

Johnson returned soon after with the cheese.

"What's this mess? I thought I asked for cheese."

"You did, sir, but ..." started Johnson.

"Never mind, never mind. How about that cold orange juice? It must be ready by now."

Johnson returned with the glass of orange juice. Lord Bingley picked up the glass and brought it to his lips but nothing came out.

"What the dickens? What's happened to it, Johnson? It won't even come out now."

"No sir, it's because ..." started Johnson.

Source: *Science Comprehension and Writing Response Centres*, Upper Primary, Blake Education.

TERM 2 ENGLISH

Write or circle the correct answers.

① **What is another word for catastrophe?**

  a experience   b disaster   c comedy

② **What happened to the chocolate that was left in the window?**

_____

③ **Why do you think this happened?**

_____

_____

_____

④ **What happened to the orange juice after it was put into the freezer?**

  a It melted.

  b It froze solid.

  c It evaporated.

⑤ **Why do you think Johnson never got to explain what happened to any of the foods?**

  a Lord Bingley was an impatient man and wouldn't wait for Johnson to answer.

  b Johnson was a butler and wasn't allowed to answer.

  c Johnson didn't know the answers to Lord Bingley's questions.

My Book Review

Title _____

Author _____

Rating ☆☆☆☆☆

Comment _____

_____

Score 2 points for each correct answer!

SCORE **/10** (0-2) (4-8) (10)

Number & Algebra

AC9M5N09

TERM 2 MATHS

Budgets

A **budget** is a plan for how much money to spend on something. You can make a budget for a birthday party, for example.

Max receives $20 pocket money each month. He uses it to pay for regular items each month.

Birthday party budget	
food	$100
party bags	$70
paper plates and cups	$30
birthday cake	$50
balloons	$5
Total	**$255**

My monthly budget	
book	$4.99
lollies	$2.00
karate lesson	$8.50

Use Max's budget to answer the questions. Show your working out. Don't forget to round the money to the nearest 5 cents.

① What is the total amount Max spends on regular items each month?

_____

② How much money does he have left over each month?

_____

③ How much 'left over' money in total will Max have if he saves it all for one year?

_____

④ Max wants to buy a watch that costs $19.99. How many months will it take him to save for the watch using his 'left over' money?

_____

_____

Max's school is having a fund-raising event to pay for some new sports equipment. Max's class is making kites to sell.

This is the budget for each kite:

Kite budget	
ball of string	$5.40
bamboo sticks	$3.50
brown paper	$2.50
stickers for decoration	$1.00

Use the kite budget to answer the questions. Show your working out.

⑤ How much will each kite cost to make?

_____

⑥ They need to sell the kites for more than it costs to make them. They want to make $7.60 profit on each kite. What will be the price of each kite?

_____

⑦ On the day, they sell 10 kites. How much money did they receive?

_____

⑧ How much profit did they make on selling the 10 kites?

_____

Score 2 points for each correct answer! **SCORE** /16 (0-6) (8-12) (14-16)

Statistics & Probability

AC9M5P02

Chance experiment

Melanie wanted to find out the chances of pulling out marbles of a particular colour from a bag. Here are the marbles she put inside the bag:

Answer the questions about Melanie's experiment.

① How many marbles were there altogether?

_____

We can write the chance of picking a red marble from the bag as a fraction, $\frac{3}{12}$. 3 out of the 12 marbles were red.

Complete the table for the other colours of marbles.

	Outcome	Number	Fraction
	red	3	$\frac{3}{12}$
②	purple		
③	dark blue		
④	light blue		
⑤	yellow		
⑥	pink		
⑦	green		

⑧ What is the total of all the fractions in the table? ____

⑨ Which coloured marbles have the same chance of being picked out as yellow?

_____

⑩ Which coloured marbles have the same chance of being picked as purple?

_____

⑪ Which coloured marble is most likely to be picked? _____

Use the spinner to answer the questions.

⑫ How many sections is the spinner divided into?

_____

⑬ Write the chance of spinning orange as a fraction.

_____

⑭ What are the chances of **not** spinning orange?

_____

⑮ Write the chance of spinning yellow as a fraction.

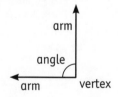

_____

⑯ Write the chance of spinning blue as a fraction.

_____

⑰ Write the chance of spinning red as a fraction.

_____

Score 2 points for each correct answer! **SCORE** /34 0-14 16-28 30-34

Measurement & Space

AC9M5M04

Comparing angles

This is a **right angle**:

arm

angle

arm   vertex

An **angle** is made up of two **arms** (or **rays**) and a **vertex**.

A curved line or curved arrow is used to show the amount of turn needed to form the angle.

Estimate if these angles are **equal to**, **less than** or **greater than** a right angle. Write the correct answer above each angle.

① _____

② _____

③ _____

④ _____

⑤ _____

⑥ _____

⑦ _____

⑧ _____

Score 2 points for each correct answer! **SCORE** /16 0-6 8-12 14-16

Problem Solving

AC9M5N09

Shopping budget

Sam has some birthday money to spend. She plans to spend two-eighths on shoes, three-eighths on T-shirts and three-eighths on books. She has $36 for books.

① How much money does Sam have altogether?

_____

② How much does Sam spend on shoes?

_____

③ How much money does Sam spend on T-shirts?

_____

Grammar & Punctuation

AC9E5LA08

Words from other languages

Australian English, like other languages throughout the world, has been influenced by other languages. Some of the words we use today come from foreign languages.

One of the most important influences on Australian English has been Aboriginal languages. About 400 Aboriginal words have been adopted by Australian English. Most of these words are the names of places, plants and animals, for example, Canberra, kangaroo, boomerang.

Here are some words that have come from other languages. Circle the word that answers each question correctly.

① This word comes from Swahili, an African language, and means 'an expedition to see wild animals'.

   a journey   **c** safari

   b holiday   **d** travel

② This word comes from the Greek 'alpha' and 'beta', the first two letters of the Greek alphabet.

   a alphanumeric   **c** beater

   b alphabet   **d** alpine

③ This word comes from the Malay word 'bambu'.

   a bamboozle   **c** bamboo

   b banana   **d** ban

④ This word comes from an Australian Aboriginal word and means 'a small pool in an intermittent stream'.

   a river   **c** creek

   b billabong   **d** puddle

⑤ This word comes from Japanese and means 'a gigantic sea wave'.

   a flood   **c** tsunami

   b ocean   **d** waveband

Phonic Knowledge & Spelling

AC9E5LY09, AC9E5LY10

Words beginning with ex– and out–

Say each word in the word bank. The prefixes **ex–** and **out–** mean 'out of'.

Word Bank

expand	explode	export	expose
exhibit	extend	extreme	exempt
outbreak	outburst	outfit	outdoor
outskirts	outline	outlet	outlandish

Choose words from the word bank to complete these sentences.

① Everyone except me went to see the
   _____ at the museum.

② I did not expect Mum to buy me a new
   _____ for the party.

③ We had to accept that it would take a long time to reach the _____
   of the city.

Match these tricky words in the box to their correct meaning.

accept   expect   except

④ to take something that is offered to you:
   _____

⑤ not including: _____

⑥ to think that something will happen:

   _____

Add the suffix –ion to these verbs to change them into nouns. You will need to change or add some letters. You may need to use a dictionary to help you.

Example: examine – examination

⑦ exhibit   _____

⑧ expand   _____

⑨ extend   _____

⑩ exempt   _____

TARGETING HOMEWORK 5 © PASCAL PRESS ISBN 9781925726473

Fires - Damage and Benefits

Informative text – Explanation
Author – Ian Rohr

Fires cause widespread damage to human, animal and plant communities. Surprisingly, they can also have some benefits.

Damage

An intensely hot **firestorm** kills off huge areas of vegetation and the wildlife that lives there. Some of these will not recover. High-intensity fires also lead to soil erosion where there are no roots to hold the soil in place.

Animals that cannot get away from the fire will die from the heat, or the smoke. Some animals will survive but for them there is now less food available and less shelter from predators and **feral** animals.

Fire also destroys farms and houses. Fire damage can be very costly. In addition, the heavy smoke clouds from major fires can cause breathing difficulties.

Source: *Fire and Drought*, Go Facts, Blake Education.

Benefits

Many Australian plants are adapted to fire, having seeds that only **germinate** after a fire. Most areas will regenerate completely after a fire. The fire's heat forces fruits to open, releasing their seeds. The ash that is left provides nutrients for the soil. Fires also **eradicate** plant diseases.

When a fire goes through an area, it removes old and dead plants, so new growth can occur. Low-intensity fires reduce the amount of fuel in an area. This limits the likelihood of more damaging high-intensity fires.

TERM 2 ENGLISH

Write or circle the correct answers.

① **What is a firestorm?**

   a a fire cause by a storm

   b a very intense and destructive fire

   c We are not told.

② **What is a feral animal?**

   a a domestic animal, such as a cat, that has gone wild

   b an animal that has survived a fire

   c an animal that lives in a forest

③ **List 4 things that fires cause damage to.**

_____

_____

_____

_____

④ **What does germinate mean?**

   a to burn in a fire

   b We are not told.

   c to grow from a seed

Find words in the text that have these meanings.

⑤ to get rid of: e_____

⑥ make less: r_____

⑦ **List 4 benefits of fires.**

_____

_____

_____

_____

Score 2 points for each correct answer!

SCORE /14

My Book Review

Title _____

Author _____

Rating ☆☆☆☆☆

Comment _____

_____

Number & Algebra

AC9M5N07, AC9M5A02

Equivalent number sentences

Equivalent means **equal.** In an equivalent number sentence, both sides of the equal sign have the **same value** – the answers are the same.

Example: 5 × 4 = 40 ÷ 2
    5 × 4 = 20 and 40 ÷ 2 = 20

Complete the number sentences to solve these questions.

① What number when multiplied by 4 has the same answer as double 16?

_____ × 4 = 2 × 16

② What number can be divided by 9 so that the answer is the same as 36 ÷ 6?

_____ ÷ 9 = 36 ÷ 6

③ When a number is multiplied by 5, the answer will be the same as 100 divided by 4. What is the number?

5 × _____ = 100 ÷ 4

④ If 56 is divided by a number, it equals double 2, plus double 2. What is the number?

56 ÷ _____ = 2 × 2 + 2 × 2

Fill in the blanks in these equivalent number sentences.

⑤ 8 × _____ = 4 × 10

⑥ 80 ÷ 8 = 100 ÷ _____

⑦ _____ × 6 = 3 × 10

⑧ _____ ÷ 7 = 64 ÷ 8

⑨ 45 ÷ 5 = _____ × 3

⑩ 25 × 4 = 200 ÷ _____

⑪ 5 × _____ = 90 ÷ 3

⑫ _____ ÷ 4 = 6 × 6

⑬ 100 × 9 = _____ × 300

Circle the correct number to solve these equivalent number sentences.

⑭ 303 ÷ ___ = 10 × 10 + 1

   a 1   b 2   c 3   d 4

⑮ 63 × 2 = 252 ÷ ___

   a 1   b 2   c 3   d 4

⑯ 6 × 12 = 8 × ___

   a 4   b 5   c 8   d 9

⑰ ___ ÷ 10 = 25 × 4

   a 1000 b 2000 c 3000 d 4000

Score 2 points for each correct answer!   SCORE **/34**   (0-14) (16-28) (30-34)

Statistics & Probability

There are no statistics & probability activities in this unit.

Measurement & Space

AC9M5M04

Measuring angles

Angles are measured in **degrees** using an instrument called a **protractor.**

This protractor measures angles up to **180°.**

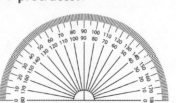

This protractor measures angles up to **360°.**

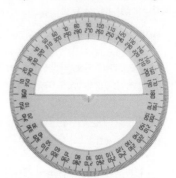

This is a **right angle.** It measures **90°.**

A **straight line** measures **180°.**

A **complete revolution** measures **360°.**

Most protractors have two scales.

The **outer scale** goes clockwise from 0° to 180°.

The **inner scale** goes anticlockwise from 0° to 180°.

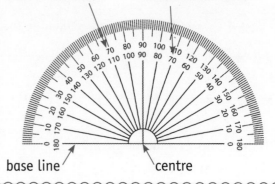

base line   centre

How to measure an angle:

- Place the midpoint of the protractor on the vertex of the angle.
- Line up one arm of the angle with the base line of the protractor.
- Read the degrees where the other arm of the angle crosses the scale.

Examples:

This angle measures 90°.

This angle measures 127°.

Make sure you read the degrees from the correct scale.

Read and record the size of the angles.

① _____

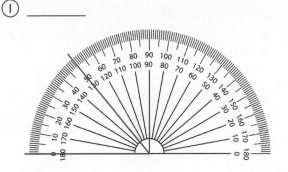

② _____

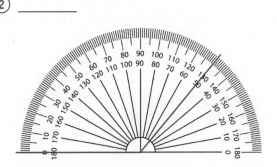

③ _____

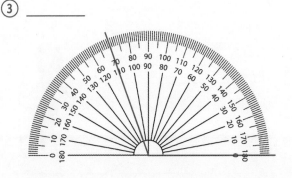

④ _____

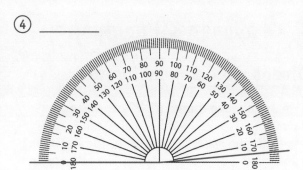

⑤ _____

⑥ _____

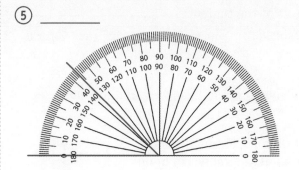

Score 2 points for each correct answer!   **SCORE**   **/12**   (0-4)   (6-8)   (10-12)

Problem Solving

AC9M5M04

Angle puzzles

① There are three angles on a straight line. One angle measures 75°. The other two angles are both multiples of 5. What are all the possibilities for the other two angles?
Remember: a straight line measures 180°.

_____

_____

_____

_____

② An ice skater is trying to spin a full 360°. She only manages to turn 170°. How many more degrees does she need to turn in order to make one complete revolution?

Grammar & Punctuation

AC9E5LA03

TERM 2 ENGLISH

Direct speech punctuation

We use **speech marks ("...")** to write someone's spoken words — also called direct speech. The speech marks go at the beginning and ending of what was said. The first spoken word always has a **capital letter** and a **comma** marks off the spoken words from the rest of the sentence.

Examples: Thomas announced, "The school fair is now open."

"The school fair is now open," announced Thomas.

NOTE: If the sentence has a **question mark (?)** or an **exclamation mark (!)**, you do not use a comma.

Rewrite these sentences. Put in the capital letters, speech marks, full stops and commas where necessary.

① go away! shouted the angry boy

_____

_____

② Terry asked are you going to Tom's birthday

_____

_____

More direct speech punctuation

When the spoken words in the sentence are split, you put a comma after the first chunk of speech, and you also put a comma after the speaking verb.

Example: "I can't wait," Paul **said**, "to meet your brother."

The first part of the spoken sentence begins with a capital letter, but the second part does not because it is a continuation of the same sentence.

Add the missing speech marks, capital letters, full stops and commas to these sentences.

③ on Saturday announced Jake we will get up early

④ my mother replied Anna is a superb cook

Phonic Knowledge & Spelling

AC9E5LY09, AC9E5LY10

Words ending in –al and –el

Say each word in the word bank. The suffix **–al** most often forms an **adjective**. Words that end in the suffix **–el** are most often **nouns or verbs**.

Word Bank

normal	rural	vital	vocal
legal	fatal	brutal	casual
shovel	shrivel	snivel	cancel
caramel	channel	rebel	novel

Choose words from the word bank to complete these sentences.

① The picture showed how the river had cut a _____ into the landscape.

② The trouble with eating _____ is that you always want more!

③ It is _____ to feel tired after strenuous physical activity.

④ It is _____ that we keep our personal belongings safe.

Adding –ly

Many adjectives that end in **–al** can be changed to adverbs by adding **–ly**.
Examples: normal, normally   vital, vitally

Add –ly to these adjectives to change them to adverbs. Write the new words.

⑤ physical _____

⑥ oral _____

⑦ vocal _____

⑧ mental _____

⑨ casual _____

⑩ formal _____

Score 2 points for each correct answer! SCORE /8   (0-2) (4-6) (8)

Score 2 points for each correct answer! SCORE /20   (0-8) (10-14) (16-20)

TARGETING HOMEWORK 5 © PASCAL PRESS ISBN 9781925726473

The Talking Hands Guesthouse

Imaginative text – Narrative
Author – Patricia Bernard

TERM 2 ENGLISH

Sujan noticed his mother waving to him from the step of their café, the smallest one in Pokhara. He saw her mouth opening and closing, but he didn't hear her. He had never heard his mother's voice – or anyone else's – because he was deaf.

Sujan stopped sweeping, put his broom aside, and taking the shopping list from his mother, he set off down Lakeside Road.

The vegetable and fish markets were beside Phewa Lake, the second largest lake in Nepal. Sujan loved the lake's mirrored surface, its multi-coloured fishing boats and its pretty pagoda island. He loved the smell of the fresh fruit and vegetables laid out in rows. Women from the country left home at dawn to reach the Pokhara market in time.

Sujan thought shopping for his mother, Dawa, was the best part of working at the café. He didn't like serving the customers. He couldn't read their lips if they looked away or they spoke a foreign language. He didn't like having to show them the message written on a piece of cardboard that explained he was deaf.

Dawa was a refugee from Tibet. She spoke Tibetan, Nepalese and a little English. When she was three years old, China sent troops

into Tibet and claimed it as its own. The Tibetan leader, the Dalai Lama, fled the country to India along with thousands of red-robed Buddhist monks.

Many ordinary Tibetans left as well, including Dawa's parents. They walked across the snow-covered Mahalangur Himal Mountains into Nepal with Dawa wrapped in a yak skin. They spent the rest of their lives in a refugee camp.

When Dawa was eighteen years old, she met Kalden, a Sherpa trekking guide. Kalden had brought a group of tourists into the refugee camp to see the Tibetan jewellery shops. A year later Dawa and Kalden married and moved closer to Phewa Lake, where most of the Sherpa guides lived.

The young couple discovered Sujan was deaf not long after he was born.

Source: *The Talking Hands Guesthouse*, Sparklers, Blake Education.

Write or circle the correct answers.

1. **This is a story set in:**

   a Tibet.   b China.   c Nepal.

2. **What is a refugee?**

   a a person from another country

   b a person who has been forced to leave their country due to war or a disaster

   c a person from Nepal

3. **Explain why Dawa became a refugee.**

   _____

   _____

4. **Name the languages that Dawa can speak.**

   _____

Match the words in the box to their meanings.

| pagoda   yak   sherpa |

5. a Hindu or Buddhist temple in the shape of a tower: _____

6. a mountaineering guide from Tibet or Nepal: _____

7. a large wild ox with shaggy hair: _____

My Book Review

Title _____

Author _____

Rating ☆☆☆☆☆

Comment _____

_____

Score 2 points for each correct answer!

SCORE **/14** (0-4) (6-10) (12-14)

Number & Algebra

AC9M5N07

Divisibility tests

> A number is **divisible** by another number if it can be divided into that number without a remainder.
>
> For example, 24 is divisible by 2. 24 can be divided by 2 twelve times with no remainder.
>
> **Divisibility test for 2**
>
> You can work out if a number is divisible by 2 by looking at the final digit. If the number ends in 0, 2, 4, 6 or 8, then it is divisible by 2.

Are these numbers divisible by 2?
Write yes or no.

① 69 _____   ⑤ 1560 _____
② 56 _____   ⑥ 4565 _____
③ 112 _____   ⑦ 12 422 _____
④ 307 _____   ⑧ 1 548 234 _____

> **Divisibility test for 3**
>
> If the sum of the digits of a number is divisible by 3, then the entire number is divisible by 3.
>
> *Example*: Is 243 divisible by 3?
>
> 2 + 4 + 3 = 9
>
> 9 is divisible by 3, so the entire number, 243, is divisible by 3.

Are these numbers divisible by 3?
Write yes or no.

⑨ 232 _____   ⑫ 128 647 _____
⑩ 1242 _____   ⑬ 142 581 _____
⑪ 13 704 _____   ⑭ 1 278 555 _____

> **Divisibility test for 4**
>
> If the last two digits of a number are divisible by 4, then the entire number is divisible by 4.

Are these numbers divisible by 4?
Write yes or no.

⑮ 408 _____
⑯ 567 _____
⑰ 6578 _____
⑱ 21 560 _____
⑲ 156 712 _____
⑳ 5 687 31 _____

> **Divisibility test for 5**
>
> If a number ends in 0 or 5, then it is divisible by 5.

Are these numbers divisible by 5?
Write yes or no.

㉑ 45 _____
㉒ 78 _____
㉓ 220 _____
㉔ 7424 _____
㉕ 1543 _____
㉖ 56 205 _____
㉗ 567 800 _____
㉘ 1 249 321 _____

> **Divisibility test for 6**
>
> For a number to be divisible by 6, it must be divisible by 2 **and** 3.
>
> *Example*: Is 146 262 divisible by 6?
>
> It ends in 2, so it must be divisible by 2.
>
> Next, add the digits:
>
> 1 + 4 + 6 + 2 + 6 + 2 = 21.
>
> 21 is divisible by 3.
>
> So 146 262 is divisible by 6.

Are these numbers divisible by 6?
Write yes or no.

㉙ 342 _____
㉚ 800 _____
㉛ 6363 _____
㉜ 24 588 _____
㉝ 185 726 _____
㉞ 3 457 230 _____

Score 2 points for each correct answer! **SCORE**  /68 (0-32) (34-62) (64-68)

Statistics & Probability

AC9M5ST01, AC9M5ST03

Presenting data

Lena carried out a survey to find out the favourite sandwich filling for the students in her class.

Here is a frequency table of Lena's results: She used this data to make a pie chart.

Filling	No. of students
Tomato	10
Ham	6
Cheese	8
Salad	3
Tuna	5

TARGETING HOMEWORK 5 © PASCAL PRESS ISBN 9781925726473

① **Use the colour key to colour the pie chart so that it matches the results in the table.**

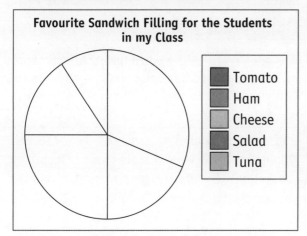

Favourite Sandwich Filling for the Students in my Class

Colour key:
- Tomato
- Ham
- Cheese
- Salad
- Tuna

Use Lena's results to answer the questions.

② How many students did Lena survey in total?

_____

③ Which filling was exactly ¼ of the total?

_____

④ What information can you get from the frequency table that you cannot get from the pie chart?

_____

_____

Measurement & Space

AC9M5M01

Measuring temperature

Gabriel Fahrenheit (1686–1736) developed the Fahrenheit scale to measure temperature. He set the freezing point of water at 32 degrees and the boiling point at 212 degrees. Some countries still use the Fahrenheit scale today, including the Bahamas, Belize, Cayman Islands, Palau and the USA.

Around 1743, Anders Celsius (1701–1744) invented the Celsius scale. He set the freezing temperature for water at 0 degrees and the boiling temperature at 100 degrees.

The Celsius scale is known as a Universal System Unit. It is used in science and in most countries.

This thermometer shows the Fahrenheit and Celsius scales.

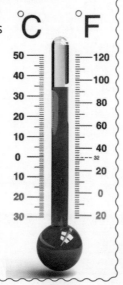

Use the thermometer to convert these Fahrenheit temperatures to degrees Celsius.

① 32° F = _____ °C   ④ 120° F = _____ °C
② 50° F = _____ °C
③ 70° F = _____ °C

Write true or false.

⑤ The boiling point of water is 212 °F.

_____

⑥ 0 °F is colder than 0 °C. _____

⑦ The freezing point of water is 0 °C.

_____

⑧ 50 °C is cooler than 100 °F. _____

⑨ Most countries use the Fahrenheit scale.

_____

⑩ The Celsius scale is used in science.

_____

⑪ The boiling point of water is 100 °C.

_____

Problem Solving

AC9M5N02

Divisibility tests

Use divisibility tests to solve this problem.

Jon's school raised $3584 to share between some local charities. Will they be able to share the money equally between:

① 2 charities?
   a Yes   **b** No
   How do you know?

   _____

② 3 charities?
   a Yes   **b** No
   How do you know?

   _____

③ 4 charities?
   a Yes   **b** No
   How do you know?

   _____

④ 5 charities?
   a Yes   **b** No
   How do you know?

   _____

⑤ 6 charities?
   a Yes   **b** No
   How do you know?

   _____

Grammar & Punctuation

AC9E5LA03

Direct and reported speech

We can write what a speaker says in a text in two ways:

Direct speech: We repeat the words spoken by the speaker.

Example: "We will be flying to New York next week," said Terri.

Reported speech: We report the words spoken by the speaker.

Example: Terri said that she would be flying to New York next week.

Speech marks ("...") are not required in reported speech.

To write reported speech, we usually change the **tense** of the spoken words.

Example:

present tense – "I <u>am baking</u> a cake for Sam's birthday," said the chef.

past tense – The chef said that he <u>was baking</u> a cake for Sam's birthday.

Rewrite these sentences as reported speech.

① "I am taking my first driving lesson today," said Tanya.

_____

_____

② "I'll wash up," offered Michael.

_____

_____

Rewrite these sentences as direct speech.

③ The man said that he was going to be late.

_____

_____

④ Dad asked me if I wanted to go fishing tomorrow.

_____

_____

⑤ My neighbour asked me to look after her cat.

_____

_____

TERM 2 ENGLISH

Phonic Knowledge & Spelling

AC9E5LY09, AC9E5LY10

Compound words

Say each word in the word bank. All the words in the list are compound words — they have two words joined together to make one word.

Word Bank

crossword	cardboard	cupcake	headfirst
highlands	stopover	storehouse	sugarcane
basketball	blindfold	blackcurrant	frostbite
fingernails	dashboard	database	download

Choose words from the word bank to complete these sentences.

① My aunty uses a lot of _____ for her craft work.

② When I clenched my fist, my _____ dug into my palm.

③ I baked a _____ but when I decorated it, it looked ghastly!

④ The diver went _____ down a deep shaft filled with water.

Make compound words beginning with cross from these words. Write the new words.

⑤ _____wind

⑥ _____way

⑦ _____roads

⑧ _____bones

⑨ _____over

⑩ _____fire

Match words from the box to create compound words.

horse	storm	house	paper
light	cycle	day	hopper

⑪ thunder_____

⑫ news_____

⑬ light_____

⑭ flash_____

⑮ birth_____

⑯ motor_____

⑰ sea_____

⑱ grass_____

TERM 2 ENGLISH

Sustaining the Land

Informative text – Report
Author – Lisa Nicol

Aboriginal peoples' connection to country helps them sustain the land.

For more than 50 000 years, the land gave Aboriginal peoples everything they needed – food, water, building materials, clothing and medicines. The way they worked with the land was guided by their spiritual connection to it. They had a duty to look after it. This responsibility is passed down in their law.

Aboriginal peoples know a lot about the land, plants and animals. They use them carefully, so there is always enough food. For example, when collecting seeds they leave some behind for new plants to grow. When hunting they don't kill young animals or mothers carrying young. They eat a variety of foods, so that no single food source runs out.

Aboriginal peoples also lit fires to manage their country. Fire-stick farming is planned burning of the land throughout the year to ensure plenty of food. It takes into account seasons, cycles of plant growth, the natural movement of water and the needs of animals. For example, Aboriginal people burn the land in patches. Burning encourages fresh shoots and creates grasslands. This attracts animals, such as wallabies and wombats, which makes them easier to hunt. The unburned patches provide shelter for other animals.

Fish River Station is a 180 000 hectare reserve, about 150 kilometres south of Darwin in the Northern Territory. Aboriginal rangers are managing the land to protect it from large,

destructive bushfires.

An old cattle station, Fish River is mainly **savanna** country. The land is prone to bushfires because of the cycle of wet and dry seasons. Since the British arrived, bushfires have become bigger and more destructive. They threaten people, animals and property. They destroy **biodiversity** and damage the land.

Traditionally, Aboriginal peoples burned early in the dry season. These early, controlled burns reduced the build-up of fuel. They also created **firebreaks**, which prevented uncontrollable fires later in the dry seasons.

Fish River's rangers burn the land to protect it. They light fires with drip torches and fire dropped from helicopters. They also use satellite images and maps to monitor the fires. They call the combination of traditional ways and modern technology "two toolkits".

The rangers have reduced the area burned by destructive bushfires from 35 per cent to just 1 per cent.

Source: *People and the Land*, Go Facts, Blake Education.

Write or circle the correct answers.

① **Another word for sustaining is:**
   a helping.   b working.   c ruining.

② **Give one example of how Aboriginal peoples ensure there is enough food to eat on their land.**

_____

_____

③ **What is the name used for the planned burning of land by Aboriginal peoples?**
   a bushfire
   b fire-stick farming
   c patch burning

Which words in the text have these meanings?

④ a system of rules: l_____

⑤ a place that gives protection from weather or enemies: sh_____

⑥ a grassy plain with few trees: s_____

⑦ **What is a firebreak?**
   a a break in a bushfire
   b a strip of bare land that helps to prevent the spread of fire

⑧ **What is two toolkits?**

Score 2 points for each correct answer!   **SCORE** /16   0-6   8-12   14-16

My Book Review

Title _____

Author _____

Rating ☆☆☆☆☆

Comment _____

_____

Number & Algebra

AC9M5N01

Decimal place value

Examples:
- Thirteen and five tenths can be written using numerals as **13.5**.
- Five hundred and sixty-two and twenty-four hundredths can be written using numerals as **562.24**.

Write these numbers using numerals.

① twenty-two and eight tenths

_____

② thirty-six and fifteen hundredths

_____

③ four hundred and eighty-one and forty-five hundredths

_____

④ two thousand, nine hundred and one hundred and thirty-two thousandths

_____

Write the place values for these numbers.

Example:

763.258 =

7 hundreds
6 tens
3 ones
2 tenths
5 hundredths
8 thousandths

⑥ 406.349 =

__ hundreds
__ tens
__ ones
__ tenths
__ hundredths
__ thousandths

⑤ 98.45 =

__ hundreds
__ tens
__ ones
__ tenths
__ hundredths
__ thousandths

⑦ 69.08 =

__ hundreds
__ tens
__ ones
__ tenths
__ hundredths
__ thousandths

Circle the number in the ones place in these amounts.

⑧ $65.35

⑨ $149.30

⑩ $760.95

⑪ $1 589.99

⑫ $62 785.20

⑬ $697 551.99

Circle the tens of dollars in these amounts.

⑭ $54.30

⑮ $236.99

⑯ $1 589.40

⑰ $44 895.45

⑱ $156 784.20

⑲ $1 567 843.00

Circle the tenths of a dollar in these amounts.

⑳ $6.99

㉑ $25.30

㉒ $159.25

㉓ $3 698.30

㉔ $25 698.70

㉕ $188 456.95

Ascending and descending order

When numbers are arranged in **ascending** order, they are arranged from the smallest number to the largest number.

Example: 0.5, 1.8, 12.5, 12.67, 236.12

When numbers are arranged in **descending** order, they are arranged from the largest number to the smallest number.

Example: 236.12, 12.67, 12.5, 1.8, 0.5

㉖ Write these numbers in ascending order.
345, 3.126, 8.9, 55

_____

㉗ Write these numbers in descending order.
123.6, 6.359, 24.08, 0.589

_____

Score 2 points for each correct answer! SCORE /54 0-24 26-48 50-54

Statistics & Probability

There are no statistics & probability activities in this unit.

Measurement & Space

AC9M5M01

Writing length using decimal notation

100 centimetres (cm) = 1 metre (m)

This means that **centimetres** are **hundredths** of a metre.

Examples:

3 metres 32 centimetres = 3.32 m

5 metres 6 centimetres = 5.06 m

Write the decimal numbers beside the matching measurements.

0.07	0.85	3.15	12.6

① 85 centimetres = _____

② 12 metres 60 centimetres = _____

③ 3 metres 15 centimetres = _____

④ 0 metres 7 centimetres = _____

Write the measurements in decimal form.

⑤ 4 metres 25 centimetres = _____

⑥ 5 metres 74 centimetres = _____

⑦ 10 metres 8 centimetres = _____

⑧ 62 centimetres = _____

Calculate the perimeter of these shapes. Write the answers in decimal notation.

⑨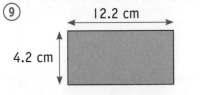

Perimeter = _____

12.2 cm
4.2 cm

⑩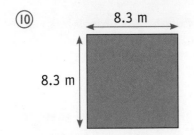

Perimeter = _____

8.3 m
8.3 m

---

10 millimetres (mm) = 1 centimetre (cm)

To convert cm to mm, you multiply by 10. The easy way to do this is to move the decimal point one place to the right.

Examples:

14.0 cm = 140 mm (14.0 is the same as 14)
25.6 cm = 256 mm
3.56 cm = 35.6 mm

Convert these measurements from cm to mm.

⑪ 15.0 cm = _____ mm

⑫ 1.6 cm = _____ mm

⑬ 25.2 cm = _____ mm

⑭ 2.56 cm = _____ mm

⑮ 345.2 cm = _____ mm

⑯ 24 cm = _____ mm

To convert **mm** to **cm**, you divide by 10. The easy way to do this is to move the decimal point one place to the left.

Examples:

7 mm = 0.7 cm   56 mm = 5.6 cm
156 mm = 15.6 cm   12.5 mm = 1.25 cm

Convert these measurements from mm to cm.

⑰ 5 mm = _____ cm

⑱ 38 mm = _____ cm

⑲ 341 mm = _____ cm

⑳ 25.5 mm = _____ cm

㉑ 1578 mm = _____ cm

㉒ 3470 mm = _____ cm

Score 2 points for each correct answer! SCORE **/44** (0-20) (22-38) (40-44)

Problem Solving

AC9M5SP01

Match it

Josie decorated six cubes with red lines.

Diagrams a to f show the **top views** of the cubes. Write the letter of the matching top view above each cube. The first one has been done for you.

① f   ②   ③

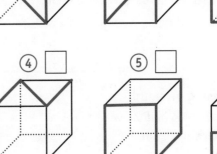

④   ⑤   ⑥

Top views

a   b   c

d   e   f

Grammar & Punctuation

Circle the possessive pronoun. Write what the pronoun 'owns'.

① That bicycle is hers, but she gave it to me.

_____

Circle the pronoun. Write if it is 1st, 2nd or 3rd person.

② She told them to sing louder. _____

③ Why are you upset? _____

Circle the verbs in these sentences. <u>Underline</u> the adverbs.

④ We'll go now and they can join us later.

⑤ We eventually reached the motel after a long drive.

Circle the correct word in brackets to complete the sentence.

⑥ Ben sings (more   most) confidently than me.

Rewrite this sentence. Put in the capital letters, speech marks, full stops and commas where necessary.

⑦ have they arrived yet? asked tim

_____

_____

Rewrite this sentence as reported speech.

⑧ "I'll mow the lawns," offered Dad.

_____

_____

Rewrite this sentence as direct speech.

⑨ Michael said that he was going to be late.

_____

_____

Add the missing pronoun.

⑩ When Mum and Dad went to London, _____ stayed with our aunt.

Circle the correct pronoun in brackets.

⑪ Reece and (me   I) like to go swimming.

Score 2 points for each correct answer! **SCORE** **/22** (0-8) (10-16) (18-22)

Phonic Knowledge & Spelling

Write these words in the plural. Remember your rules!

① cherry _____

② child _____

③ chimney _____

④ chateau _____

Write the plurals of these words.

⑤ ox _____

⑥ mattress _____

Circle the synonym.

⑦ **elect:**   play   vote   release   decline

Write advice or advise to complete these sentences.

⑧ She acted on my _____ not to buy that house.

⑨ He will _____ me about which pet to choose.

Write the antonyms of these words using either –ful or –less. Write the new word.

⑩ fearless _____

⑪ harmful _____

Add –ly to these adjectives to change them to adverbs. Write the new words.

⑫ visual _____

⑬ physical _____

Match the words from the box to make compound words.

| ache   horse   day   light |

⑭ sea_____   ⑰ birth_____

⑮ flash_____

⑯ tooth_____

These words all begin with 'ch'. Sort the words into the correct beginning sound.

| chef   chord   chateau chilli   chrome   children |

⑱ 'tch' sound

_____   _____

⑲ 'k' sound

_____   _____

⑳ 'sh' sound

_____

Score 2 points for each correct answer! **SCORE** **/40** (0-18) (20-34) (36-40)

TARGETING HOMEWORK 5 © PASCAL PRESS ISBN 9781925726473

South Australia 1826

Informative text – Explanation
Author – Lisa Nicol

In 1831 the British minister in charge of Great Britain's colonies received a plan. It was titled *Proposal to His Majesty's Government for founding a colony on the Southern Coast of Australia.* It was a plan for a very different British colony — one without convicts.

British politician and **entrepreneur** Edward Gibbon Wakefield proposed to sell land to free settlers. Money raised from land sales would pay for tickets to the colony for honest farm workers, not convicts. Within four years, the British Parliament had passed the *South Australia Act* and the first land was offered for sale.

Between February and July 1836, nine ships left Great Britain bound for the newly created **province** of South Australia. In November, 636 settlers went ashore at Holdfast Bay (now Glenelg) and the province was proclaimed on 28 December. A town was laid out by surveyor Colonel William Light. It was named Adelaide, after the **consort** of the British king.

Source: *Australia: Colonies*, Go Facts: Australian History, Blake Education.

TERM 2 ENGLISH

Write or circle the correct answers.

1. Who came up with the plan to settle South Australia?

_____

2. In what way was this planned settlement different to other settlements?

_____
_____

3. When was the *South Australia Act* passed?

_____

Which words in the text have these meanings?

4. a member of Parliament: p_____
5. an administrative region or area of a country: p_____
6. to go to the shore: a_____
7. the wife or husband of the king or queen: c_____

8. Was Great Britain ruled by a king or a queen at this time?

_____

9. Who was the surveyor who laid out the town of Adelaide?

_____

10. What was the original name of Glenelg?

_____

11. What does **proclaimed** mean?
   a settled
   b officially announced
   c sold

Score 2 points for each correct answer!

SCORE /22   0-8   10-16   18-22

My Book Review

Title _____

Author _____

Rating ☆☆☆☆☆

Comment _____
_____

Number & Algebra

Use the lattice method to calculate this multiplication.

① 543 × 42 = _____

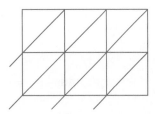

Circle the largest number.

② a 1.5   b 1.468   c 1.23

③ a 0.8   b 1.8   c 1.679

Write >, < or = to make these statements true.

④ 0.60 ___ 0.6

⑤ 1.30 ___ 1.50

⑥ $\frac{7}{10}$ ___ 0.7

⑦ 2.3 ___ 2.1345

⑧ $\frac{24}{100}$ ___ 0.25

⑨ 2.003 ___ 2.03

Write the number of squares coloured blue as a fraction and as a percentage.

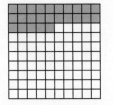
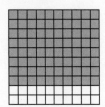

⑩ fraction = ____

⑪ percentage = _____

⑫ fraction = ____

⑬ percentage = _____

Use the number lines to help you work out the answers.

⑭ $1\frac{2}{6} + \frac{5}{6}$ = _____

⑮ $1\frac{2}{10} - \frac{8}{10}$ = _____

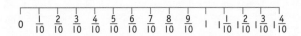

Li's class is making bookmarks to sell at a fund-raising event. This is the budget for each bookmark:

card	$0.20
stickers	$1.00
sticky-back plastic	$0.50

Use the bookmark budget to answer the questions. Show your working out.

⑯ How much will each bookmark cost to make?

_____

⑰ They want to make $1.60 profit on each bookmark. What will the price be?

_____

Complete these equivalent number sentences.

⑱ 200 ÷ _____ = 5 × 4

⑲ 35 × 2 = 280 ÷ _____

Are these numbers divisible by 4? Write yes or no.

⑳ 113 _____

㉑ 2 490 _____

㉒ 542 781 _____

㉓ 8 672 516 _____

Write these numbers using numerals.

㉔ thirty-six and nine tenths _____

㉕ five hundred and forty-one and fifty-five hundredths _____

㉖ Write these numbers in ascending order.

290, 2.904, 5.6, 52

_____

㉗ Write these numbers in descending order.

223.6, 6.231, 22.08, 0.359

_____

Score 2 points for each correct answer!   SCORE **/54** (0-24) (26-48) (50-54)

Statistics & Probability

Decide where the events should go on the probability line. Write 0, 0.25, 0.5, 0.75 or 1.

Impossible   Certain

0   0.25   0.5   0.75   1

① You roll a regular die and get a 10. _____

② You will have a drink tomorrow. _____

③ Everyone in your class will eat a banana tomorrow. _____

Jennie asked the players in the school netball teams how many goals they scored in a season. Here are Jennie's results:

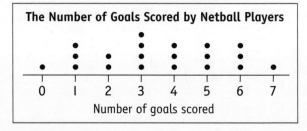

The Number of Goals Scored by Netball Players

Number of goals scored

TARGETING HOMEWORK 5 © PASCAL PRESS ISBN 9781925726473

Use the dot plot to answer the questions.

④ How many players did Jennie survey?

_____

⑤ How many players scored 3 goals or more?

_____

⑥ Which number of goals was the most common? _____

Use this spinner to answer the questions.

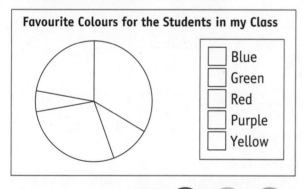

⑦ How many sections is the spinner divided into? ____

⑧ Write the chance of spinning blue as a fraction. ____

⑨ Write the chance of **not** spinning blue. ____

⑩ Write the chance of spinning yellow or green as a fraction. ____

Eli carried out a survey to find out the favourite colours of the students in his class. The frequency table shows his results.

Eli used this data to make a pie chart.

Colour	No. of students
Blue	12
Green	4
Red	10
Purple	2
Yellow	8

⑪ **Colour the pie chart to match the data in the table.**

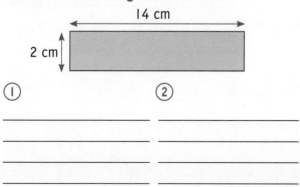

Favourite Colours for the Students in my Class

☐ Blue
☐ Green
☐ Red
☐ Purple
☐ Yellow

Score 2 points for each correct answer! SCORE **/22** (0-8) (10-16) (18-22)

Measurement & Space

Calculate the perimeter. Show two different methods for working out the answer.

14 cm

2 cm

① _____

_____

_____

② _____

_____

_____

What 3D object could each net fold to make?

③ _____

_____

④ _____

Estimate if these angles are equal to, less than or greater than a right angle. Write the correct answer above each angle.

⑤ _____

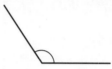

⑥ _____

Read and record the size of the angles.

⑦ _____

⑧ _____

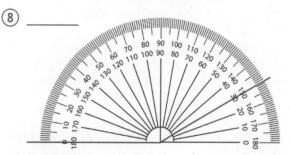

Use the thermometer to convert the Fahrenheit temperatures to degrees Celsius.

⑨ 32 °F = _____ °C

⑩ 50 °F = _____ °C

Convert these measurements from cm to mm.

⑪ 18 cm = _____ mm

⑫ 4.6 cm = _____ mm

⑬ 35.2 cm = _____ mm

Convert these measurements from mm to cm.

⑭ 5 mm = _____ cm

⑮ 38.5 mm = _____ cm

⑯ 3 417 mm = _____ cm

Score 2 points for each correct answer! SCORE **/32** (0-14) (16-26) (28-32)

Grammar & Punctuation

AC9E5LA05

Active and passive voice

> **Active voice:** <u>The subject</u> is *doing the action* of the **verb**.
>
> *Examples:* <u>Naomi</u> **ate** an ice cream.
> <u>The police officer</u> **arrested** the thief.
>
> **Passive voice:** *The object of the action* becomes <u>the subject</u> of the sentence. The verb in passive has two parts — **'be' + past participle.**
> *Examples:*
> <u>The ice cream</u> **was eaten** by Naomi.
> <u>The thief</u> **was arrested** by the police officer.

Are these sentences active or passive? Write A or P.

① The zebra **was attacked** by a lion. ____

② Max **is riding** his bike. ____

③ I **will read** my new book tomorrow. ____

④ The house **was destroyed** by the cyclone.

____

Writing in the active voice

> When we write, it is generally better to choose active rather than passive verbs. It makes the message clearer and easier to understand.

Rewrite these passive voice sentences in the active voice.

⑤ The letter was written by Rocco.

_____

⑥ The rules are being explained to us by the coach.

_____

_____

Change these active voice sentences to passive voice.

⑦ Janine scored a goal.

_____

⑧ Hundreds of spectators are watching the athletics.

_____

_____

Phonic Knowledge & Spelling

AC9E5LY09, AC9E5LY10

Words that end in –id and –ide

Say each word in the word bank. We emphasise the first syllable of the words that end in **–id**. We emphasise the second syllable in the words that end in **–ide**.

Word Bank

avid	valid	vivid	livid
candid	rigid	solid	squalid
reside	provide	confide	divide
decide	subside	pesticide	homicide

Choose words from the word bank to complete these sentences.

① I truly believe we should

_____ free food for the homeless.

② She hopes to one day fulfil her dream to _____ in London.

③ The insect had _____ colours on its wings.

Write words from the word bank that match these clues.

④ stiff and hard to bend:

_____

⑤ very dirty and unpleasant:

_____

⑥ very angry:

_____

Choose which suffixes you can add to the words below. Write the new words. Remember your spelling rules!

–ed, –ing, –ly, –ent, –ence

⑦ rigid _____

_____

⑧ decide _____

_____

⑨ confide _____

_____

Score 2 points for each correct answer! **SCORE** /16 (0-6) (8-12) (14-16)

Score 2 points for each correct answer! **SCORE** /18 (0-6) (8-14) (16-18)

Bound for New South Wales

Historical narrative text
Author – Merryn Whitfield
Illustrator – Steve Hunter

Sarah stood quietly in the shade of an overhanging branch. She had done her best to make herself look presentable for the reverend, but she knew it was a hopeless task. Clutching her infant to her chest, she murmured soothing sounds to quieten him.

"Ahem ..." Her thoughts were disturbed by a polite cough coming from the makeshift pulpit. Reverend Richard Johnson, pastor for the First Fleet, was staring at Sarah. His displeasure at her inattention was obvious.

"We, His Humble servants, are gathered here today in the sight of our most merciful Father. We ask Him to forgive our sins ..." As the reverend continued, Sarah once again allowed her thoughts to wander.

She had grown up in Worchester, a small country village, three days' walk from London. Yet at the tender age of 18 she was forced to leave all that she knew. At the point of starvation, alone, dressed in threadbare rags, she had done what so many before her had. The words of the judge in the court of Old Bailey still echoed in her ears: "You have been found guilty of felony, stealing a half loaf of bread with a value of 3 pence. As a result, I sentence you to seven years of hard labour in the penal colony of New South Wales."

So here she was, in a strange and unwelcoming land with nothing but the rags on her back and a babe in her arms.

"... and protect him from the evils of sin so that he may become an honest and pious man." With that, Reverend Johnson dipped his fingers in the blood-warm water and wiped them across the infant's head. "May your sins be cleansed. May you start your life anew in the eyes of God."

As Sarah stood there holding her infant son, she thought about what the reverend said. She was surprised to find that there was much truth in it. Back in England, she had been an illiterate peasant with no home, no family and no chance of a decent life. But here things were different. Here there was a chance, a chance for freedom, land and independence. Here there was hope, hope for her son and his future.

Maybe, just maybe, she too could start anew in the colony of New South Wales.

Source: *Writing Centres: Imaginative Texts –*
Upper Primary, Blake Education.

TERM 3 ENGLISH

Write or circle the correct answers.

1. Why was Sarah sent to New South Wales?

    _____

2. Why did Sarah think it was 'a hopeless task' trying to make herself look presentable for the reverend?

    a She hated being clean and tidy.

    b She had just spent many months at sea in squalid conditions.

    c She didn't know how to look after herself.

3. What is a **felony**?

    a stealing

    b being poor

    c a serious crime

Find words in the text that have these meanings.

4. temporary: m_____

5. thin and tattered: th_____

6. in the wrong: g_____

7. unable to read or write: i_____

8. What did Reverend Johnson say that gave hope to Sarah?

    _____

    _____

Score 2 points for each correct answer!   SCORE /16   0-6   8-12   14-16

My Book Review

Title _____

Author _____

Rating ☆☆☆☆☆

Comment _____

_____

Number & Algebra

AC9M5N07, AC9M5N08

Rounding to the nearest 1000

When you round to the nearest 1000, look at the last three digits. If they are **less than 500**, you round the number **down**. If the last three digits are **500 or more**, round the number **up**.

The easy way to do this is to look at the number in the hundreds place. If the digit is 0, 1, 2, 3 or 4, round down. If the digit is 5, 6, 7, 8 or 9, round up.

Examples:

1424 has a 4 in the hundreds place ↓ so round it down to 1000.

1668 has a 6 in the hundreds place so round it up to 2000.

Round these numbers to the nearest 1000.

① 7043 _____
② 3860 _____
③ 8100 _____
④ 1213 _____
⑤ 5900 _____
⑥ 4501 _____
⑦ 9050 _____
⑧ 4703 _____
⑨ 9821 _____

If the number you are rounding is in the tens of thousands or more, you still look at the digit in the hundreds place when rounding to the nearest 1000.

Examples:

34 579 rounded to nearest 1000 is 35 000.

563 100 rounded to nearest 1000 is 563 000.

4 783 854 rounded to nearest 1000 is 4 784 000.

Round these numbers to the nearest 1000.

⑩ 15 698 _____
⑪ 26 024 _____
⑫ 55 700 _____
⑬ 134 209 _____
⑭ 872 567 _____
⑮ 502 328 _____
⑯ 5 675 431 _____
⑰ 6 842 800 _____

Round these numerals to the nearest 1000 and quickly estimate the answer. Circle the correct estimate.

⑱ 4569 + 1230
  a 5000   b 6000   c 7000

⑲ 4320 + 4590
  a 7000   b 8000   c 9000

⑳ 12 360 + 22 600
  a 35 000   b 36 000   c 37 000

㉑ 8239 – 2560
  a 4000   b 5000   c 6000

㉒ 10 236 – 6800
  a 2000   b 3000   c 4000

㉓ 435 329 – 221 682
  a 210 000   b 212 000   c 213 000

Score 2 points for each correct answer!

SCORE /46   0-20   22-40   42-46

Statistics & Probability

AC9M5ST01, AC9M5ST03

Survey results

Stella asked the students in her class about their pets. Here are the results of her survey.

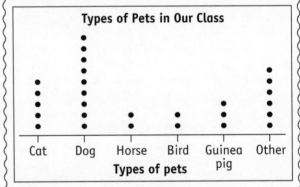

Types of Pets in Our Class

Cat   Dog   Horse   Bird   Guinea pig   Other

Types of pets

Who looks after your pets?

Always me	IIII
Always other family members	HHH IIII
Shared between family members	HHH HHH IIII

Use Stella's data to answer the questions.

① Which type of pet was the most popular?

  _____

② How many students have a cat? _____

③ How many students did Stella survey? _____

④ 5 students in Stella's class do not have a pet. How many students are there in Stella's class? _____

TARGETING HOMEWORK 5 © PASCAL PRESS ISBN 9781925726473

⑤ Is it true that most families in Stella's class share the responsibility of looking after their pets?

　　a　yes　　b　no

Do you think Stella asked these questions when she carried out her survey? Write yes or no.

⑥ What is your favourite pet?　　_____

⑦ Do you like dogs or cats best?　　_____

⑧ What type of pet do you have?　　_____

⑨ When did you get your pet?　　_____

⑩ Do you look after your pet?　　_____

⑪ Do you have a pet?　　_____

⑫ Who looks after your pet – always you, always other family members, or shared between family members?　　_____

Score 2 points for each correct answer! **SCORE** **/24** (0-10) (12-18) (20-24)

Measurement & Space

AC9M5M03

24-hour clock

Write the matching 24-hour times from the box. The analogue times are all pm.

| 14:30 | 16:15 | 21:15 | 23:45 |

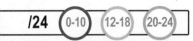

① _____　　　　③ _____

② _____　　　　④ _____

How much time has passed between the times shown on these clocks?

⑤ clock 1 and clock 3

_____

⑥ clock 4 and clock 3

_____

⑦ clock 3 and clock 2

_____

Use the flight timetable to answer the questions.

Depart Newtown	Arrive Oldtown	Airline	Frequency
09:50	11:05	KingAir	daily
11:25	12:40	JetOne	daily
14:00	15:15	KingAir	Fri/Sat
15:20	16:35	JetOne	daily
19:25	20:40	KingAir	M/T/W
20:00	21:15	JetOne	daily

⑧ How long does it take to fly from Newtown to Oldtown?

_____

⑨ Could I catch a 14:00 plane to Oldtown on a Monday?

_____

⑩ Which airline would get me to Oldtown in time for a meeting at noon on Monday?

_____

⑪ Tad missed the 11:25 flight. He only flies with JetOne. How long will it be until the next flight?

_____

Score 2 points for each correct answer! **SCORE** **/22** (0-8) (10-16) (18-22)

Problem Solving

AC9M5M03

Time puzzle

Work out the pattern in the times shown on these clocks.

① What is the pattern?

_____

_____

② What time should the next clock in the pattern show?

_____

Grammar & Punctuation

AC9E5LA05

Compound sentences

Remember! A simple sentence has a subject and a verb.

A **compound sentence** is two simple sentences joined together by a **conjunction**. Each sentence has a subject and a verb.

Example:

subject　verb　　conjunction　subject　verb
Megan <u>went</u> yesterday **and I** <u>am going</u> tomorrow.

Conjunctions include: and, but, so, or, nor, for, yet.

Join these sentences together by choosing the most suitable conjunction from those listed above.

① Alex was supposed to walk the dog, _____ he watched TV all afternoon.

② Jon needs to study harder, _____ he will not pass his exams.

③ Jackie loves singing _____ she also loves dancing.

④ I went to my nan's house, _____ I could help her with the gardening.

Subjects in compound sentences

Each part of a compound sentence has a **subject**. Sometimes it is the same and sometimes it is different.

Examples:

Jack went fishing **but he** didn't catch any fish. (same subject)

I went to town early **and Sam** came in later. (different subject)

If the subject is the same, the subject in the second part of the sentence is often replaced by a **pronoun**.

Example: subject　　　conjunction　pronoun
Kate loves to play netball **and** <u>she</u> loves to go swimming.

Replace the subject in the second part of the sentence with a suitable pronoun. Rewrite the sentence.

⑤ The penguins waddled up the beach **and** the penguins went into their burrows.

_____

_____

⑥ The dog can eat tinned food **or** the dog can eat dry food.

_____

_____

Score 2 points for each correct answer! **SCORE** **/12**　(0-4)　(6-8)　(10-12)

Phonic Knowledge & Spelling

AC9E5LY09, AC9E5LY10

Words ending in –ect and –ict

Say each word in the word bank. These words have endings that are similar so you need to use your eyes and ears when learning to spell them.

Word Bank

elect	reject	project	object
inject	inspect	respect	reflect
strict	district	inflict	afflict
conflict	contradict	predict	verdict

Choose words from the word bank to complete these sentences.

① We tried to _____ what the questions might be in the science test.

② You should _____ his answer even if you disagree with it.

③ The jury's _____ was guilty.

④ The doctor had to

_____

the vaccine into my arm.

Words that can be confused

The words **afflict** and **inflict** can be easily confused.

Afflict: if something afflicts you, it causes you suffering

Inflict: to make or force someone to suffer something

Circle the correct word so that these sentences make sense.

⑤ It was obvious that the animal was (inflicted　afflicted) by a disease.

⑥ The robber (inflicted　afflicted) a terrible injury on the man.

⑦ The school was (inflicted　afflicted) by an outbreak of flu.

⑧ The doctor suspected that the injury was self- (inflicted　afflicted).

Score 2 points for each correct answer! **SCORE** **/16**　(0-6)　(8-12)　(14-16)

Convict Life

Informative text – Report
Authors – Frances Mackay and Catherine Gordon

Daily life

The lives of the convicts were strictly controlled. They were sent to Australia as punishment, so they were expected to work hard from sunrise to sunset. Male convicts cleared land for farming, chopped down trees for building, made bricks, and built roads and government buildings. Female convicts often worked as servants for officials or were sent to institutions known as 'female factories', where they completed daily tasks like laundry and cleaning the barracks.

Food

When the settlers first arrived in Australia, they had to bring supplies with them or have them shipped from England. By the early 1800s, a lot of the food settlers ate was grown in Australia. In 1811, the weekly ration for convicts in New South Wales was 7 pounds of salt beef, 4 pounds of pork, 6 pounds of wheat and 15 pounds of corn.

Typical meals for convicts

- Breakfast – porridge made from oatmeal and water, bread
- Lunch – bread roll, dried and salted meat
- Dinner – bread roll

Punishments

If the convicts were badly behaved, they could be punished. Sometimes they were flogged with a whip called a cat-o'-nine-tails. They could be put into stocks or leg irons, or into a dark cell in solitary confinement. If the convicts continued to misbehave, they could be sent to a penal colony such as Norfolk Island or Port Arthur. Sometimes convicts were hanged. It paid to be a well-behaved convict, however. After four years of good behaviour, prisoners who had been sentenced to seven years' transportation were granted a Ticket of Leave, which allowed them to work for themselves. Some convicts were also pardoned and allowed to return to England.

Source: *Australian History Centres*, Upper Primary, Blake Education.

TERM 3 ENGLISH

Write or circle the correct answers.

① **Name three types of work male convicts did in the new colony.**

_____

_____

② **Name three types of work female convicts did in the new colony.**

_____

_____

③ **What is a ration?**

a a shopping list

b an amount each person is allowed when there is a shortage

c a menu

Find words in the text that have these meanings.

④ people in charge: o_____

⑤ places where people work or live together: i_____

⑥ buildings where soldiers live: b_____

⑦ declared free from guilt: p_____

⑧ **Name four ways in which convicts could be punished.**

_____

_____

⑨ **What does solitary confinement mean?**

a a convict prison

b a dark cell

c to be kept alone in a cell away from other convicts

Score 2 points for each correct answer!

SCORE **/18** (0-6) (8-14) (16-18)

My Book Review

Title _____

Author _____

Rating ☆☆☆☆☆

Comment _____

_____

Number & Algebra

AC9M5N07

Division

The ÷ sign means **divide**. When we are dividing, we can split the number we are dividing into smaller numbers.

Example: 161 ÷ 7

• Use ×7 number facts to take away smaller 'chunks'.

• 10 × 70 = 70. Take this away from 161.

• Keep taking 70 until you cannot.

• 3 × 7 = 21

• Then add: 10 + 10 + 3 = 23.

• 161 ÷ 7 = 23

```
          10 + 10 + 3 = 23
       7 ) 161
          – 70     10 lots of 7
            91
          – 70     10 lots of 7
            21
          – 21     3 lots of 7
             0
```

Use the **chunking method** to complete these divisions.

① 175 ÷ 5 = _____

```
    5 ) 175
       – 50    10 × 5 = 50
       ____

       ____

       ____

       ____
```

② 252 ÷ 6 = _____

```
    6 ) 252
       ____

       ____

       ____

       ____
```

Sometimes, you get a remainder when you divide. *Example:* 189 ÷ 4

```
          10 + 10 + 10 + 10 + 7 = 47 r 1
       4 ) 189
          – 40     10 × 4 = 40
           149
          – 40     10 × 4 = 40
           109
          – 40     10 × 4 = 40
            69
          – 40     10 × 4 = 40
            29
          – 28     7 × 4 = 40
             1     There is 1 left over.
```

Use the **chunking method** to complete these divisions.

③ 182 ÷ 5 = _____

```
    5 ) 182
       ____

       ____

       ____

       ____

       ____
```

④ 215 ÷ 7 = _____

```
    7 ) 215
       ____

       ____

       ____

       ____

       ____
```

Score 2 points for each correct answer! SCORE /8   0-2   4-6   8

Statistics & Probability

There are no statistics & probability activities in this unit.

TARGETING HOMEWORK 5 © PASCAL PRESS ISBN 9781925726473

Measurement & Space

AC9M5M04

Rotation

When a shape is **turned**, it is called a **rotation**.

- **Clockwise** turns are in the same direction as the hands on a clock turn: ↻
- **Anticlockwise** turns are in the opposite direction: ↺

We can use **degrees** to describe the size of the turn.

The kite has rotated 90° clockwise.

The kite has rotated 90° anticlockwise.

The kite has rotated 180°.

Which rotation would get the shape to fit into the cut-out? Circle the correct answer.

①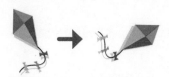

- a 45° clockwise
- b 45° anticlockwise
- c 90° clockwise
- d 90° anticlockwise

②

- a 45° clockwise
- b 45° anticlockwise
- c 90° clockwise
- d 90° anticlockwise

③

- a 45° clockwise
- b 45° anticlockwise
- c 90° clockwise
- d 90° anticlockwise

④

- a 180° clockwise
- b 45° anticlockwise
- c 450° clockwise
- d 90° anticlockwise

⑤

- a 180° clockwise
- b 360° clockwise
- c 90° clockwise
- d 45° clockwise

⑥

- a 90° clockwise
- b 90° anticlockwise
- c 45° clockwise
- d 45° anticlockwise

Score 2 points for each correct answer! **SCORE** /12 0-4 6-8 10-12

Problem Solving

AC9M5N09

Make it add up

Write the numbers 1 to 16 in the grid so that all the rows and columns add to make 34.

You can only use each number once.

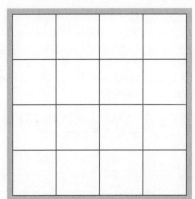

TERM 3 MATHS

81

Grammar & Punctuation

AC9E5LA08

Replacing dull verbs with more precise verbs

Some verbs are dull and overused.

Example: The old lady **laughed**.

We can make the meaning of the sentence clearer by using more precise verbs.

Examples:

The old lady **cackled**.
The old lady **giggled**.
The old lady **chortled**.
The old lady **guffawed**.

Find two precise verbs in the box that match with each common verb.

observe	reflect	guzzle	slice
inquire	devour	dash	sip
scurry	munch	snip	
contemplate	glimpse	question	

① cut

_____ _____

② think

_____ _____

③ ask

_____ _____

④ run

_____ _____

⑤ see

_____ _____

⑥ drink

_____ _____

⑦ eat

_____ _____

Circle the verb that more precisely describes the action in these sentences.

⑧ The baker (sliced diced segmented) the bread to make a sandwich loaf.

⑨ The doctor closely (looked at examined viewed) the very sick patient.

⑩ Jenna was (exhausted tired weary) after her marathon race.

Phonic Knowledge & Spelling

AC9E5LY09, AC9E5LY10

Words that end in –age

Say each word in the word bank. They all end in the suffix **–age**. Some of these words are nouns and some are verbs.

Word Bank

package	postage	cottage	courage
marriage	village	vintage	voyage
average	advantage	bandage	breakage
engage	manage	hostage	rummage

Choose words from the word bank to complete these sentences.

① We made up a rhyme about a witch that lived in an old _____.

② It is an _____ to have a sense of rhythm when dancing.

③ I bought my outfit for the 1920s costume party at the _____ shop.

④ The gangsters held the _____ captive for a ransom.

Make compound words ending in age. Write the new words.

⑤ teen _____

⑥ sew _____

⑦ volt _____

⑧ dam _____

Add endings to the words in brackets to complete the sentences. Write the new words.

⑨ Please make sure the item is _____ correctly before posting it. (package)

⑩ The new owner was _____ the hotel very well. (manage)

Welcome back

Imaginative text – Narrative
Author – Lisa Thompson, **Illustrator** – Ned Culic

"I don't believe it!" cried Hannah as she entered the bus shelter. "What are you doing here? You're supposed to be gone! You changed schools! Remember?"

Hannah threw her arms up in disbelief.

"Let me guess. They found out exactly how much of a pain you are and they knocked you back. Great. Just great! I was so looking forward to this school term without you. It was going to be a Josh-free zone! It was going to be really peaceful!"

"Peaceful? Who wants peace?" Josh smirked. "I'm happy to see you too, Hannah. Look, I've even brought you a little something." He took his hand from his pocket and a spider bounced on the floor, its legs shaking jelly-like in the air.

Hannah let out an almighty scream. "AHHHHHHHHHHHHHHH." It shook the bus shelter.

Josh danced around, laughing. Finally he reached over and picked up the rubber spider.

"I love it. You're such a lung horn!" laughed Josh. He held out the rubber spider.

"You'd scream at anything. No Brainer, it's not even real. Someone like you should be able to see that."

Hannah's face went red with anger. "How many times do I have to tell you? Don't call me that!"

"What? No Brainer?"

Hannah's face went even redder. "Look, Super Pain, just keep your dumb pranks away from me."

She took a few deep breaths. "You know you're getting very unoriginal, Josh. You did the spider thing last term. What else is on today's list? Another reptile rampage at recess?"

Source: *Assignment Fiasco*, Sparklers, Blake Education.

TERM 3 ENGLISH

Write or circle the correct answers.

① **What type of text is this?**

  a historical recount   c narrative

  b personal recount   d explanation

② **What type of word is peaceful?**

  a noun   c adjective

  b verb   d adverb

③ **What type of person is Josh?**

  a a prankster

  b popular at school

  c easy to get along with

④ **Which is the odd word?**

  a joked   c laughed

  b sniggered   d smirked

⑤ **What name did Josh call Hannah that upset her?**

_____

⑥ **How did Hannah's face show that she was really angry?**

_____

Find words in the text that have these meanings.

⑦ smiled in a silly way: s_____

⑧ powerful: a_____

⑨ riot: r_____

Score 2 points for each correct answer!

SCORE **/18**   0-6   8-14   16-18

My Book Review

Title _____

Author _____

Rating ☆☆☆☆☆

Comment _____

_____

Number & Algebra

AC9M5N04

Calculating percentages

Percent means **out of 100**.

$1\% = \frac{1}{100}$ or 1 out of 100.

To calculate 1% of a number, divide it by 100.

Examples:

1% of 200 = 2

1% of 500 = 5

1% of 456 = 4.56

1% of 23 = 0.23

Remember – to divide by 100, move the decimal point two places to the left.

Calculate 1% of these numbers.

① 1% of 300 = _____

② 1% of 800 = _____

③ 1% of 1000 = _____

④ 1% of 763 = _____

⑤ 1% of 78 = _____

⑥ 1% of 5 = _____

To calculate 10% of a number, divide it by 10. Calculate 10% of these numbers.

⑦ 10% of 50 = _____

⑧ 10% of 60 = _____

⑨ 10% of 1000 = _____

⑩ 10% of 429 = _____

⑪ 10% of 48 = _____

⑫ 10% of 7 = _____

Calculating GST

GST is a tax on most goods and services in Australia. The GST is currently 10%.

Here is an invoice for some building work:

Perfect Plumbing Racecourse Drive, Newtown	
Invoice	
Connect waste and water services for a new shower and toilet	
Net amount	$909.50
GST	$90.95
Total incl. GST	**$1000.45**

The invoice shows that the cost of the work has 10% added for GST.

Calculate the GST that would be added to these amounts. Then work out the total cost.

net amount: $58.00

⑬ GST _____

⑭ Total _____

net amount: $365.00

⑮ GST _____

⑯ Total _____

net amount: $125.50

⑰ GST _____

⑱ Total _____

net amount: $1456.30

⑲ GST _____

⑳ Total _____

Score 2 points for each correct answer!

SCORE /40   0-18   20-34   36-40

Statistics & Probability

AC9M5P02

Spinner probability

Use these spinners to answer the questions.

Spinner 1   Spinner 2

What probabilities do these symbols have of being fairly spun? Circle the correct answer.

① ▲   a $\frac{1}{3}$ b $\frac{1}{6}$ c $\frac{3}{6}$ d $\frac{3}{1}$

② ♥   a $\frac{2}{6}$ b $\frac{1}{6}$ c $\frac{1}{2}$ d $\frac{2}{3}$

③ ✖   a $\frac{1}{2}$ b 0   c 1   d $\frac{2}{10}$

④ ▶   a $\frac{1}{3}$ b $\frac{3}{10}$ c $\frac{3}{1}$ d $\frac{1}{4}$

⑤ ◆   a $\frac{4}{14}$ b $\frac{4}{10}$ c $\frac{1}{2}$ d $\frac{1}{4}$

Using only the numbers 1 to 6, complete the spinners so that they match the probability statements that describe them.

⑥ • The chances of getting a 1 is 0.

• You are more likely to get a 2 than a 3.

• You have no chance of spinning a 4.

TARGETING HOMEWORK 5 © PASCAL PRESS ISBN 9781925726473

⑦ • You are certain to get a number less than 4.
• There is a $\frac{1}{8}$ chance of spinning a 2.
• You are more likely to spin a 3 than a 1.

⑧ • You are twice as likely to land on a 4 than a 3.
• There is no chance of spinning a 2 or a 6.
• There is a $\frac{2}{8}$ chance of spinning a 5.

Score 2 points for each correct answer! SCORE **/16** (0-6) (8-12) (14-16)

Measurement & Space

AC9M5SP01

Front, side and top views

These are the views of a car from the top, side and front:

Top

Side

Front

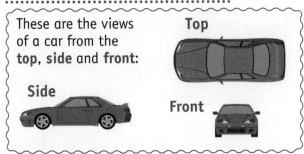

Write the letters of the matching views from the box for each of these objects. *Hint*: you need to use one view more than once.

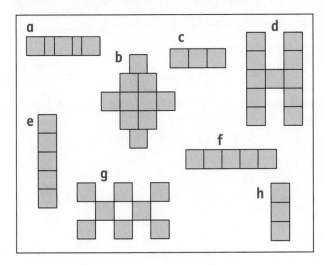

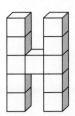

① front view: ___
② side view: ___
③ top view: ___

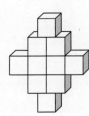

④ front view: ___
⑤ side view: ___
⑥ top view: ___

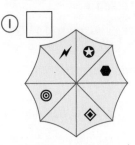

⑦ front view: ___
⑧ side view: ___
⑨ top view: ___

Score 2 points for each correct answer! SCORE **/18** (0-6) (8-14) (16-18)

Problem Solving

AC9M5SP03

Match it!

Write the letter of the matching side view beside each umbrella top view.

① ☐

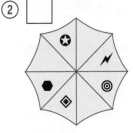

a

② ☐

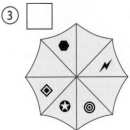

b

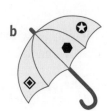

③ ☐

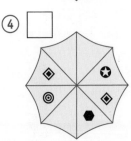

c

④ ☐

d

Grammar & Punctuation

AC9E5LA05

Complex sentences

A **complex sentence** has two (or more) clauses:

• **main clause** which contains the main idea. This clause makes sense on its own and is a complete sentence.

Example: I wore my raincoat.

• **subordinate clause** which adds more information about the main idea. A <u>subordinate clause</u> would not make sense on its own.

Example: I wore my raincoat <u>because it had started to rain</u>.

A subordinate clause can be at the beginning, middle or end of the sentence.

Circle the main clause and underline the subordinate clause in these sentences.

① Unless you have another idea, we will play basketball this afternoon.

② I like to eat lunch outside when the sun is shining.

③ Nathan, who was born in Sydney, decided to move to Adelaide.

④ Since his car broke down, my uncle catches the bus to work.

⑤ The wicked witch, who lives in the forest, slowly opened the cottage door.

Match the correct main clauses to the correct subordinate clauses. Write the correct letters (a–e) on the lines.

    a you can have an ice-cream.
    b Ali sat up to watch TV.
    c Jack saw three kangaroos.
    d whenever she thinks of her gran.
    e because he has improved his handwriting.

⑥ While looking through the window, ___

⑦ Ryan received a certificate ___

⑧ Amy feels happy ___

⑨ Although it was late, ___

⑩ If you eat all your dinner, ___

Phonic Knowledge & Spelling

AC9E5LY09, AC9E5LY10

Suffixes –or and –er

Say each word in the word bank. The suffix **–er** and **–or** in these words has the meaning of 'one who', so one who boards is a board**er**, one who instructs is an instruct**or**.

Word Bank

busker	jogger	lodger	dressmaker
butcher	plumber	ranger	boarder
ambassador	actor	author	conductor
director	editor	instructor	senator

Choose words from the word bank to complete these sentences.

① Meanwhile, the _____ waited nervously for his movie audition.

② The _____ did a good job therefore she would probably be voted in again.

③ I sometimes get a _____ to make me some new clothes.

④ The _____ said we can use the bathroom whenever we want.

Name the following people. All the words end in –er or –or.

⑤ one who dances _____

⑥ one who narrates a story _____

⑦ one who invents things _____

⑧ one who sails boats _____

Add the correct suffix to the word in brackets to complete the sentences. Choose from –er, –or, –ed, –ing and –y. Write the new word.

⑨ We went to the _____ to buy a birthday cake. (baker)

⑩ She was _____ the school newspaper. (edit)

⑪ I go _____ in the park every Saturday. (jog)

⑫ The boy was _____ by his previous teacher. (tutor)

Effects of Introduced Plants and Animals

Informative text – Report
Authors – Frances Mackay and Catherine Gordon

Australia is well known for its unique plants and animals — many of them are found nowhere else in the world.

During the 1800s, people from Europe began arriving in Australia in great numbers. Some people thought the Australian environment was strange and needed to look more like the one back in Britain. Acclimatisation Societies were set up to import plants and animals to Australia to make the landscape look more familiar.

Some of these imported species had a devastating effect on our native plants and animals. These changes still have an impact on our environment today.

Prickly pear

This plant was brought to Australia to use as hedging and to establish a cochineal dye industry. The red dye is created using insects found on the prickly pear.

The plant spread very quickly, and by 1920 millions of hectares in Queensland and New South Wales were infested with it. It made the land useless for farming.

In 1926, scientists found a way to control the plant — they released a moth called *Cactoblastis cactorum*. The caterpillars of this moth eat the prickly pear.

European rabbit

Rabbits were brought to Australia on the Frist Fleet to be bred for food. In 1859, some rabbits were released from a farm. They quickly grew in numbers and spread to most parts of Australia. They are considered to be one of Australia's main pests.

Rabbits cause damage to farm crops. They threaten the survival of native animals by eating many native plants and reducing the amount of food available.

Source: *Australian History Centres*, Upper Primary, Blake Education.

TERM 3 ENGLISH

Write or circle the correct answers.

① **What does acclimatisation mean?**

a discovering new species

b importing plants and animals

c adapting to a new climate and environment

② **Why did the European settlers want to bring new plants and animals to Australia?**

_____

_____

③ **The settlers wanted to establish a cochineal dye industry in Australia. What plant or animal did they introduce to do this?**

_____

_____

④ **What did this plant or animal do to the environment?**

_____

_____

⑤ **How was the problem solved?**

_____

_____

Which words in the text have these meanings?

⑥ being the only one of its kind; unlike anything else: u_____

⑦ to bring goods in from another country: i_____

⑧ highly destructive or damaging: d_____

⑨ overrun, inundated: i_____

My Book Review

Title _____

Author _____

Rating ☆☆☆☆☆

Comment _____

_____

Score 2 points for each correct answer!

SCORE /18 (0-6) (8-14) (16-18)

Number & Algebra

AC9M5N06

Area model of multiplication

Here is another method for multiplication. It is called the **area method**.

Example: 13 × 23

• First, expand **13** into 10 + 3 and expand **23** into 20 + 3:

	20	+	3
10			
+ 3			

• Multiply the numbers outside the grid like this:

	20	+	3
10	10 × 20 = **200**		10 × 3 = **30**
+ 3	3 × 20 = **60**		3 × 3 = **9**

• Add:

	20	+	3
10	10 × 20 = **200**		10 × 3 = **30**
+ 3	3 × 20 = **60**		3 × 3 = **9**

200 + 30 = **230**

60 + 9 = **69**

_____

299

13 × 23 = 299

It is called the **area method** because you can show the problem in a diagram like this:

←———— 23 ————→

10 × 20 = **200**

10 × 3 = **30**

13

3 × 3 = **9**

3 × 20 = **60**

Use the area method to complete these multiplications.

① 35 × 24 = _____

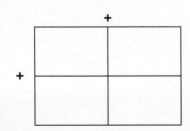

② 46 × 37 = _____

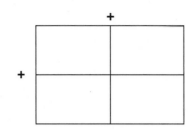

③ 64 × 48 = _____

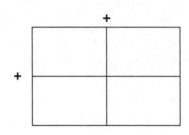

④ 51 × 77 = _____

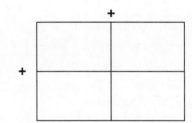

⑤ 84 × 29 = _____

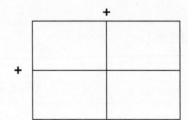

Score 2 points for each correct answer!

SCORE /10   0-2 4-8 10

Statistics & Probability

There are no statistics & probability activities in this unit.

TARGETING HOMEWORK 5 © PASCAL PRESS ISBN 9781925726473

Measurement & Space

AC9M5SP03

Tessellation

Some shapes fit together to cover an area without leaving any gaps. These shapes **tessellate**.

Write true or false.

① This triangle will tessellate. _____

② A square will tessellate. _____

③ A regular pentagon will tessellate. _____

④ A regular hexagon will tessellate. _____

⑤ A regular heptagon will tessellate. _____

⑥ A regular octagon will tessellate. _____

Sometimes, two shapes can be joined together to make a shape that will tessellate.

Which combinations of two shapes shown in Questions 1 to 6 can be put together to tessellate? Draw them in the space below.

⑦ _____ and _____.

⑧ _____ and _____.

Problem Solving

AC9M5SP03

Making shapes

Cutting a hexagon in half like this makes two pieces that are the same shape and size.

Can these shapes be made from the two halves of the hexagon? Answer yes or no.

① _____

② _____

③ _____

④ _____

⑤ _____

TERM 3 MATHS

Grammar & Punctuation

AC9E5LA06

Adjectival clauses

An **adjectival clause** follows the noun it describes and is part of a noun group. It begins with *who* (to describe people) or *which* or *that* (to describe things).

Use **which** when adding **extra** but not essential information.

Example:
noun ⌐ adjectival clause
The house, <u>which we saw earlier</u>, had a magnificent garden.

Use **that** when adding **essential** information.

Example:
noun ⌐ adjectival clause
The house <u>that was built in 1842</u> is now up for sale.

Underline the adjectival clause and circle the noun or noun group it describes.

① The purse that you found belongs to my sister.

② Melbourne, which I love to visit, is the capital of Victoria.

③ Kerry ate all the grapes that were left in the fruit bowl.

Using commas with adjectival clauses

Place commas around an adjectival clause ONLY if the clause contains *extra* (not essential) information.

Example: Alexander Fleming, <u>who was a scientist</u>, discovered penicillin.

Clauses beginning with 'that' never need a comma because they always contain essential information.

Example: The girl <u>**that** fell over</u> had to go to hospital.

Put in all the commas where they are necessary.

④ Libby is the girl who bakes the cakes.

⑤ The car which was blue belonged to my neighbour.

⑥ Danielle who lives in Adelaide is a pharmacist.

Phonic Knowledge & Spelling

AC9E5LY09, AC9E5LY10

Words with the suffix –ly

Say each word in the word bank. They are all **adverbs**. They say more about 'how' or 'how long' something is done.

Word Bank

gently	genuinely	gingerly	centrally
civilly	quietly	quickly	quarterly
politely	presently	privately	honestly
heavily	terribly	tenderly	busily

Choose words from the word bank to complete these sentences.

① We are _____ looking forward to riding our bikes tomorrow.

② Yesterday it rained _____ during the afternoon.

③ Tonight I want everyone to wait _____ backstage.

Changing adjectives to adverbs

Most adjectives add –ly to make an adverb. If the adjective ends in **y**, change the **y** to **i** before adding –ly.

Complete these sentences. Choose words from the box and add –ly.

fortunate gentle immediate awkward noise

④ The people in the protest march voiced their anger _____.

⑤ _____ Jason was not badly hurt after his fall.

⑥ The vet _____ lifted the injured dog into the van.

⑦ She rang the police _____ after the accident.

⑧ The man perched himself _____ on the slippery new sofa.

AC9E5LY04, AC9E5LY05

Jed

Imaginative text – Narrative
Author – Kathryn England

On a moonlit night, among the trees of a sparsely timbered paddock, the dingo and the working dog faced each other.

The dingo was creamy-fawn with a sleek hide and amber eyes. She hunted alone; she had lost her mate months earlier, after he'd eaten a poisoned bait. But she wasn't hungry this day. She had spent the morning curled nose to tail in her lair, a dark space behind fallen boulders at the edge of a valley. During the afternoon she had emerged and lay stretched out in the lacy shade of acacia shrubs, enjoying dappled sun on her back and the sweet scent of spring grass. When darkness fell, she had made her way up the valley wall and along a ridge.

The working dog, a kelpie, had been fed in the usual way, at the usual time. He'd waited patiently at the back door for the sounds that told him food was coming —

the scraping back of chairs at the dining table, the click of dishes being collected and stacked. When footsteps approached the back door, he was ready with eager eyes and a wagging tail. His food dish was set down and he made short work of the soft parts of his meal, saving the hard piece until last. After gnawing the bone for almost an hour, he padded over to his kennel and settled down on his blanket, ready for sleep.

That was when he heard it: a thin, mournful thread of sound winding through the night. He'd heard the cry before. It was a female dingo. But it was too far away to bother him. He growled softly, head on his paws, but didn't stir. He'd been asleep an hour when he heard the cry again, closer this time. He leaped to his feet, wide awake now, and waited for the answering cry of a male. It did not come.

Source: *Jed*, Blake's Novels, Blake Education.

TERM 3 ENGLISH

Write or circle the correct answers.

① **What does sparsely timbered mean?**

a many trees

b few trees

c special trees

② **List the words and phrases used to describe what the dingo looked like.**

_____

Which words in the text have these meanings?

③ glossy: s_____

④ honey-yellow colour: a_____

⑤ an animal's den: l_____

⑥ **Which is the odd word?**

a keen   c eager

b interested   d disinterested

⑦ **What two signals did the dog recognise that told him he was going to be fed?**

_____

⑧ **What is another way of saying 'he made short work of the soft parts of his meal'?**

_____

⑨ **What did the dog do when he heard the dingo's cry again?**

_____

Score 2 points for each correct answer! | SCORE **/18** (0-6) (8-14) (16-18)

My Book Review

Title _____

Author _____

Rating ☆☆☆☆☆

Comment _____

_____

UNIT 21

Number & Algebra

AC9M5N05

Fraction word problems

Solve these word problems using fractions.
Draw a diagram or write a number sentence to
help you. Show your working out.

At Su's party, three cakes were each cut into
12 pieces. At the end of the party, the chocolate
cake had three pieces left over, the cream cake
had two pieces left and the ice-cream cake had
one piece left.

① What fraction of the chocolate cake was
eaten?

_____

② What fraction of the cream cake was eaten?

_____

③ What fraction of the ice-cream cake was
eaten?

_____

A large pizza was ordered for a party.
It was cut into sixteenths. Cam ate 4 pieces,
David ate 5 pieces and Mandy ate 3 pieces.

④ What fraction of the pizza did Cam eat?

_____

⑤ What fraction of the pizza did Mandy and
David eat?

_____

⑥ How much more did Mandy and David eat
than Cam?

_____

⑦ What fraction of the pizza was left over?

_____

At the party, Luke and Tom shared a chocolate
bar. Luke ate $\frac{1}{2}$ and Tom ate $\frac{3}{12}$.

⑧ Who ate more?

_____

⑨ How much was left over?

_____

There were 15 children at the party. 8 children
were 9 years old, 4 children were 10 years old
and 3 children were 8 years old. 8 children
were boys.

⑩ What fraction of the children were
10 years old?

_____

⑪ What fraction of the children were under
10 years old?

_____

⑫ What fraction of the children were girls?

_____

Score 2 points for
each correct answer!   SCORE **/24** (0-10) (12-18) (20-24)

Statistics & Probability

AC9M5P02

Playing card probability

Use the playing cards to answer the questions.
Write your answers as fractions.

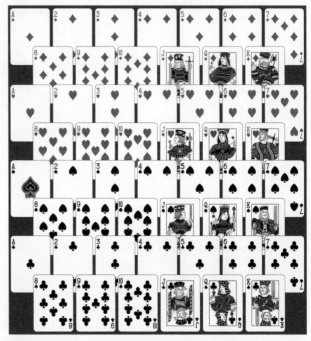

If the cards are stacked in a deck or placed
face down, what is the probability of:

① picking a ten of clubs? _____

② picking a Jack? _____

③ picking a heart? _____

④ picking a 2, 3, 4 or 5? _____

⑤ **not** picking a King? _____

⑥ picking a picture card? _____

⑦ **not** picking a club or a spade? _____

⑧ picking a 6, 7, 8, 9 or 10? _____

⑨ picking a 14? _____

⑩ **not** picking a picture card? _____

Score 2 points for
each correct answer!   SCORE **/20**

TERM 3 MATHS

92

TARGETING HOMEWORK 5 © PASCAL PRESS ISBN 9781925726473

Measurement & Space

AC9M5P02

Map directions

This is a map of where these children live:

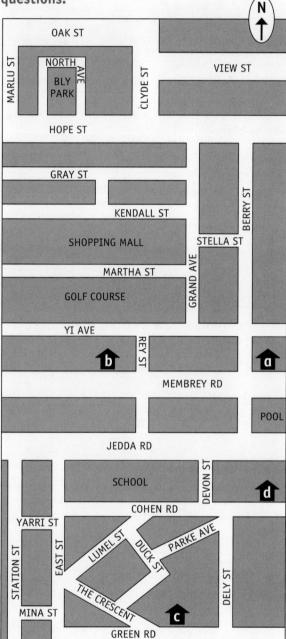 Mirri, 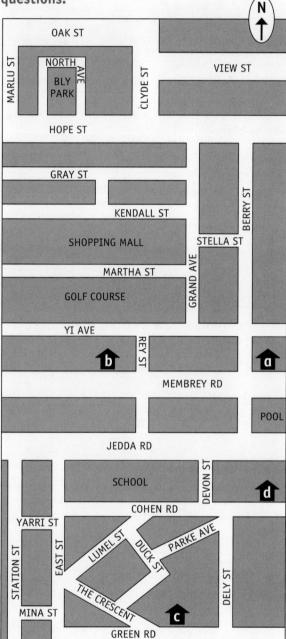 Kim, Bella, Adam.

Use the map to answer the following questions.

① What is the name of the road that Mirri and Kim live in?

_____

② Mirri walks down Berry Street to get to the school. What does she pass on the way?

_____

③ Name the streets that border the school.

_____
_____

④ Complete these directions for Kim to walk from his house to Bly Park.

Kim walks along Membrey Road and turns _____ into Rey Street. Then he turns _____, and left into _____ _____. He walks north, passing _____ Street, _____ Street and Gray Street on his left. At the end of the avenue, he turns _____ into Hope Street and continues along this street until he arrives at Bly Park.

⑤ **Bella is going to visit her friend Mirri. Complete the directions for her journey.**

Bella walks east along _____ _____ and turns left into _____ Street. She walks north to Cohen Road, turns _____, then continues north along _____ Street. She turns right into Jedda Road and then left into _____ Street. She passes the pool and turns right into _____ _____. Mirri's house is on the left.

⑥ **Describe the shortest route for Adam to walk from his home to the golf course.**

_____
_____
_____
_____
_____
_____

Score 2 points for each correct answer! SCORE 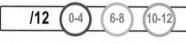 /12 ⓪-4 6-8 10-12

Problem Solving

AC9M5N07

Bouncing ball!

A ball is dropped from a height of 125 m.

Each time it hits the ground, it bounces up to $\frac{3}{5}$ of the height it fell.

① How high will the ball bounce on the second bounce?

_____

② How high will the ball bounce on the fourth bounce?

_____

Grammar & Punctuation

AC9E5LA06

Noun clauses

> A **noun clause** does the work of a noun. It sits within the main clause.
>
> Noun clauses begin with: who, which, what, when, where, why, how, if, that.
>
> A noun clause can be:
> • a subject – **What Jayne said** upset me.
> • an object – I don't know **what I'll do** if we can't go.

Underline the noun clauses in these sentences.

① Ask the teacher if this is correct.

② I don't understand why he did that.

③ That office is where my dad works.

④ That he should behave like that is very unusual.

Noun clauses that begin with 'that'

> The conjunction **that** is often omitted from noun clauses to improve the flow of speaking or writing.
>
> *Example:*
> Mum said **that** she was feeling very happy.
> Mum said she was feeling very happy.

Rewrite these sentences without that.

⑤ She said that she was good at skating.

_____

_____

⑥ I didn't know that he could play the piano.

_____

_____

⑦ Are you sure that you want this puppy?

_____

_____

⑧ Ned said that the movie was awful.

_____

_____

Phonic Knowledge & Spelling

AC9E5LY09, AC9E5LY10

Prefixes pre– and pro–

Say each word in the word bank. The prefix **pre–** often means 'before'. The prefix **pro–** often means 'for' or 'in favour of'.

Word Bank

prefer	prepare	pretend	presume
present	prevent	preview	prehistoric
protect	protest	produce	promote
proceed	propose	profile	profession

Choose words from the word bank to complete these sentences.

① We had to _____ to exit the room at noon.

② There was no entrance at the front so we had to _____ that it was at the back.

③ The police tried to _____ entry to the street by setting up a roadblock.

Some words are easily confused with others. Match the words in the box to their correct meanings.

proceed	precede	perfect

④ ideal, without fault: _____

⑤ to get going, make a start: _____

⑥ to come before, lead up to: _____

Add –ed and –ing by writing the new words. Remember your rules!

⑦ prepare
  add –ed: _____
  add –ing: _____

⑧ preserve
  add –ed: _____
  add –ing: _____

⑨ prevent
  add –ed: _____
  add –ing: _____

⑩ protest
  add –ed: _____
  add –ing: _____

The Hunter or the Hunted?

By Lachlan Scott

Persuasive text – Interview
Author – Merryn Whitfield

Imagine being attacked by a great white shark and living to tell about it. Would you then go back into shark-infested waters to teach others to understand the creature that nearly killed you? Well, Reece Foxtrot did just that.

Lachlan Scott: Hi Reece. I bet you're glad to be here today.

Reece Foxtrot: That's for sure, mate.

LS: I'm certain that the memory of what occurred that fateful day will haunt you forever. Could you take us through what happened before the attack?

RF: Well, it was a great day — perfect boating weather. So some friends and I decided to go spear fishing off the point. It's a great spot that only the locals know about. I went down first. I was just about to take aim at a fish when it happened.

LS: Did you get any sort of warning?

RF: None at all. It was like being hit by a train from behind. I lost my mask and my spear gun in that first moment.

LS: Crikey! That must have been terrifying! I get goose bumps even imagining it.

RF: To be honest, it all happens so quick you don't have time to think. You just go into survival mode, I guess.

LS: Did the shark let go then?

RF: Unfortunately no. It came back like a bad smell. I clawed at its eyes and tried to kick it away as it swam towards me. But in a way, I was lucky. The shark grabbed the fish I had already caught that were tied to a loop on my belt. Once the belt snapped, I floated up to the surface.

LS: You were lucky you didn't drown!

RF: Yeah. My friends quickly dragged me into the dinghy, and once we got back to the beach they drove me to hospital where the doctors and nurses did a remarkable job saving my life.

LS: Most people would hate sharks after something like that.

RF: I did for a while. But I began to realise that I was in their territory. The more I learned about them, the more determined I was to help save them. Did you know that humans kill around 100 million sharks each year? I want to stop that from happening.

LS: That's very admirable. I'm not sure I would even be able to have a bath after such an experience. Let alone go back in the ocean and save the creature that tried to eat me. Thanks for sharing your remarkable story with us today.

RF: It's been my pleasure.

Source: *Writing Centres: Persuasive Texts* – Upper Primary, Blake Education.

Write or circle the correct answers.

1 **Where might this have happened?**

 a on a radio or television program

 b in a magazine

 c at a police station

2 **The text includes informal language. Circle the phrases below that are informal.**

 a That's for sure, mate.

 b I did for a while.

 c Crikey! That must have been terrifying!

3 **How did Reece describe what it felt like when the shark attacked him?**

_____

4 **How did Reece's friends help save him?**

_____

Score 2 points for each correct answer! | **SCORE** /8 | 0-2 | 4-6 | 8

My Book Review

Title _____

Author _____

Rating ☆☆☆☆☆

Comment _____

Number & Algebra

AC9M5N10

Number patterns

Complete these number patterns.

① Add 20 to the previous number.

_____, 65, _____, _____, _____

② Subtract 25 from the previous number.

_____, 85, _____, _____, _____

③ Add 0.5 to the previous number.

_____, 5.5, _____, _____, _____

④ Subtract 0.5 from the previous number.

_____, 7.0, _____, _____, _____

⑤ Add $\frac{1}{3}$ to the previous number.

_____, $\frac{2}{3}$, _____, _____, _____

⑥ Subtract $\frac{3}{8}$ from the previous number.

_____, $\frac{7}{8}$, _____, _____

Fill in the blanks in these number patterns. Follow the rules.

⑦ **Rule: + 1.5**

24.5, _____, _____, _____, 30.5

⑧ **Rule: − 1.5**

80.0, _____, _____, _____, 74.0

⑨ **Rule: + 4.3**

235.1, _____, _____, _____, 252.3

⑩ **Rule: − 1.3**

564.5, _____, _____, _____, 559.3

Work out the rule for these number patterns.

⑪ 550, 450, 350, 250, 150, 50

Rule: _____

⑫ 60, 62.5, 65, 67.5, 70, 72.5

Rule: _____

⑬ 100, 110.25, 120.5, 130.75, 141

Rule: _____

⑭ 10, 9.75, 9.5, 9.25, 9, 8.75, 8.5

Rule: _____

⑮ 80, 77.4, 74.8, 72.2, 69.6, 67, 64.4

Rule: _____

Are these patterns correct or incorrect? Circle the correct answer.

⑯ **Rule: + $1\frac{1}{4}$**

13, $14\frac{1}{4}$, $15\frac{1}{2}$, $16\frac{3}{4}$, $18\frac{1}{4}$

a correct   b incorrect

⑰ **Rule: − $1\frac{2}{5}$**

$20\frac{4}{5}$, $19\frac{2}{5}$, 18, $17\frac{3}{5}$, $16\frac{1}{5}$

a correct   b incorrect

⑱ **Rule: + $5\frac{3}{8}$**

$10\frac{1}{8}$, $15\frac{4}{8}$, $20\frac{7}{8}$, $26\frac{2}{8}$, $31\frac{5}{8}$

a correct   b incorrect

⑲ **Rule: + $2\frac{3}{10}$**

$90\frac{1}{10}$, $92\frac{4}{10}$, $94\frac{7}{10}$, 97

a correct   b incorrect

⑳ **Rule: − $4\frac{3}{4}$**

75, $70\frac{1}{4}$, $65\frac{1}{2}$, $60\frac{3}{4}$

a correct

b incorrect

Score 2 points for each correct answer! **SCORE** | **/40** | (0-18) (20-34) (36-40)

Statistics & Probability

There are no statistics & probability activities in this unit.

Measurement & Space

AC9M5M03

Timetables

Use the flight timetable below to answer the following questions.

Flight	Departs Melbourne	Arrives Sydney	Departs Sydney	Arrives Canberra
Flight 1	8:45	10:20	11:20	12:05
Flight 2	11:25	12:50	13:30	15:25
Flight 3	13:40	No stop-over		16:30

① Show the departure times from Melbourne on these analogue clocks.

a Flight 1   **c** Flight 3

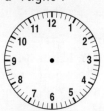 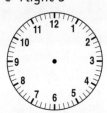

b Flight 2

② How long is each stopover?

a Flight 1 _____

b Flight 2 _____

③ Show the Canberra arrival times on these 12-hour digital clocks.

a Flight 1   **b** Flight 2   **c** Flight 3

④ How long does the quickest journey take? Answer in hours and minutes.

_____

⑤ If you were 5 minutes late for Flight 1, how long would you have to wait to catch Flight 2?

_____

⑥ How much later than Flight 1 does Flight 3 leave Melbourne?

_____

⑦ Flight 4 leaves Melbourne at 18:00. Fill in this flight timetable to show when Flight 4 might arrive at Sydney and then depart from Sydney and arrive at Canberra.

Flight	Departs Melbourne	Arrives Sydney	Departs	Arrives Canberra
Flight 4	18:00			

Identical shapes

Can you figure out how to make identical shapes from these groups of squares? For example, this shape is divided into three identical shapes of squares:

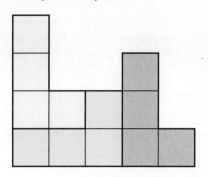

① Colour the squares to divide this shape into four identical shapes of squares.

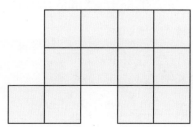

② Colour the squares to divide this shape into five identical shapes of squares.

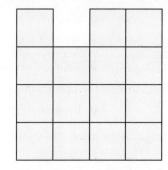

③ Colour the squares to divide this shape into six identical shapes of squares.

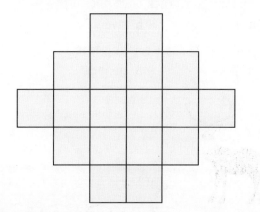

TERM 3 MATHS

Score 2 points for each correct answer!   SCORE **/14**   (0-4) (6-10) (12-14)

Grammar & Punctuation

AC9E5LA08

Words with different meanings

Some words can have very different meanings, depending on how they are used.
The word **set** for example has over 400 different meanings!

Match the meanings of set in the box to the sentences. Write the correct letters (a–f) on the lines.

   a to spread open to the wind
   b to be ready to run
   c to arrange properly
   d to become firm
   e to be unwilling to change
   f to fix at a certain time

① We put the jelly in the fridge to **set**. ____

② He is **set** in his ways. ____

③ The alarm was **set** for 7 am. ____

④ Ready! **Set**! Go! ____

⑤ Jai **set** the table ready for dinner. ____

⑥ The sailors **set** the sails. ____

Circle the correct meaning of the word in bold.

⑦ Can you **spot** the deer over there?
   a see   **b** place

⑧ The bus driver had to **park** the bus first.
   a garden   **b** steer into place

⑨ He decided to **run** for presidency.
   a jog   **b** be a candidate

⑩ The students were **kind** to the new girl.
   a type   **b** helpful

⑪ The pilot will **fly** us to Brisbane.
   a lure   **b** move through the air

⑫ He started to **rock** back and forth.
   a music   **b** sway

⑬ Dad had to pay a parking **fine**.
   a thin   **b** penalty

Score 2 points for each correct answer! SCORE **/26** (0-10) (12-20) (22-26)

Phonic Knowledge & Spelling

AC9E5LY09, AC9E5LY10

Letter team 'qu'

Say each word in the word bank. They all contain the letter team **qu**. The letter **q** is always followed by **u**. The letters **qu** can make two different sounds: 'kwa' as in 'quick' and the 'k' sound as in 'mosquito'.

Word Bank

quiz	quest	quilt	quote
quarry	quarrel	queue	quay
quaver	quantity	quality	qualify
quadrant	quarter	require	equipment

Choose words from the word bank to complete these sentences.

① The bed _____ ended up at a funny angle by morning.

② Mum obtained a _____ from the dressmaker to make an angel costume.

③ The hungry cat tried to catch a fish from the _____, but all was quiet.

④ The spelling _____ was quite difficult but I passed it.

Match the words in the box to their meanings.

quiver	quarry	quaver	quadrant
quay	quest	quote	

⑤ a place beside the water for ferries or ships:
_____

⑥ a place where stone is dug out:
_____

⑦ a certain price for a job:
_____

⑧ a quarter of a circle:
_____

⑨ a search:
_____

⑩ a case for holding arrows:
_____

⑪ a trembling sound: _____

Score 2 points for each correct answer! SCORE **/22** (0-8) (10-16) (18-22)

TARGETING HOMEWORK 5 © PASCAL PRESS ISBN 9781925726473

Planet under Threat

Informative text – Discussion
Author – Ian Rohr

Earth's natural resources sustain the many, diverse forms of life on the planet. But humans are polluting and exhausting these resources.

Natural resources

Our natural resources are forests, water, soil, minerals, plants, animals and **fossil fuels**. Some natural resources can be partly renewed; for example, forests can be replanted and soil damage can be repaired. Other resources are not **renewable**; when they are all used up, they are gone forever.

Many animal and plant species have become endangered as their natural habitats continue to be destroyed. Fresh water in rivers and lakes is under threat from irrigation, which reduces flow, and soil run-off, which pollutes them.

Damaging the environment

Carbon dioxide is a gas that occurs naturally in the atmosphere. The amount of carbon dioxide in the atmosphere is increasing because people are removing forests, which absorb carbon dioxide, and burning fossil fuels, which generate carbon dioxide. Increased carbon dioxide has caused the Earth's atmosphere and oceans to heat up. This is called **global warming**.

Conservation and sustainability

What can be done to help the planet? Conservation is choosing to not use up or **contaminate** the planet's natural resources. It is working to protect, restore and sustain our environment.

Sustainability is using the planet's resources in a responsible and planned way, so that they will last longer. It is development that benefits the current generation without disadvantaging future generations.

Source: *Conservation*, Go Facts, Blake Education.

Write or circle the correct answers.

① List seven natural resources found on our planet.

_____

_____

_____

② What are **fossil fuels**?

a old types of fuels

b fuels formed from animal and plant remains from millions of years ago

c fuels used to burn fossils

③ Which is an example of a **renewable resource**?

a cutting down trees to build houses

b using coal to generate electricity

c replanting forests that have been cut down

④ Give two reasons why carbon dioxide levels are increasing in our atmosphere.

_____

_____

Are these statements fact or opinion?

⑤ Humans are polluting the earth.

_____

⑥ Humans don't care about looking after the planet. _____

⑦ We don't need to worry about future generations. _____

Which words in the text have these meanings?

⑧ able to be replaced:
r_____

⑨ the air around the earth:
a_____

⑩ threatened with extinction:
e_____

⑪ using the earth's resources in a responsible way: s_____

Score 2 points for each correct answer!

SCORE **/22** (0-8) (10-16) (18-22)

My Book Review

Title _____

Author _____

Rating ☆☆☆☆☆

Comment _____

_____

Number & Algebra

AC9M5N10, AC9M5A01

Number patterns and puzzles

The rule for this **function machine** is × 20.

IN	OUT
4	80
8	160
10	200
20	400
100	2000

× 20

This means you multiply each number in the **In** column by 20 to get the answer in the **Out** column.

Work out the rule for each function machine and write it in the box. Then complete the function machine. *Hint*: All the rules are either multiplication or division.

① Rule: _____

IN	OUT
50	5
200	20
80	
1000	
300	

④ Rule: _____

IN	OUT
2	2000
2.7	2700
40	
41.2	
13	

② Rule: _____

IN	OUT
7	70
8.5	85
24.5	
62.5	
75.2	

⑤ Rule: _____

IN	OUT
9000	9
5670	5.67
8000	
678	
12 000	

③ Rule: _____

IN	OUT
64	8
80	10
640	
800	
160	

⑥ Rule: _____

IN	OUT
7	35
10	50
25	
500	
5000	

Write these questions as number sentences. Include the answers.

⑦ What number multiplied by 5 equals 1000 ÷ 10?

_____

⑧ What number divided by 7 equals 64 divided by 8?

_____

⑨ If you divide 500 by 10, you get the same answer as multiplying what by 2?

_____

⑩ What number can be multiplied by 3 to equal 6 000 divided by 100?

_____

Score 2 points for each correct answer!

SCORE **/20** (0-8) (10-14) (16-20)

Statistics & Probability

AC9M5ST01, AC9M5ST03

Interpreting data

These are the results of cricket test matches played by international teams.

Team	Matches	Won	Lost	Drawn	% Won
Australia	744	350	194	200	47.00
Bangladesh	73	3	63	7	4.11
England	926	329	267	330	35.53
India	464	114	147	203	24.57
New Zealand	375	71	153	151	18.93
Pakistan		115	101	154	31.08
South Africa		131	126	112	35.50
Sri Lanka		64	76	75	29.77
West Indies		156	162	167	32.10
Zimbabwe		9	52	26	10.34

Use the data to answer the questions.

Australia played a total of 744 matches. Calculate how many matches these teams played.

① Pakistan _____

② South Africa _____

③ Sri Lanka _____

④ West Indies _____

⑤ Zimbabwe _____

⑥ Which team won the most matches?

_____

TARGETING HOMEWORK 5 © PASCAL PRESS ISBN 9781925726473

Which teams won more matches than they lost?

⑦ _____

⑧ _____

⑨ _____

⑩ _____

⑪ How many more matches did England win than Pakistan? _____

⑫ Which team had the smallest number of draws?

_____

⑬ Which team lost the most matches?

_____

Score 2 points for each correct answer! **SCORE** **/26** (0-10) (12-20) (22-26)

Measurement & Space

AC9M5M01, AC9M5N07

Making biscuits

Ava is making biscuits to sell at the school fair.

Ingredients
125 g butter
50 g caster sugar
1 egg
50 g plain flour
50 g wholemeal flour
20 g cornflour
50 g currants
25 g mixed peel
plus a little milk, cinnamon and ground ginger

Shopping price list

250 g butter	$2.50
500 g caster sugar	$2.00
6 eggs	$3.00
1 kg plain flour	$3.00
1 kg wholemeal flour	$3.00
300 g cornflour	$2.25
300 g currants	$3.00
200 g mixed peel	$1.60
milk, cinnamon, ground ginger	donated free

The recipe makes 20 biscuits. Ava needs to work out how much it costs to make one biscuit in order to decide how much to sell the biscuits for.

Calculate the cost of the ingredients to make 20 biscuits, using the shopping price list. You may need a calculator.

Example: **cost of butter**
The recipe needs 125 g of butter.
125 g is half of 250 g, so divide the cost of $2.50 by 2.
The cost of butter is **$1.25**.

① cost of caster sugar

_____

② cost of egg

_____

③ cost of plain flour

_____

④ cost of wholemeal flour

_____

⑤ cost of cornflour

_____

⑥ cost of currants

_____

⑦ cost of mixed peel

_____

⑧ What is the total cost to make 20 biscuits?

_____

⑨ What is the approximate cost of one biscuit?
a $0.10   **b** $0.15   **c** $0.25

⑩ Ava wants to make 5 cents profit on each biscuit. How much will she sell each one for?

_____

Score 2 points for each correct answer! **SCORE** **/20** (0-8) (10-14) (16-20)

Problem Solving

AC9M5N07

Sale day!

Calculate the sale prices for each item of clothing. Complete the table.

Garment	Original price	10% off price	20% off price
T-shirt	$15.00	$13.50	$12.00
Dress			
Shorts			
Jeans			
Shirt			
Jumper			

Grammar & Punctuation

AC9E5LA02

Points of view

> Look at this point of view: This book is boring.
>
> A statement such as this is called a **bare assertion** because it doesn't tell us who made the statement or on what basis the point of view has been made. More concise points of view could include:
>
> - **In my opinion**, the book is boring.
> - **Most book reviewers consider** this book to be boring.
> - **Sue and Michael think** this book is boring.
> - **It is generally agreed** that this book is boring.

Match each bare assertion in the box to a suitable beginning that tells us who could have made that opinion. Write letters a–c on the lines.

    a this bicycle is the safest.

    b this holiday is the cheapest.

    c budgies make the best bird pets.

① Ted's pet shop claims that ... _____

② FlyNow Holidays guarantee ... _____

③ Road Safety experts say ... _____

Underline three bare assertions in this paragraph.

④–⑥ The school concert was held last night. It was a sellout with over 100 tickets sold. It was the best concert ever. The school choir sang three songs, accompanied by Mr Jackson on the piano. The song choice was better than last year. Nyall played the guitar and Max played the violin. The teachers did a funny play about Sinbad the Sailor. Supper was superb.

Phonic Knowledge & Spelling

AC9E5LY08, AC9E5LY09, AC9E5LY10

Suffix –en and prefix en–

Say each word in the word bank. All the words either begin or end with **en**. The **prefix en–** means 'in' or 'into'. The **suffix –en** means 'make' or 'cause'.

Word Bank

enrol	enlist	enthral	encounter
engulf	enforce	enclose	envelop
lengthen	widen	broaden	harden
loosen	listen	glisten	threaten

Choose words from the word bank to complete these sentences.

① When I _____ to someone talk about food, it makes me feel hungry.

② Dad had to _____ his belt just enough to feel comfortable.

③ We had to _____ the help of volunteers to help us address all the envelopes.

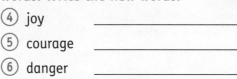

Add the prefix en– to these words. Write the new words.

④ joy _____

⑤ courage _____

⑥ danger _____

⑦ rich _____

Letter team 'ough'

> The letter team **ough** can make different sounds as in the following words: bough, enough, ought, thorough, hiccough, through, dough, cough.

Write four words from the box that have the same ough sound as 'fought' (aw).

enough	although	rough	ought	tough
thought	plough	brought	bought	drought

⑧ _____

⑨ _____

⑩ _____

⑪ _____

TARGETING HOMEWORK 5 © PASCAL PRESS ISBN 9781925726473

Brace Yourself

Imaginative text – Narrative
Author – Sally Murphy

Call me Garth. My parents did. They looked at me, lying all tiny and pathetic in the hospital, and said, "Let's call him Garth." It could have been worse. Dad was keen on me being Garp, from some movie he'd seen, but Mum wouldn't let him. All my life I've been surrounded by kids with normal names, like Mitchell and Brodie and Ben, and I've been stuck with the uncool label of Garth.

It kind of fits because at first glance I'm a bit uncool looking — skinny, spiky hair, freckles. But I'm not uncool on the inside. On the inside I'm waaaaay cool. Pity the rest of the world can't see that. If they could, I'd be the coolest kid in my school, maybe in my whole town. Which would be a big help because I'm new to the town *and* the school.

And the reason I'm new? It's all Dad's fault. Dad and his midlife crisis.

One night he came home from work and announced over dinner,

"Well, I've resigned." Just like that. He'd had a cool job as a lawyer. Lots of money, nice car, and a great townhouse in East Perth. Then one morning he looked at himself in the mirror and started to worry that he's getting old and hasn't done enough with his life.

Brace yourself, Garth: your life is in for big changes.

The next thing we were looking at a house in a town I'd never heard of. I was hoping like crazy Dad wouldn't buy it. Dad and the real estate agent were ignoring me and raving about the pressed tin ceilings — whatever they were — and the fireplace.

"So what do you think?" Dad finally asked, as if he valued my opinion. As soon as I opened my mouth, he said, "Great. That's settled then. We'll take it."

Brace yourself, Garth: these are *really* big changes.

Source: *Brace Yourself*, Blake's Novels, Blake Education.

TERM 3 ENGLISH

Write or circle the correct answers.

1. **The story is written in the first person as if Garth is talking directly to the reader. What effect does this have?**

   a It helps the reader to relate more easily to Garth.

   b It makes the story difficult to understand.

   c It makes it harder for the reader to relate to Garth.

2. **Where did Garth used to live?**

   _____

3. **What does pathetic mean in this story?**

   a cute

   b weak and useless

   c old

4. **What is a midlife crisis?**

   a making a bad decision

   b something bad that happens when you are older

   c a feeling that you haven't done enough with your life when you reach middle age

5. **What does 'Brace yourself, Garth' mean?**

   a Garth has to wear braces.

   b Garth is telling himself to be prepared for what will happen next.

   c Dad is telling Garth to get ready for the move.

6. **Which line in the text tells you that Garth's dad didn't consult with him about choosing the new house?**

   _____

Score 2 points for each correct answer!

SCORE /12   0-4   6-8   10-12

My Book Review

Title _____

Author _____

Rating ☆☆☆☆☆

Comment _____

_____

Number & Algebra

AC9M5N01

Rounding decimal numbers

> **What is 3.16 rounded to the nearest tenth?**
>
> When rounding decimal numbers, we look at the digits after the decimal point.
>
> When you round to tenths, you leave one digit after the decimal point.
>
> *Example*: **Round 3.16 to the nearest tenth.**
>
> In **3.16**, the 1 is in the tenths column. We want to know if 3.16 is closer to 3.1 or 3.2. So we look at the next digit, 6. This is higher than 5, so we round up to **3.2**.
>
> Remember the rounding rules:
> • Round **down** the digits 0, 1, 2, 3 and 4.
> • Round **up** the digits 5, 6, 7, 8 and 9.

Round these numbers to the nearest tenth. Circle the correct answer.

1. 2.34
   a 2.2   b 2.3   c 2.4   d 2.5
2. 5.17
   a 5.0   b 5.1   c 5.2   d 5.3
3. 24.23
   a 24.0   b 24.1   c 24.2   d 24.3
4. 156.49
   a 156.3   b 156.4   c 156.5   d 156.6
5. 1.345
   a 1.2   b 1.3   c 1.4   d 1.5
6. 5.069
   a 5.0   b 5.1   c 5.2   d 5.3

Rounding to the nearest hundredth

> When you round to hundredths, you leave two digits after the decimal point.
>
> *Example*:
>   Round 3.478 to the nearest hundredth.
>
> First find the digit in the hundredths place: **7**.
>
> Then look at the next digit to the right: **8**. This is higher than 5, so we round up to **3.48**.

Round these numbers to the nearest hundredth. Circle the correct answer.

7. 2.347
   a. 2.35   b. 2.36   c. 2.25   d. 2.26

8. 7.333
   a 7.32   b 7.33   c 7.34   d 7.31
9. 12.759
   a 12.75   b 12.76   c 12.77   d 12.74
10. 156.213
    a 156.20   b 156.21   c 156.23   d 156.22
11. 1.6578
    a 1.64   b 1.65   c 1.66   d 1.67
12. 5.9221
    a 5.82   b 5.92   c 5.93   d 5.94

Score 2 points for each correct answer!   **SCORE** /24   0-10   12-18   20-24

Statistics & Probability

There are no statistics & probability activities in this unit.

Measurement & Space

AC9M5M03

Days, hours, minutes and seconds

> 60 seconds = 1 minute
> 60 minutes = 1 hour
> 24 hours = 1 day

Circle the longest period of time.

1. a 1 hour
   b 75 minutes
   c 1 hour 10 minutes
2. a 1 min 30 sec
   b 100 sec
   c 2 minutes
3. a 180 sec
   b 2 minutes
   c 2 minutes 29 sec
4. a 4 hours
   b 300 minutes
   c 280 minutes

Complete these time conversions.

5. 120 minutes = _____ hours
6. 3 _____ = 180 seconds
7. 48 _____ = 2 days
8. 300 _____ = 5 minutes
9. 5 hours = _____ minutes
10. 1 day = _____ minutes

TARGETING HOMEWORK 5 © PASCAL PRESS ISBN 9781925726473

Use the clocks to answer the following questions. Write the correct answers.

A

C

B

D

(11) How many minutes is clock A away from 12 o'clock?

_____

(12) How many minutes is clock B away from 10 o'clock?

_____

(13) How many minutes is clock C away from 4:55?

_____

(14) How many hours and minutes past noon is clock D?

_____

(15) How many hours and minutes before noon is clock D?

_____

(16) What time did clock B show 90 minutes earlier? Answer in digital time.

_____

(17) What time will clock D show in 200 minutes time? Answer in digital time.

_____

(18) What is the difference in minutes between the times shown on clock C and clock B?

_____

Write these times in hours and minutes.

(19) 250 minutes = _____

(20) 360 minutes = _____

(21) 125 minutes = _____

(22) 174 minutes = _____

(23) 132 minutes = _____

(24) 345 minutes = _____

Score 2 points for each correct answer!

SCORE **/48** (0-22) (24-42) (44-48)

Equal shares

Ruby, Talia and Ash have 13 beetle collector cards to share. Because they can't share 13 cards equally, they decide to share so that the total card values are equal.

The values for the 13 cards are:

50	1000	550	250	75
200	600	75	60	125
240	50	175		

What will be the values of the cards for each equal share?

Hint: To get started, you could add the numbers and divide by three to find out what each share should total. Or, you could make the cards and move them around into different groups until you find the answer.

(1) Write the numbers for each equal share.

_____

_____

_____

(2) How did you solve the problem?

_____

_____

(3) If you had to solve a similar problem, what would you try first?

_____

_____

(4) If the children wanted to share the cards among four people so that the total card values are equal, could they? Why or why not?

_____

_____

TERM 3 MATHS

Grammar & Punctuation

Are these sentences active or passive? Write A or P.

① The bike **was ridden** by Max. _____

② Max **is riding** his bike. _____

Join these sentences with the most suitable conjunction: and, but, so, or, nor, for, yet.

③ She was supposed to wash the dishes, _____ she played outside instead.

④ Jackie needs to practise harder, _____ she will not pass her piano exams.

Replace the subject in the second part of the sentence with a suitable pronoun. Rewrite the sentence.

⑤ The rabbits hopped across the grass **and** the rabbits disappeared into their burrows.

_____

_____

_____

Circle the verb that more precisely describes the action.

⑥ My mum (made   did   decorated) my birthday cake with lavish icing.

Underline the main clause and circle the subordinate clause.

⑦ Will, who plays for the Rosetown Tigers, won the Player of the Year Award.

Underline the adjectival clause and circle the noun or noun group it describes.

⑧ Maxwell, who lives next door, looked after our cat today.

Put in commas where necessary.

⑨ The beach which is near us has been contaminated with oil.

Underline the noun clause.

⑩ Mum asked if I could help her.

Circle the word/phrase that matches the correct meaning of the word in bold.

⑪ The jelly soon **set** in the fridge.

   a grouped   **b** firmed up

⑫ Underline the sentence that is a bare assertion.

   a That cake is the best.

   b Three prominent chefs agreed that cake was the best.

Phonic Knowledge & Spelling

Add the suffixes by writing the words.

① confide   **add –ed** _____

                  add –ing _____

                  add –ent _____

Circle the correct word so that the sentence makes sense.

② The burglar (inflicted   afflicted) a terrible injury on the policeman.

Make compound words ending in –age. Write the words.

③ teen   _____

④ sew   _____

⑤ dam   _____

⑥ volt   _____

Name the people. The words end in –er or –or.

⑦ one who narrates a story: _____

⑧ one who sings: _____

Add the correct suffix to the word in brackets. Write the new word.

   –er   –or   –ed   –ing   –y

⑨ She was _____ the school newspaper. (edit)

Add –ly to these words.

⑩ easy   _____

⑪ fortunate   _____

Add –ed and –ing. Write the new words.

⑫ preserve _____ _____

Circle the words that have the same sound as the 'ough' in thought.

⑬ ought   through   fought   rough

   plough   tough   bought

Choose the correct word to complete each sentence.

| quiver   quarry   quaver |

⑭ The bowman pulled an arrow out from his _____.

⑮ The workmen dug the stone from the local _____.

Score 2 points for each correct answer! **SCORE** **/24**

Score 2 points for each correct answer! **SCORE** **/30**

TARGETING HOMEWORK 5 © PASCAL PRESS ISBN 9781925726473

Reading & Comprehension

Jessica Mauboy, 1989–

Informative text – Biography
Author – Lisa Nicol

Jessica Mauboy is an award-winning musician and actor. She is one of Australia's most successful and popular pop singers.

Jessica Mauboy was born in Darwin. Her father is from West Timor in Indonesia and her mother is from the Kuku Yalanji people of North Queensland. Mauboy grew up with music. Her father played guitar and her mother sang. Mauboy sang in the backyard with her four sisters, and in the church choir with her grandmother.

Mauboy first came to public attention as runner-up on the television show *Australian Idol*. Not long after, she signed a recording contract. She has released four CDs that have included the hits "Saturday Night", "Inescapable", "Pop a Bottle (Fill Me Up)", "Never Be the Same" and "Can I Get a Moment?" Her single "Burn" went to number one on the music charts.

As well as her singing career, Mauboy has starred in two films: *Bran Nue Dae* (2010) and *The Sapphires* (2012). Both films tell stories about Indigenous Australians.

Source: *Great Indigenous Australians*, Go Facts, Blake Education.

TERM 3 ENGLISH

Write or circle the correct answers.

1. Where was Jessica Mauboy born?

_____

2. Name two ways her family helped to develop her interest in music.

_____

_____

3. What does **public attention** mean?

  a to make people aware of something or someone

  b to make a fool of yourself

4. Name two of Mauboy's hit songs.

_____

_____

5. Which film did Mauboy star in, in 2012?

_____

6. Which is the odd word out?

  a liked

  b popular

  c unpopular

  d admired

7. What is a **recording contract**?

  a an agreement with a company that produces records and CDs

  b an agreement with radio stations to play your records

8. Which of Mauboy's songs went to number one on the music charts?

_____

9. How old was Jessica Mauboy in 2018?

_____

10. What does **indigenous** mean?

  a someone who lives in Australia

  b native to a particular place

Score 2 points for each correct answer!

SCORE /20 0-8 10-14 16-20

Number & Algebra

Round to the nearest 1000.

① 6052 _____   ③ 23 570 _____

② 9821 _____   ④ 568 740 _____

⑤ Use the **chunking method** to solve this division.

135 ÷ 5 = _____

5 ⟌ 135

_____

_____

_____

Mentally calculate these percentages.

⑥ 1% of 202 = _____

⑦ 1% of 540 = _____

⑧ 1% of 2000 = _____

⑨ 10% of 70 = _____

⑩ 10% of 843 = _____

⑪ 10% of 1000 = _____

⑫ Use the area method to multiply these numbers.

25 × 24 = _____

There were 12 children at a party. 6 children were 9 years old, 4 were 10 years old and 2 were 8 years old. 8 children were girls.

⑬ What fraction of the children were aged 10?

_____

⑭ What fraction of the children were under 10 years old?

_____

⑮ What fraction of the children were boys?

_____

Complete these number patterns.

⑯ Add 20 to the previous number.

_____, 45, _____, _____, _____

⑰ Subtract 0.5 from the previous number

_____, 6.0, _____, _____, _____

⑱ What's the rule?

50, 52.5, 55, 57.5, 60

Rule = _____

Round to the nearest tenth.

⑲ 27.23 _____   ⑳ 256.49 _____

Round to the nearest hundredth.

㉑ 4.347 _____   ㉒ 15.759 _____

Score 2 points for each correct answer!

SCORE  /44 (0-20) (22-38) (40-44)

Statistics & Probability

Statistics & Probability

① Using only the numbers 1 to 6, complete the spinner so that it matches the probability statements.

- You are certain to get a number lower than 5.
- You are twice as likely to get a 2 as a 1.
- You have a 3 in 8 chance of getting a 3.
- You have an equal chance of spinning a 4 and a 2.

Circle the correct answer based on fair spins of this spinner.

② What is the chance of number 1 being spun?

a $\frac{1}{3}$ b $\frac{3}{6}$ c $\frac{1}{6}$ d $\frac{6}{1}$

③ What is the chance of either 2 or 4 being spun?

a $\frac{2}{4}$ b $\frac{2}{6}$ c $\frac{4}{2}$ d $\frac{1}{6}$

④ What is the chance of 7 being spun?

a $\frac{1}{6}$ b $\frac{6}{6}$ c 0   d 1

Use the data for the pie-eating competition to answer the following questions.

	Pie flavour				
Contestant	Apple	Berry	Cherry	Date	Egg
Maya	6	1	5	4	0
Tim	3	5	3	3	8
Ellin	1	7	0	4	4
Henry	9	2	0	2	7
Song	4	6	1	6	5
Max	2	8	2	11	1

TARGETING HOMEWORK 5 © PASCAL PRESS ISBN 9781925726473

TERM 3 MATHS

⑤ Who ate the most pies? _____

⑥ Which two contestants ate the fewest pies?
_____

⑦ How many Egg pies were eaten? _____

⑧ What pie flavour was eaten the most?
_____

⑨ What pie flavour was eaten the least?
_____

⑩ How many pies were eaten altogether?
_____

⑪ How many more Apple pies were eaten than Cherry pies?
_____

⑫ Did Song eat more pies than Henry? _____

Measurement & Space

Write or circle the correct answers.

Which rotation would get the shape to fit into the cut-out?

①
a 45° anticlockwise
b 45° clockwise
c 90° anticlockwise
d 90° clockwise

②
a 90° clockwise
b 135° anticlockwise
c 135° clockwise
d 90° anticlockwise

What do these 2D faces look like? Circle the correct answers.

③ Face A
a   b   c

④ Face B
a   b   c

⑤ Face C
a   b   c

Answer the questions about this rectangular prism.

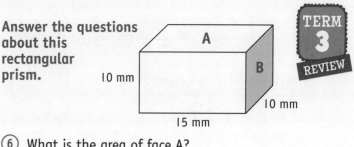

10 mm
10 mm
15 mm

⑥ What is the area of face A?
_____

⑦ What is the area of face B?
_____

⑧ To make up a cordial drink, you need $\frac{1}{5}$ cordial and 80% water. Circle the jug that shows the correct amount of cordial.

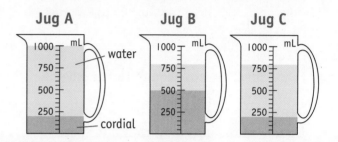

Jug A   Jug B   Jug C
1000 mL   1000 mL   1000 mL
750   750   750
500   500   500
250   250   250
water
cordial

Complete these time conversions.

⑨ 180 minutes = _____ hours

⑩ 3 _____ = 180 seconds

⑪ 72 _____ = 3 days

⑫ 240 _____ = 4 minutes

Circle the best description of the 24-hour digital time.

⑬ **13:09**
a thirteen minutes past nine
b almost ten minutes past one in the afternoon
c nearly half past one
d close to ten past three in the afternoon

⑭ **16:45**
a three quarters of an hour past six
b nearly seven o'clock
c quarter to five pm
d quarter to six am

⑮ How much time has elapsed between the two digital clocks above?
_____

⑯ 1 kg of flour costs $3.00.
How much is 250 g worth? _____

⑰ 400 g of raisins costs $8.00.
How much is 50 g worth? _____

UNIT 25

Grammar & Punctuation

AC9E5LA08

Adverbial clauses

An **adverbial clause** gives more information about the main idea by saying **how, when, where** and **why** things are happening. It begins with a conjunction and can be placed anywhere in the sentence.

A **comma** is placed *after* an adverbial clause at the beginning of a sentence.

Example: conjunction

When I turn 12, our family is travelling to Europe.
comma

No comma is needed if the clause is at the end of the sentence.

Example: conjunction

Our family is travelling to Europe **when** I turn 12.
no comma

Underline the adverbial clause in these sentences.

① After I have walked the dog, I will read my book.

② If Dad calls, tell him I am on my way.

③ Though it was not her chore, Elisa washed up.

④ We played on the beach until the sun set.

⑤ As it was wet outside, we all played indoors.

Punctuate these sentences with capitals, commas, full stops and question marks.

⑥ because no-one was home the thieves broke into the house

⑦ after the match we went to the pizza restaurant

⑧ when she arrives make sure to tell alice the good news

⑨ will you vacuum the floor while I do the dishes

⑩ if they win today the hammersmith tigers will win the cup

Phonic Knowledge & Spelling

AC9E5LY09, AC9E5LY10

Prefixes mis– and dis–

Say each word in the word bank. The prefix **mis–** means 'wrongly'. The prefix **dis–** means 'not' or 'opposite'.

Word Bank

mistake	misplace	misprint	mistrust
mislead	misjudge	misbehave	misinterpret
disturb	discover	discard	disappear
distract	disobey	dishonest	dismantle

Choose words from the word bank to complete these sentences.

① It was a _____ to wander off the track because we got lost.

② I wonder what it must be like to _____ a new animal species.

③ I agree that it is better to be honest than _____.

④ "If you _____, there will be a suitable punishment!"

Write antonyms for the words using the prefix mis– or dis– words. Remember! Antonyms are words with the opposite meaning.

⑤ fortune _____

⑥ continue _____

⑦ able _____

⑧ understand _____

Match the words in the box with their meanings.

dismantle	misplace	misinterpret
disappear	misprint	

⑨ to take something apart: _____

⑩ to interpret something incorrectly: _____

⑪ to stop being visible: _____

⑫ to put something in the wrong place: _____

⑬ to make an error in printing: _____

TERM 4 ENGLISH

Score 2 points for each correct answer! **SCORE** **/20** (0-8) (10-14) (16-20)

Score 2 points for each correct answer! **SCORE** **/26** (0-10) (12-20) (22-26)

TARGETING HOMEWORK 5 © PASCAL PRESS ISBN 9781925726473

Our Solar System

Informative text – Report
Author – Frances Mackay

Our solar system includes the Sun, which is a star, and all the objects that orbit around it, including the planets, moons and asteroids. Scientists estimate that the edge of the solar system is about 15 billion kilometres from the Sun.

The Sun's diameter is 109 times larger than the Earth's. The Sun is mostly composed of the gases hydrogen and helium. Light from the Sun takes eight minutes to reach Earth. The Sun orbits around the centre of the Milky Way galaxy, taking 225 000 000 years to complete a full orbit!

Our solar system consists of eight planets, four inner planets: Mercury, Venus, Earth and Mars, and four outer planets: Jupiter, Saturn, Uranus and Neptune. The four inner planets are smaller and made mostly from rock and metal. The four outer planets are much larger and are made up of gases. There are also five dwarf plants: Pluto, Ceres, Eris, Makemake and Haumea. Pluto used to be considered one of the planets in our solar system but it was downgraded to a dwarf planet in 2006.

A mnemonic to help you remember the names of the planets in order is: My Very Educated Mother Just Served Us Noodles.

Note – the planets in this diagram have not been drawn to scale.

Between Mars and Jupiter is the asteroid belt. The asteroid belt contains millions of asteroids, some of them no larger than boulders, while others are much larger. One of the dwarf plants, Ceres, is found in this belt.

Our planet, Earth, is 149 600 000 kilometres from the Sun. The average surface temperature of the Earth is 22 °C, whereas the Sun's average is 6000 °C. It takes 365¼ days for Earth to orbit the Sun. The planet closest in size to Earth is Venus.

Mercury is the smallest planet, not much larger than Earth's Moon. Jupiter is the largest planet — it is so large that all the planets could fit inside it! Jupiter takes 11.9 years to orbit the Sun.

Write or circle the correct box answers.

1. **What is the Sun?**
   - a a planet
   - b our solar system
   - c a star

2. **Which is the odd word?**
   - a estimate
   - b approximate
   - c guess
   - d certain

3. **What gases is the Sun made from?**

   _____

4. **Name the five dwarf planets in our solar system.**

   _____
   _____
   _____

5. **Which word in the text means 'demoted to a lower level of importance'?**

   _____

6. **Name the two planets closest to Earth.**

   _____
   _____

Score 2 points for each correct answer! **SCORE** **/12** (0-4) (6-8) (10-12)

My Book Review

Title _____

Author _____

Rating ☆☆☆☆☆

Comment _____
_____

TERM 4 ENGLISH

UNIT 25

Number & Algebra

AC9M5N01

Decimal numbers

Write these numbers.

① 6 thousand + 5 hundreds + 4 tens + 6 ones + 4 tenths

_____

② 12 thousands + 8 hundreds + 2 tens + 4 ones + 5 tenths + 2 thousandths

_____

③ 78 thousands + 5 tens + 8 thousandths

_____

④ 345 thousands + 9 hundreds + 2 ones + 48 hundredths

_____

Write these numbers on the number line.

⑤ 4.0 ⑧ 3.50
⑥ 3.05 ⑨ 1.04
⑦ 0.40 ⑩ 1.4

Circle the decimal number that is between the two given numbers.

⑪ 336.34 and 337.09
a 336.08   c 337.03
b 337.35   d 336.25

⑫ 5023.76 and 5024.13
a 5024.08   c 5023.58
b 5023.08   d 5024.18

⑬ 32 456.52 and 32 457.19
a 32 456.32   c 32 456.64
b 32 457.91   d 32 457.20

Write these numbers in descending order (from largest to smallest).

⑭ 1.3, 1.11. 1.26, 1.32

_____

⑮ 0.09, 0.01, 0.04, 0.10

_____

⑯ 25.62, 25.7, 25.72, 25.06

_____

Statistics & Probability

AC9M5P01, AC9M5P02

Probability scale

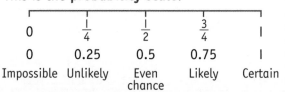

Things that are certain to happen have a probability of 1. Things that are impossible have a probability of 0.

Write the numbers 1 to 7 above the correct arrows to show the probability of each of the following events.

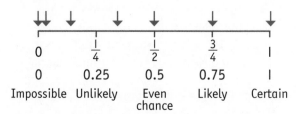

① All the water in the oceans will dry up next week.
② You will eat some food today.
③ You roll a dice and get a 1 or 2.
④ You will become a billionaire.
⑤ You will travel to another country one day.
⑥ You toss a coin and get a tail.
⑦ You will pull a King out of a deck of cards.

When there are two possibilities for an event, the probability of the possibilities totals 1.
Example: If there's a 1 in 3 chance that you will go swimming tomorrow, there's a 2 in 3 chance that you will **not** go swimming tomorrow.

What chances do the following events have of occurring?

⑧ rolling 6 on a regular die _____
⑨ rolling 1 to 5 on a regular die _____
⑩ picking out a blue marble from a bag of 5 blue marbles _____
⑪ picking out a red marble from a bag of 5 blue marbles _____
⑫ picking out a red marble from a bag of 5 red marbles and 2 blue marbles _____
⑬ picking out a blue marble from a bag of 5 red marbles and 2 blue marbles _____

Score 2 points for each correct answer! SCORE /32

Score 2 points for each correct answer! SCORE /26

112

TARGETING HOMEWORK 5 © PASCAL PRESS ISBN 9781925726473

Measurement & Space

AC9M5M04

Using a full circle protractor

This is how to use a full circle or 360° protractor:

- Place the centre of the protractor on the vertex of the angle.
- Line up one arm of the angle with the 0° on the protractor.
- Count up from 0° to the other arm of the angle.

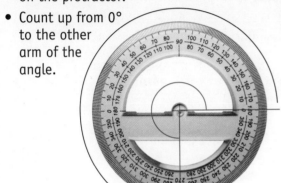

270°

Read and record the size of the angles.

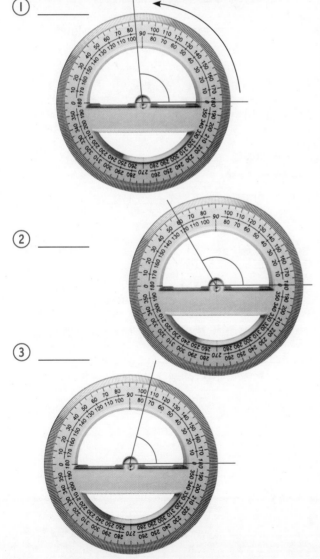

① _____

② _____

③ _____

④ _____

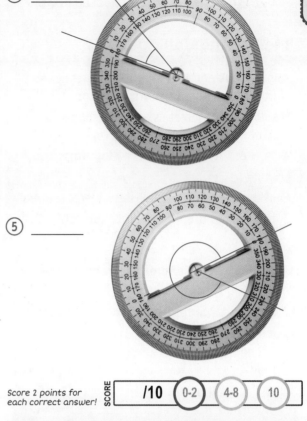

⑤ _____

Score 2 points for each correct answer! **SCORE** **/10** (0-2) (4-8) (10)

Problem Solving

AC9M5M04

Angles in a triangle

The three angles in a triangle add up to 180°.

This means that if we know the size of two angles, we can calculate the third angle:

50° + 75° = 125°

180° − 125° = 55°

So, the third angle is 55°.

Calculate the missing angle in these triangles.

① _____
_____

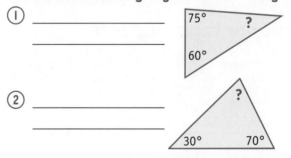

75°   ?

60°

② _____
_____

?

30°   70°

③ _____
_____

?

25°   20°

④ _____
_____

?   42°

87°

TERM 4 MATHS

Grammar & Punctuation

AC9E5LY10

Tricky singular nouns

Some nouns end in **s** and look like they are plural, but in fact they are **singular**.

Examples: mathematics, politics, baked beans, social studies, news, mumps, United States

With these words, you use a **singular verb**.

Examples:

Mathematics **is** my favourite subject. (correct)

Mathematics **are** my favourite subject. (incorrect)

Circle the correct form of the verb in these sentences.

① The United States (has   have) a large population.

② Baked beans (is   are) my favourite snack food.

③ The news (have   has) an important item on tonight.

Tricky plural nouns

Some nouns are always in the **plural** form and use a **plural verb**.

Examples: scissors, jeans, savings, pyjamas, shorts, oats, police, barracks

Circle the correct form of the verb in these sentences.

④ The police (have   has) surrounded the house.

⑤ Her clothes (was   were) too casual for the job interview.

⑥ Oats (is   are) good to eat for breakfast.

Titles of books and films

Titles of books and films are always treated as **singular**, even though the title sounds plural.

Example: The Birds **is** a classic horror film.

Circle the correct form of the verb in these sentences.

⑦ *Great Expectations* (are   is) a book written by Charles Dickens.

⑧ *Gremlins* (are   is) available on DVD.

⑨ *The Witches* (was   were) written by Roald Dahl.

Score 2 points for each correct answer! **SCORE** **/18** (0-6) (8-14) (16-18)

Phonic Knowledge & Spelling

AC9E5LY09, AC9E5LY10

Suffix –ion

Say each word in the word bank. They all end in the noun suffix –ion. Words with this suffix usually end in –ion, –tion or –sion.

Word Bank

action	auction	selection	attention
operation	pollution	exploration	exception
tension	vision	division	decision
cushion	fashion	passion	session

Choose words from the word bank to complete these sentences.

① My nan made a _____ cover for our sofa.

② My parents sold our house at _____ to the highest bidder.

③ The selection of

_____ clothing in the shop was exceptional.

Changing verbs to nouns

When verbs end in **–ate**, you drop the **e** before adding **–ion** to make a noun.

Examples: operate, operation
navigate, navigation

Change these verbs to nouns by adding –ion. Write the new word.

④ illustrate _____

⑤ punctuate _____

⑥ decorate _____

⑦ irrigate _____

Word families

These words are in the same **word family**: act, react, reaction, action, actor.

Write the words that are in the same family.

tensile   tension   selective   vision   selection
intense   interview   preview   preselect

⑧ tense _____

_____   _____

⑨ view _____

_____   _____

⑩ select _____

_____   _____

Score 2 points for each correct answer! **SCORE** **/20** (0-8) (10-14) (16-20)

TARGETING HOMEWORK 5 © PASCAL PRESS ISBN 9781925726473

Ecology by J J Barber

Informative text – Explanation
Author – Frances Mackay

Extract from Chapter 2 – What are resources?

What are resources?

Natural resources

Natural resources are things that are found in nature. They have not been made by humans. Natural resources include water, land, soils, rocks, minerals, plants, animals and fossil fuels. Humans depend on natural resources to survive, and a decline in one resource can have a huge impact on another. For example, a lack of rainfall in an area can cause rivers to dry up. When the water disappears from rivers, plants and animals die and humans can no longer water their crops in order to grow the food they need. Many plant and animal species have already become extinct or are endangered as their natural habitats are being destroyed by human activities. Sustainability is using our natural resources in a responsible way so they will last longer.

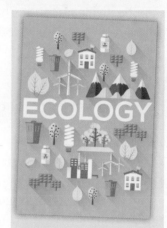

Human resources

Human resources are the people who make up the workforce that produces goods and services for us to use. Human resources can vary in quantity around the world — some places have more people than others. Human resources can also vary in the quality of knowledge and effort required to produce things — some countries have more highly trained or skilled people to do the work than other countries.

Capital resources

Capital resources are the goods made and used to produce other goods and services. Capital resources include such things as tools, equipment, machinery and buildings. The quantity and quality of capital resources varies greatly from one country to another. Some countries have access to better quality equipment, infrastructure and technological development than other countries.

Contents

Write or circle the correct answers.

Name the chapter where you might find information on the following.

① how manufacturing affects our environment

_____

② how pollution can be prevented

_____

Under which subheading do you find the following information?

③ how countries vary in the quantity of equipment they have

_____

④ a definition of human resources

_____

⑤ a list of natural resources

_____

What type of resource are these? Natural (N), Human (H) or Capital (C)?

⑥ a scientist _____

⑦ forest _____

⑧ factory _____

⑨ **Endangered** means:

  a a dangerous habit.

  b something that is dangerous.

  c at risk of becoming extinct.

My Book Review

Title _____

Author _____

Rating ☆☆☆☆☆

Comment _____

_____

Score 2 points for each correct answer!

SCORE **/18** (0-6) (8-14) (16-18)

TERM 4 ENGLISH

Number & Algebra

AC9M5N02

More divisibility tests

A number is **divisible** by another number if it can be divided into that number of parts without a remainder. For example, **36** is divisible by **6**. 36 can be divided into 6 parts of 6, with no remainder.

Divisibility test for 7

This is a bit tricky, but you can work out if a number is divisible by 7 by doing the following steps.

Example: Is 1603 divisible by 7?

Step 1: Remove the last digit.
Take off the 3 to leave 160.

Step 2: Double the digit you removed and take this away from the number left over in step 1.
Double 3 = 6
Take 6 from 160 = 154

Step 3: Continue steps 1 and 2 until only one digit remains. If this digit is 0 or 7, then the number is divisible by 7.
Take off the 4 from 154 to leave 15.
Double 4 = 8
Take 8 from 15 = 7
1603 is divisible by 7.

Are these numbers divisible by 7?
Show your working and circle yes or no.

① 1562   a yes   b no

_____

_____

② 1680   a yes   b no

_____

_____

③ 2546   a yes   b no

_____

_____

_____

Divisibility test for 9

Add all the digits in the number. If the answer is divisible by 9, then the whole number is divisible by 9.

Examples:

504   5 + 0 + 4 = 9. ✔ divisible by 9.

7407   7 + 4 + 0 + 7 = 18. ✔ divisible by 9.

Are these numbers divisible by 9?
Show your working and circle yes or no.

④ 1702   a yes   b no

_____

⑤ 522   a yes   b no

_____

⑥ 7479   a yes   b no

_____

⑦ 1689   a yes   b no

_____

⑧ 5688   a yes   b no

_____

Divisibility test for 10

This is the easiest one of all! If a number ends in 0, then it is divisible by 10.

Are these numbers divisible by 10?
Write yes or no.

⑨ 56 _____   ⑫ 9999 _____

⑩ 500 _____   ⑬ 10 000 _____

⑪ 1240 _____   ⑭ 45 600 _____

Divisibility test for 11

Subtract the last digit from the rest of the number. If the answer is divisible by 11, then the whole number is divisible by 11.

Example: Is 253 divisible by 11?

Subtract 3 from 25 = 22
22 is divisible by 11, so 253 is divisible by 11.

Are these numbers divisible by 11?
Show your working and circle yes or no.

⑮ 374   a yes   b no

⑯ 5112   a yes   b no

⑰ 352   a yes   b no

⑱ 4015   a yes   b no

⑲ 2348   a yes   b no

Score 2 points for each correct answer!   SCORE   /38   0-16   18-32   34-38

Statistics & Probability

There are no statistics & probability activities in this unit.

TARGETING HOMEWORK 5 © PASCAL PRESS ISBN 9781925726473

Measurement & Space

AC9M5M01

Capacity

> Remember: 1000 millilitres = 1 litre
> 1000 mL = 1 L

Use arrows to mark these measurements on the measuring container. 500 mL is marked as an example.

① 750 mL   ⑥ 4250 mL

② 1.25 L   ⑦ 4.75 L

③ 2250 mL   ⑧ 5500 mL

④ 2.75 L   ⑨ 5750 mL

⑤ 3.5 L   ⑩ 6.25 L

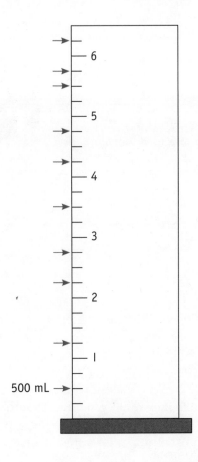

Look at the capacity of each container.

a   0.25 L

b   0.5 L

c   2 L

d   2.5 L

e   3.25 L   f   4.5 L

Write the letters of the containers you could use to exactly make up each measurement.

> *Example:*
> Container **a** holds 0.25 L.
> Container **b** holds 0.5 L.
> You could fill container **a** twice and container **b** once to make up 1 L:
> 0.25 + 0.25 + 0.5 = 1.
>
> 1 L = [**a**] + [**a**] + [**b**]

⑪ 750 mL = ☐ + ☐

⑫ 1.25 L = ☐ + ☐ + ☐

⑬ 2250 mL = ☐ + ☐

⑭ 2.75 L = ☐ + ☐ + ☐

⑮ 3.5 L = ☐ + ☐ + ☐

⑯ 4250 mL = ☐ + ☐ + ☐

⑰ 4.75 L = ☐ + ☐

⑱ 5500 mL = ☐ + ☐ + ☐

⑲ 5750 mL = ☐ + ☐ + ☐

⑳ 6.25 L = ☐ + ☐ + ☐ + ☐

Score 2 points for each correct answer!

SCORE /40   (0-18)   (20-34)   (36-40)

Problem Solving

AC9M5M01, AC9M5N09

Keeping goldfish happy

Goldfish each need 6 litres of water to stay healthy in a tank.

Calculate how many goldfish you can keep in the following tanks.

① 60 litre tank

_____

② 180 litre tank

_____

③ 480 litre tank

_____

④ 1450 litre tank

_____

TERM 4 MATHS

Grammar & Punctuation

AC9E5LA09, AC9E5LY04

Commas

We use **commas** in the following ways:

- to separate items in a list, e.g. We bought eggs, milk, butter, cheese and bread.
- to set off introductory words at the beginning of a sentence, e.g. Well, that was interesting!
- before and after interruptions in a sentence, e.g. The Melbourne Show, I think, is the best one.
- to separate connectives from the rest of the sentence, e.g. Firstly, I think we should go there together.
- to separate prepositional phrases from the rest of the sentence, e.g. After the game, we celebrated the team's victory.

Cross out the incorrect comma in each sentence.

① Wow, that new game, is brilliant!

② After school, Sam and her friends explored, the riverbank.

③ The activities you could try were sculpture, drawing, painting, collage and, photography.

④ Doing homework, she thought, could sometimes, be interesting.

⑤ Finally, the endless journey through the desert, was almost over.

Mark where the 13 commas should be placed in this paragraph.

⑥–⑱ On Saturday Mum Dad and I went to the Ranelagh Show. I really enjoyed looking at the farm animals. There were sheep goats pigs cattle horses chickens geese and alpacas. Personally I liked the alpacas best but Mum preferred the goats. Dad on the other hand liked the horses especially the huge draught horses that were demonstrating how to pull a plough. After the show we went to Grandma's house for dinner. Then I fell asleep in the car on the way home.

Phonic Knowledge & Spelling

AC9E5LY04, AC9E5LY05

Prefixes in– and im–

Say each word in the word bank. The prefixes **in–** and **im–** loosely mean 'not' or 'within'.

Word Bank

income	include	invest	inform
inflate	infertile	inspire	inaccurate
imagine	immigrant	immerse	immediate
impatient	impolite	improper	improve

Choose words from the word bank to complete these sentences.

① I can't deny that I need to _____ my handwriting.

② The doctor had to _____ my brother that he needed surgery.

③ Our teacher said we have to _____ the whole class in the play.

Add in– or im– to these base words. Write the new words.

④ adequate _____

⑤ mobile _____

⑥ possible _____

⑦ capable _____

Choose verbs from the word bank that match these nouns.

⑧ imagination _____

⑨ inflation _____

Adding the suffix –sion

Look what happens when you add the suffix **–sion** to words that end in **–ade, –ide, –ode** and **–ude**: invade, invasion   decide, decision   explode, explosion   include, inclusion.

Add –sion to these words. Write the new words.

⑩ divide _____

⑪ provide _____

⑫ implode _____

⑬ erode _____

Fast food is not all junk

Persuasive text – Argument
Authors – Hazel Edwards and Goldie Alexander

Once upon a time, when your grandparents were children, there were no fast-food restaurants. Hard to imagine, isn't it? Take away the takeaway dinners and lots of working parents would be extra-tired. Lots of kids would be extra-disappointed too!

What is junk food?

Junk is another word for rubbish: something you throw away because it has no use. That's not how we should think about food. Food is essential fuel. Junk food contains very little nutritional value. It doesn't have much that is actually good for you, such as vitamins, protein or fibre. What it usually does contain is lots of salt, fat, sugar and even chemicals. Lollies, salty, deep-fried chips and fizzy drinks all qualify as junk food.

What about fast food?

Fast food is just what it sounds like — food that is ready in a hurry. Fast food has been prepared for you to save you the time it takes to cook. That doesn't mean it has to be junk. Many fast-food companies produce low-fat, low-sugar foods and many restaurants offer takeaway service for tasty, healthy meals.

So what's the problem?

The problem is the choices you make, not the food itself. There's no problem if you most often choose foods with good nutritional value and eat junk food only rarely.

Source: *Why weight?*, Health & Understanding, Blake Education.

Write or circle the correct answers.

① **What does 'Food is essential fuel' mean?**

   a Food is an important type of petrol.

   b Food is essential to keep our bodies working.

   c Food needs to be eaten every day.

Are these statements fact or opinion? Write F or O.

② Junk food contains very little nutritional value. ____

③ Chips and fizzy drinks are the best types of fast foods. ____

④ Fast food doesn't have to be junk food. ____

⑤ **Explain the difference between junk food and fast food.**

_____

_____

_____

Match the words in the box to their meanings.

| essential | rarely | chemicals | low-sugar |

⑥ very little sugar: _____

⑦ not often: _____

⑧ something you must have or do:

   _____

⑨ substances made by humans in a laboratory:

   _____

⑩ **Give three examples of junk food from the text.**

_____

_____

⑪ **How often does the author suggest you eat junk food?**

   a daily   b once a week   c rarely

Score 2 points for each correct answer!   **SCORE** /22   0-8   10-16   18-22

My Book Review

Title _____

Author _____

Rating ☆☆☆☆☆

Comment _____

_____

Number & Algebra

AC9M5N03

Fraction number lines

Use the number line to help you decide if these fractions are **less than 1, equal to 1** or **greater than 1**. Write **< 1, = 1** or **> 1**.

① $\frac{10}{10}$ _____

② $1\frac{1}{5}$ _____

③ $\frac{15}{10}$ _____

④ $\frac{3}{5}$ _____

⑤ $\frac{1}{2}$ _____

⑥ $\frac{10}{5}$ _____

⑦ $\frac{4}{10}$ _____

⑧ $\frac{20}{10}$ _____

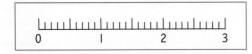

Use the number line to help you solve these.

⑨ $1\frac{4}{10} + \frac{5}{10} =$ _____

⑩ $\frac{2}{5} + \frac{3}{5} =$ _____

⑪ $1\frac{1}{2} + 1\frac{1}{2} =$ _____

⑫ $\frac{9}{10} + \frac{5}{10} =$ _____

⑬ $1 - \frac{3}{10} =$ _____

⑭ $2\frac{3}{10} - \frac{8}{10} =$ _____

⑮ $3 - \frac{3}{5} =$ _____

⑯ $2\frac{9}{10} - \frac{1}{2} =$ _____

⑰ Write these fractions in **descending** order (from largest to smallest).

$\frac{1}{2}$, $1\frac{7}{10}$, $\frac{10}{10}$, $\frac{3}{10}$, $1\frac{3}{5}$, $\frac{1}{5}$

_____

⑱ Write these fractions in **ascending** order (from smallest to largest).

$\frac{16}{10}$, $\frac{3}{5}$, $\frac{1}{2}$, $1\frac{5}{10}$, $\frac{1}{5}$, $1\frac{7}{10}$

_____

Score 2 points for each correct answer! SCORE /36

Statistics & Probability

AC9M5ST01

Survey questions

When you carry out a survey, you need to ask questions. There are three types of questions:

- **Open-ended questions** – The person being surveyed (respondent) gives a full answer, using their own knowledge or feelings.

- **Multiple choice questions** – The respondent has answers to choose from.

- **Yes or no questions:** The respondent answers either yes or no.

What types of questions are these?
Write **O** for open-ended, **M** for multiple choice or **Y/N** for yes or no questions.

① ☐ How long have you lived at your address?

② ☐ Do you like swimming?

③ ☐ Do you prefer basketball, netball or hockey?

④ ☐ How often do you eat out?
- once a month   • once a week
- once a year   • never

⑤ ☐ Who is your favourite author?

⑥ ☐ Are you older than 10 years?

Survey questions can gather different types of data. Two types of data are:
- **Numerical data:** data that can be measured or counted
- **Categorical data:** data that can be arranged into categories or types

What type of data would you get if you asked these questions? Write N for numerical or C for categorical.

⑦ ☐ How old are you?

⑧ ☐ What is your favourite type of pet?

⑨ ☐ How many hours this week have you watched television?

⑩ ☐ How tall are you?

⑪ ☐ Which sports brand do you prefer?

You have been asked to conduct a survey of the students in your class to find out about the sports they play.

Write two questions that would gather numerical data.

⑫ _____
_____
_____

⑬ _____
_____
_____

Write two questions that would gather categorical data.

⑭ _____
_____
_____

TARGETING HOMEWORK 5 © PASCAL PRESS ISBN 9781925726473

⑮ _____

_____

_____

SCORE /30 (0-12) (14-24) (26-30)

Measurement & Space

AC9M5M02

Measuring length, perimeter and area

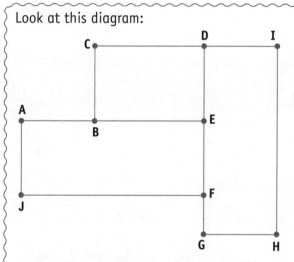

Look at this diagram:

To measure **line AB**, you measure from point A to point B. To measure **line ABC**, you measure from A to B then add on the measurement from B to C.

Use the diagram to calculate the following. You will need to use a ruler. Measure to the nearest half centimetre.

① What is the length of line AB? _____

② What is the length of line ABCD?

_____

③ What is the perimeter of rectangle AEFJ?

_____

④ What is the perimeter of rectangle DIHG?

_____

⑤ What is the area of rectangle CDEB?

_____

⑥ What is the area of rectangle DIHG?

_____

⑦ How much longer is line CDI than line BE?

_____

⑧ Which is shorter: line JF or line DF?

_____

⑨ What is the diagonal measurement from point C to point E?

_____

⑩ What is the diagonal measurement from point A to point H?

_____

SCORE /20 (0-8) (10-14) (16-20)

Problem Solving

AC9M5N09

Holiday time

Mr and Mrs Robertson are planning to take their children on a camping holiday for five days. Here is their budget:

- Caravan park:
  - Children cost $25 per night each
  - Adults cost $40 per night each
  - Total for the family for 5 nights = $775
- Campervan rental: $95 per day
- Food allowance: $100 per day

Calculate the following:

① Use the cost of the caravan park to work out how many children there are in the family.

_____

_____

_____

_____

② What is the total cost for food?

_____

③ What is the total cost for the campervan rental?

_____

④ What is the total cost of the holiday, excluding spending money?

_____

_____

TERM 4 MATHS

Grammar & Punctuation

AC9E5LA09

Using the apostrophe

Remember! The apostrophe is used for two purposes:

1. to show possession or belonging
   Examples:
   The <u>dog's bowl</u> was empty. (singular owner)
   The <u>girls' coats</u> were left in the hall. (plural owners)

2. to show that a letter or letters are missing in contractions.
   Examples: **Didn't** is short for 'did not'.
   They've is short for 'they have'.

Add the apostrophes to these sentences. Careful! There are apostrophes for possession and for contractions.

① Dont get too close to the cliffs edge!

② Samanthas mother is selling her fathers house.

③ Id like to ride Toms bike but its a bit big for me.

④ The players uniforms didnt arrive in time for the match.

⑤ The childrens paintings are on the teachers desk.

⑥ I wish theyd hurry up or well be late!

Write the correct form of plural possessive nouns.

Example: the books of the students
= the students' books

⑦ the eggs of the chickens

_____

⑧ the leaves of the trees

_____

⑨ the tools of the builders

_____

⑩ the footprints of the mice

_____

⑪ the shoes of the girls

_____

⑫ the webs of the spiders

_____

Phonic Knowledge & Spelling

AC9E5LY09, AC9E5LY10

Suffixes –ment and –ness

Say each word in the word bank. The suffix **–ment** means 'the state of', e.g. punishment is the state of being punished.

The suffix **–ness** means 'state of being', e.g. brightness is the state of being bright.

Both suffixes turn the base word into a **noun**.

Word Bank

darkness	laziness	softness	fairness
madness	selfishness	happiness	business
amendment	refreshment	movement	
management	amazement	amusement	
appointment	engagement		

Choose words from the word bank to complete these sentences.

① The _____ was started ten years ago so it has had a decade of selling online.

② Mum changed her doctor's

_____

because of her work schedule.

Antonyms

Antonyms are words opposite in meaning.
Examples: happiness, unhappiness
softness, hardness

Match the words in the box to their antonyms.

lightness	unfairness	mismanagement
unselfishness		

③ management _____

④ selfishness _____

⑤ darkness _____

⑥ fairness _____

Add –ment or –ness to make new words. Write the words.

⑦ govern _____

⑧ agree _____

⑨ sad _____

⑩ weak _____

Score 2 points for each correct answer! SCORE /24 (0-10) (12-18) (20-24)

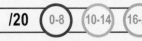

Score 2 points for each correct answer! SCORE /20 (0-8) (10-14) (16-20)

TARGETING HOMEWORK 5 © PASCAL PRESS ISBN 9781925726473

The Beautiful Spurs

Imaginative text – Narrative
Author – Kate Walker

"Aaron is coming! Aaron is home!"

Dora flew across the farmyard. She jumped onto the gate and waved wildly at a distant figure on horseback. It was her brother, Aaron, riding at an easy pace towards the farm.

Katie, Dora's older sister, hurried across the farmyard too, the hem of her skirts raising the dust. It was true, Aaron was coming! Even at a distance Katie recognised him on his big, grey horse.

She waved her straw hat. "Aaron! Aaron!"

Ben heard the name being called. He instantly threw the slops at the pigs, bucket and all. He tore across the yard, leapt the fence, and ran flat out up the road. He wanted to be the first to greet their brother.

"Aaron, you're home!" Ben called as he got closer.

Ben was so excited he ran into the shoulder of Aaron's big mare. She spooked and started back.

"Take it easy!" Aaron said. He settled his horse, and then swung his little brother up behind him, onto the horse's broad rump.

Ben began firing questions. "How long are you staying? What's happening in the city? Did you bring me anything?"

Aaron always brought presents home for everyone.

"Look in the saddlebags," Aaron replied. "There might be something in there for you." The horse walked on quietly.

Ben picked the bag on the right side of the saddle. He unbuckled its strap and, sure enough, right at the top he found a brown paper parcel tied with string.

"Is this it? Is it?" he asked. Without waiting for a reply, Ben tore the paper open. "Oh, Aaron," he gasped. "They're beautiful."

In the nest of paper lay a beautiful pair of spurs. They were made of polished brass. Etched along the shafts were delicate vines of morning glory. The straps were honey-red leather, and the eight-pointed star wheels tinkled like tiny bells. Just holding them made Ben sit up straighter on his brother's horse. He even gave the mare a none-too-gentle tap with the heels of his boots. He couldn't help himself.

Source: *The Beautiful Spurs*, Blake's Novels, Blake Education.

Write or circle the correct answers.

1. **Where does Aaron live?**
   a on the farm
   b in the city
   c in the mountains

2. **What was Ben doing when Aaron arrived?**

   _____

3. **What type of word is wildly?**
   a verb   c adverb
   b noun   d adjective

4. **What are spurs used for?**
   a to add decoration to boots
   b we are not told
   c to urge a horse forward

5. **What is a 'none-too-gentle tap'?**

   _____

Score 2 points for each correct answer!

SCORE /10 0-2 4-8 10

My Book Review

Title _____

Author _____

Rating ☆☆☆☆☆

Comment _____

_____

TERM 4 ENGLISH

Number & Algebra

AC9M5N10

Number line patterns

The number line below shows a pattern for the rule: **+ 6, – 3**. The green jumps show the first part of the rule, **+ 6**. The orange jumps show the second part of the rule, **– 3**.

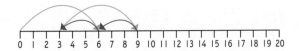

① Continue the pattern on the number line above.

Work out the rule for each of these number line patterns. Write the rule and continue the patterns.

② Write the rule: _____

③ Continue the pattern.

④ Write the number you ended up on: _____

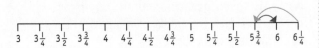

⑤ Write the rule: _____

⑥ Continue the pattern.

⑦ Write the number you ended up on: _____

⑧ Write the rule: _____

⑨ Continue the pattern.

⑩ Write the number you ended up on: _____

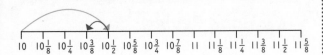

⑪ Write the rule: _____

⑫ Continue the pattern.

⑬ Write the number you ended up on: _____

TERM 4 MATHS

Statistics & Probability

There are no statistics & probability activities in this unit.

Measurement & Space

AC9M5SP03

Rotational symmetry

A shape has rotational symmetry if it looks identical in different positions when it is rotated around its centre.

This shape can be rotated to three different positions. The shape looks the same in each position. It has a rotational symmetry of order 3.

Circle the correct rotational symmetry of order for these shapes.

①
a 2
b 3
c 4
d 5

②
a 2
b 3
c 4
d 5

③
a 2
b 3
c 4
d 5

④
a 2
b 3
c 4
d 5

⑤

a 3
b 4
c 6
d 8

⑥

a 3
b 4
c 6
d 8

Complete the shapes so that they have the given order of rotational. symmetry.

⑦ order 3

⑧ order 4

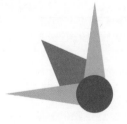

Which direction?

If you turned these shapes so that 1 pointed north, what directions would the other numbers point to? Use the compass to help you work it out.

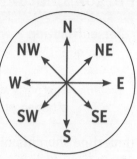

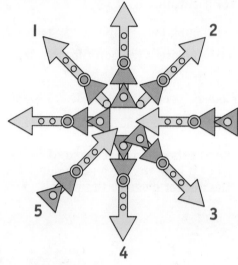

1 points **North**	
2 points _____	4 points _____
3 points _____	5 points _____

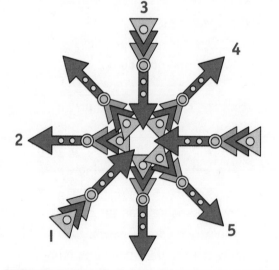

1 points **North**	
2 points _____	4 points _____
3 points _____	5 points _____

Score 2 points for each correct answer!

SCORE **/16** (0-6) (8-12) (14-16)

TERM 4 MATHS

Grammar & Punctuation

AC9E5LY06

Personification

Personification is when you give human traits, qualities or feelings to an animal or object.

thing   human trait

Example: The party **died** as soon as the music stopped playing.

Underline the animal or object that is being personified in these sentences. Then highlight the personification.

① The swimming pool invited me to jump in.

② Rain gently kissed the earth for the first time in weeks.

③ The leaves raced each other across the lawn.

④ The candle flame danced in the breeze.

⑤–⑯ **Read this poem that personifies the wind. Circle the 12 human qualities the author gives to the wind.**

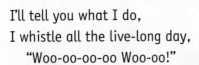

The March Wind

I come to work
  as well as play,

I'll tell you what I do,
I whistle all the live-long day,
  "Woo-oo-oo-oo Woo-oo!"

I toss the branches up and down,
  And shake them to and fro,
I whirl the leaves in flocks of brown,
  And send them high and low.

I strew the twigs upon the ground,
  The frozen earth I sweep,
I blow the children round and round,
  And wake the flowers from sleep.

Anonymous

Phonic Knowledge & Spelling

AC9E5LY08, AC9E5LY09, AC9E5LY10

Words ending in –our and –ous

Say each word in the word bank. Words ending in –our are usually nouns. The suffix –ous means 'full of'. These words are adjectives.

Word Bank

flavour	vapour	glamour	rumour
humour	honour	odour	splendour
famous	fabulous	perilous	dangerous
poisonous	jealous	generous	adventurous

Choose words from the word bank to complete these sentences.

① I would love to read the journal of a _____ person.

② Our tour guide had a _____ sense of humour.

③ Lemons have a sour _____.

The letter team our can make different sounds. Match words from the box with words that have the same 'our' sound.

court	flour	pour	your	hour	ourselves

④ sounds like 'four'

_____
_____
_____

⑤ sounds like 'sour'

_____
_____
_____

Add the suffix –ous to these words to make adjectives. Write the new words. Remember your spelling rules!

⑥ danger   _____

⑦ fame   _____

⑧ outrage   _____

⑨ luxury   _____

 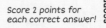

Sticks McLennon

Imaginative text – Narrative
Author – Maude Farrugia

"How could you possibly break *both* your arms!" Harriette yelled.

Her voice was so loud Samson could hear it rattling through the garage wall. He was sitting outside, waiting for his big sister Matilda, who was copping Harriette's rage inside.

Samson drew his shoulders up around his ears and tried not to listen. He was scared of Harriette Stewart even when she wasn't yelling; he was positively terrified of her when she was. He didn't want to be there. He would have much preferred to be at home, finishing off his maths assignment or tucked up in bed with his library book about stamp-collecting.

"I told you!" Matilda yelled back, waving her two plastered arms at Harriette in exasperation. "It was an accident!"

"Sometimes I wonder, Matilda, if you even want to be in this band," Harriette shot back.

Samson shook his head. There was nothing his sister wanted more than to be the drummer in Harriette's band, Harriette and The Spews. And now she had two broken arms. Because he had

become stuck on top of the monkey bars. Because he was super-scared of heights. And she'd had to rescue him. Only she slipped halfway up. And landed on his bike.

That's why he was here and had been listening to Harriette and Matilda's yelling match for the past ten minutes. And Harriette was winning.

"Well, who're we going to get to replace you, Matilda?" asked Ruth, the Spew's bass player. "The Waipatiki-West Battle of the Bands is in exactly three weeks!"

Matilda looked miserably at her two plaster-casted arms.

"Samson!" she yelled, gritting her teeth.

Samson stepped slowly into the garage. There were guitars and electrical cords strewn about the floor, and smushed drink cans and half-eaten apples lay everywhere. Slumped on the dirty brown couch in the corner of the garage were the three remaining members of Harriette and The Spews. They stared at him, open mouthed.

"No way! Not him!" said Becky, her safety pin earrings jangling against her face.

Source: *Sticks McLennon*, Blake's Novels, Blake Education.

Write or circle the correct answers.

① **Why was Harriette so angry?**

_____

_____

② **What does exasperation mean?**

a fear   b worry   c very annoyed

③ **How did Matilda break her arms?**

_____

_____

④ **Name four of the band members.**

_____

_____

⑤ **Where is the story set?**

a Australia

b New Zealand

c no clues are given in the story

Score 2 points for each correct answer!   SCORE **/10** (0-2) (4-8) (10)

My Book Review

Title _____

Author _____

Rating ☆☆☆☆☆

Comment _____

_____

Number & Algebra

AC9M5A01, AC9M5N08

Commutative law

Some operations are **commutative**. This means that it doesn't matter which number comes first when you complete the operation – the answer will be the same. Addition and multiplication are commutative.

Examples:
$12 \times 4 = 48$ $5 + 6 = 11$
$4 \times 12 = 48$ $6 + 5 = 11$

Subtraction and division are **not commutative**:

Examples:

$12 \div 4$ gives a different answer to $4 \div 12$

$25 - 10$ gives a different answer to $10 - 25$

The commutative law means that we can add and multiply numbers in any order that makes it easier to work out the answer.

Example: $23 + 19 + 7$

It's easier to first add 23 and 7 to make 30. Then add on 19 to make 49.

Estimate the result of adding the three numbers. Then write a number sentence to show the easiest order and calculate the answers.

① 24   18   6   Estimate: _____

_____

② 52   37   48   Estimate: _____

_____

③ 50   89   50   Estimate: _____

_____

④ 1000 67 4500 Estimate: _____

_____

Estimate the result of multiplying the three numbers. Then write a number sentence to show the easiest order and calculate the answers.

⑤ 5   48   2   Estimate: _____

_____

⑥ 52   4   25   Estimate: _____

_____

⑦ 100 5 10   Estimate: _____

_____

⑧ 50   73   2   Estimate: _____

_____

⑨ Did estimating first help you get the correct answers? Explain why or why not.

_____

_____

Which number sentence shows the commutative law? Circle the correct answer.

⑩ **a** $24 \times 4 = 96$
   b $24 \times 4 = 4 \times 24$
   c $24 \times \frac{1}{4} = 6$
   d $24 \times 4 = 96 \div 4$

⑪ **a** $10 \times 3 = 3 \times 10$
   b $10 \times (3 + 7) = 10 \times 3 + 10 \times 7$
   c $10 \times 3 = 30$
   d $30 = 10 \times 3$

⑫ **a** $14 + 16 + 25 = 25 + 16 + 14$
   b $25 + 16 = 14 + 25$
   c $16 + 14 + 25 = 45$
   d $45 - 16 = 45 - 14$

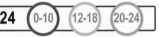

Score 2 points for each correct answer!   SCORE   **/24**   (0-10) (12-18) (20-24)

Statistics & Probability

AC9M5ST01, AC9M5ST03

Comparing data

Use the three sets of data about animals to answer the questions.

5 tallest land animals	
Giraffe	5.8 m
African elephant	3.05 m
Cape buffalo	2.9 m
Ostrich	2.74 m
Siberian tiger	2.59 m

5 fastest land animals	
Cheetah	98 km/h
Pronghorn antelope	97 km/h
Lion	84 km/h
Thomson's gazelle	82 km/h
Wildebeest	80 km/h

Five heaviest animals	
Blue whale	190 000 kg
Whale shark	11 800 kg
African elephant	5000 kg
Asian elephant	4000 kg
Rhinoceros	2200 kg

① What is the height and mass of an average African elephant?

_____

② How fast can a lion run? _____

③ How much taller is a giraffe than an ostrich?

_____

④ What is the total mass of the animals in the heaviest animals table? _____

(5) How much heavier is the blue whale than the next heaviest animal?

_____

(6) How much faster than a Thomson's gazelle is a pronghorn antelope? _____

This is an unfinished graph for one of the sets of data.

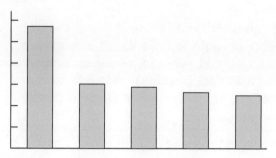

(7) Which set of data will this graph represent?

_____

(8) Complete the vertical scale on the graph above.

Score 2 points for each correct answer! | SCORE | **/16** | 0-6 | 8-12 | 14-16

Measurement & Space

AC9M5SP03

Enlarging shapes

When we enlarge a shape or drawing, we can use a **scale factor**. In this example, the smaller square has been doubled in size, so we say it has been enlarged by a **scale factor of 2**.

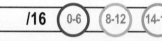

Has the smaller shape been accurately enlarged by a scale factor of 2?
Circle yes or no.

(1) a yes   b no

(3) a yes   b no

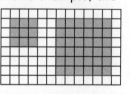

(2) a yes   b no

(4) a yes   b no

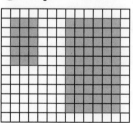

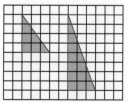

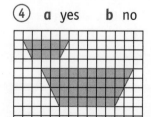

Enlarge each shape by a scale factor of 2.

(5)

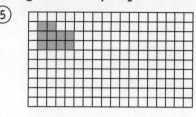

(6)

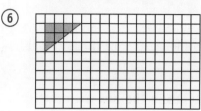

Score 2 points for each correct answer! | SCORE | **/12** | 0-4 | 6-8 | 10-12

Problem Solving

AC9M5M02

Solve it!

These shapes have been enlarged by a scale factor of 2. For each side marked **?**, work out what length that side was **before** it was enlarged. Write the correct answers on the lines.

(1) _____

8 cm · 10 cm · ?

(2) _____

? · 4 m · 8 m

(3) _____

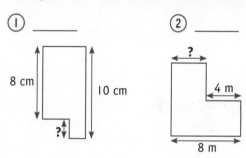

11 m · ? · 16 m

(4) _____

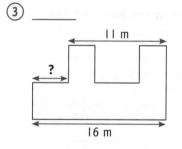

? · 6 cm · 7 cm · 12 cm · 12 cm

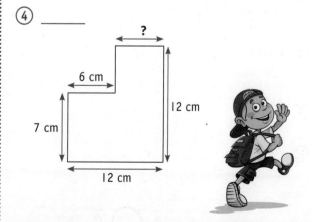

TERM 4 MATHS

Grammar & Punctuation

AC9E5LA04

Sentence beginnings

> The **beginning of a sentence** can help the reader to **predict** what the text is going to be about.
>
> For example, we know that the phrase, 'Once upon a time ...' indicates that the text will be a fairytale.

Match the text types in the box with the sentence beginnings.

> discussion   book review   instructions
> anecdote   biography

① Should students wear school uniforms?

_____

② Collect your ingredients.

_____

③ Yesterday, a funny thing happened.

_____

④ James Mason was born in Canberra in 1965.

_____

⑤ This book by JJ Ryle is the best I have ever read.

_____

Sentence endings

> When we read the **final sentence** we can also **predict** what type of text it is.

Match the text types in the box with the final sentences.

> anecdote   advertisement   movie review
> interview   fairytale

⑥ And they all lived happily ever after.

_____

⑦ Thanks, Brad, for an amazing insight into your world.

_____

⑧ Next time, I am going to go shopping with a friend!

_____

⑨ I rate this movie 9 out of 10.

_____

⑩ To obtain your discount, please bring this coupon with you.

_____

Score 2 points for each correct answer! SCORE **/20** (0-8) (10-14) (16-20)

Phonic Knowledge & Spelling

AC9E5LY09, AC9E5LY10

Suffixes –able and –ible

Say each word in the word bank. The suffixes **–able** and **–ible** mean 'able to be'. Adding these suffixes turns the base word into an **adjective**.

It can be tricky to know if you should add **–able** or **–ible** to a word, but as a general rule, you add **–able** to 'whole' or 'proper' words (such as like, like**able**) and **–ible** to words that are not whole words (such as **possible**).

Word Bank

portable	probable	likeable	reliable
changeable	miserable	comfortable	agreeable
possible	flexible	audible	visible
edible	incredible	sensible	responsible

Choose words from the word bank to complete these sentences.

① It is _____ that there are aliens living on other planets.

② The group of people we worked with were very _____ and friendly.

③ As the weather is so _____, the barbecue will probably be cancelled.

④ We will possibly end up with that sofa as it looks so _____.

Antonyms

> Remember! **Antonyms** are adjectives that describe people and things in the **opposite** way.
>
> *Example:* dark, light

Write the antonyms of these words by adding the prefix in–, im–, ir–, il–, un– or dis–.

⑤ audible   _____

⑥ mobile   _____

⑦ replaceable   _____

⑧ advantage   _____

⑨ legible   _____

⑩ comfortable   _____

Score 2 points for each correct answer! SCORE **/20** (0-8) (10-14) (16-20)

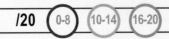

Refraction

Informative text – Explanation
Author – Janette Ellis

Refraction is the change in direction and speed of a wave as it passes into a different **medium**.

When light travelling through air enters a **denser** medium, like water or glass, it slows down and changes direction. It bends away from the surface of the new medium.

The opposite happens when light moves from a denser medium into a less dense medium. Light bends towards the border of the medium and speeds up.

Dispersion

Light refracted through a triangular prism splits into its various colours. This is called dispersion and the range of colours is called the spectrum of visible light. Red light bends the least and violet light bends the most.

Rainbows form when droplets of water in the atmosphere both reflect and refract light. A double rainbow occurs when light is reflected twice inside each water droplet. The colours in one rainbow are in reverse order to those in the other.

The straw isn't bent where it enters the water — the light bouncing off it is refracted. Light reflected from the top of the straw travels in a straight line to our eyes. Light reflected from the part that's underwater is refracted when it goes from water through glass into air.

Source: *Light*, Go Facts: Science, Blake Education.

Write or circle the correct answers.

① **What does medium mean in this text?**

a average

b the substance in which something occurs such as water or air

c a type of art material

② **What happens when light is refracted?**

a It bends straws.

b It splits into different colours.

c It changes direction and speed.

③ **Which is the odd word?**

a dense   b thick   c thin

④ **What happens when light is dispersed?**

a It splits into different colours.

b It bends straws.

c It heats up.

⑤ **Which colour of the spectrum bends the least?**

_____

⑥ **Explain how a double rainbow is formed.**

_____

_____

_____

My Book Review

Title _____

Author _____

Rating ☆☆☆☆☆

Comment _____

_____

Score 2 points for each correct answer!

SCORE **/12** (0-4) (6-8) (10-12)

TERM 4 ENGLISH

Number & Algebra

AC9M5N06

Multiplication

You can use a **vertical method** to carry out multiplication.
Example: **56 × 5**

```
      56
  ×    5
      30    5 × 6 ones
  +  250    5 × 5 tens
     280
```

Use the vertical method to multiply these numbers.

① 　 36
　× 　 3

　+ _____
　 _____

② 　 68
　× 　 3

　+ _____
　 _____

③ 　 47
　× 　 6

　+ _____
　 _____

④ 　 59
　× 　 4

　+ _____
　 _____

⑤ 　 92
　× 　 5

　+ _____
　 _____

⑥ 　 76
　× 　 7

　+ _____
　 _____

You can use the same method for larger numbers. *Example:*

```
      325
  ×     5
       25    5 × 5 ones
  +   100    5 × 2 tens
     1500    5 × 3 hundreds
     1625
```

Use the vertical method to multiply these numbers.

⑦ 　 543
　× 　　 6

　+ _____
　 _____
　 _____

⑧ 　 362
　× 　　 5

　+ _____
　 _____
　 _____

⑨ 　 479
　× 　　 4

　+ _____
　 _____
　 _____

⑩ 　 172
　× 　　 9

　+ _____
　 _____
　 _____

⑪ 　 563
　× 　　 6

　+ _____
　 _____
　 _____

⑫ 　 762
　× 　　 8

　+ _____
　 _____
　 _____

Score 2 points for each correct answer! SCORE **/24** 〔0-10〕 〔12-18〕 〔20-24〕

Statistics & Probability

There are no statistics & probability activities in this unit.

Measurement & Space

AC9M5SP01

Nets

A **net** is a flat shape that can be folded to make a **3D object**. This is the net for a cube:

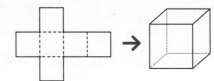

TARGETING HOMEWORK 5 © PASCAL PRESS ISBN 9781925726473

Write the letter of the 3D object that each net will fold into. Write none for the nets that have no matching 3D object.

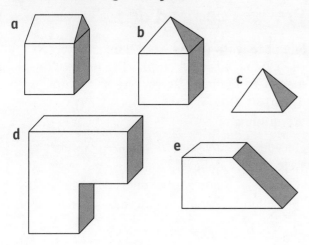

a
b
c
d
e

① _____

② _____

③ _____

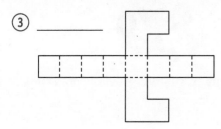

④ _____

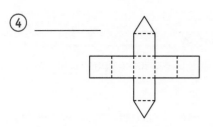

⑤ _____

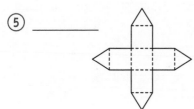

⑥ _____

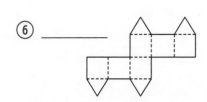

⑦ _____

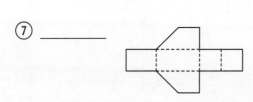

⑧ _____

Score 2 points for each correct answer!

SCORE **/16** (0-6) (8-12) (14-16)

Problem Solving

AC9M5N06

Multiplication problems

Solve these problems using the **vertical method** of multiplication.

Show your working out.

① There were 8 boxes of books. Each box has 573 books. How many books altogether?

× _____

+ _____

_____

_____

② The pet shop bought 9 boxes of pet food costing $168 each. How much did the total cost?

× _____

+ _____

_____

_____

③ There were 539 rows of 9 chairs in the hall. How many chairs in total?

× _____

+ _____

_____

_____

TERM 4 MATHS

Grammar & Punctuation

AC9E5LE02

Idioms

An **idiom** is an expression, word or phrase that has a different meaning to what the words actually say. We use idioms in our everyday speech, especially to our friends and family.

Example: He **let the cat out of the bag**.

  This expression doesn't actually mean to let a cat out of a bag, it means to tell a secret or reveal a surprise.

Match the idioms in the box to their meaning.

on the ball	spill the beans
last straw	let your hair down
hit the road	sitting on the fence

① relax, have fun:

_____

② going to leave:

_____

③ had enough:

_____

④ to be right about something:

_____

⑤ tell people secret information:

_____

⑥ undecided:

_____

Underline the idioms in the sentences. Write what they actually mean.

⑦ Last week it was raining cats and dogs.

meaning = _____

_____

⑧ They were having a ball at the concert.

meaning = _____

_____

⑨ The athlete was as fit as a fiddle.

meaning = _____

_____

Phonic Knowledge & Spelling

AC9E5LY09, AC9E5LY10

Prefixes re– and de–

Say each word in the word bank. The prefix **re–** means 'back' or 'again'. The prefix **de–** means 'to remove', 'to reverse something' or 'a departure from'.

Word Bank

recede	recycle	reduce	rehearse
release	relieve	rely	resign
declare	decrease	depend	defy
dehydrate	deposit	develop	determine

Choose words from the word bank to complete these sentences.

① We cut up our old bills with scissors before we _____ the paper.

② Our crèche tries to _____ good table manners at lunch time.

③ I think we need to _____ the amount of plastics we use.

Match the words in the box to their meanings.

defy	resign	recede

④ to go or move back: _____

⑤ to refuse to obey: _____

⑥ to voluntarily leave a job or position:

_____

Add the suffixes –ing and –ion to these words. Write the new words. Remember your spelling rules!

⑦ relate
add **–ing**: _____
add **–ion**: _____

⑧ dehydrate
add **–ing**: _____
add **–ion**: _____

⑨ reflect
add **–ing**: _____
add **–ion**: _____

Truganini (1812? – 1876)

Informative text – Biography
Authors – Frances Mackay and Catherine Gordon

Truganini was an important Tasmanian Aboriginal leader during the 1800s. She was also a negotiator and spokesperson for her people.

Truganini was born in Van Diemen's Land around 1812, and was the daughter of Mangana (Mangerner), the leader of the Recherche Bay people.

Between 1828 and 1832, many conflicts were fought between Aboriginal people and European settlers. These conflicts were referred to as the 'Black Wars'. By the time Truganini was 17, she had experienced the abduction of her sister and the murders of her mother, her fiancé and an uncle.

As a result of the conflicts, the government decided to move Aboriginal peoples to island reserves. George Augustus Robinson was responsible for the first of these missions on Bruny Island in 1829. This was where he met Truganini. Disease eventually caused the Bruny Island Mission to close in 1830, but Robinson still believed that he could help Aboriginal peoples through Christianity.

From 1830 to 1835, Truganini accompanied Robinson on his travels across Tasmania, acting as his guide and interpreter.

Robinson and Truganini managed to convince the remaining Aboriginal peoples (numbering about 160 at the time) to relocate to Flinders Island in 1835. Truganini believed that they would be safe and protected from the violence of the conflicts, but many people died from diseases caused by the poor living conditions.

Truganini and 46 other survivors were moved to Oyster Cove in 1847. By 1869, Truganini was one of only two full-blood Tasmanian Aboriginal people still alive.

Truganini died in Hobart in 1876, at the age of 64. Her skeleton was eventually put on display at the Tasmanian Museum until 1947. It was not until 1976, one hundred years after her death, that her remains were cremated and scattered in the waters close to her homeland.

Source: *Australian History Centres*, Upper Primary, Blake Education.

Write or circle the correct answers.

① **What is Van Diemen's Land called today?**

_____

② **What is a negotiator?**
  a someone who tries to find the way between one place and another
  b someone who deals with money
  c someone who acts as a peacemaker between two groups of people

③ **What did the European settlers do to members of Truganini's family by the time she was 17?**

_____

④ **Name the five places Truganini lived in throughout her lifetime.**

_____

⑤ **What was the main reason the Aboriginal peoples did not survive after they were relocated?**

_____

⑥ **Which word in the text means 'taking someone away against their will'?**
  a abduction   b cremated   c protected

⑦ **What does full-blood mean?**
  a someone who only has one race in their family history
  b The text does not tell us.
  c someone who has the right amount of blood in their body

Score 2 points for each correct answer!   **SCORE** /14   0-4   6-10   12-14

My Book Review

Title _____

Author _____

Rating ☆☆☆☆☆

Comment _____

_____

Number & Algebra

AC9M5N09

Calculating fractions of numbers

To find a **half** of a number, divide by **2**.
To find a **third** of a number, divide by **3**.
To find a **quarter** of a number, divide by **4**.

Example: $\frac{1}{4}$ of 24
$$= 24 \div 4$$
$$= 6$$

Solve the following by dividing.

① $\frac{1}{2}$ of 78 _____

② $\frac{1}{3}$ of 60 _____

③ $\frac{1}{5}$ of 300 _____

④ $\frac{1}{7}$ of 56 _____

⑤ $\frac{1}{10}$ of 500 _____

⑥ $\frac{1}{6}$ of 120 _____

⑦ $\frac{1}{8}$ of 240 _____

⑧ $\frac{1}{9}$ of 135 _____

⑨ $\frac{1}{4}$ of 100 _____

Solve the following.

⑩ $\frac{1}{6}$ of a day = _____ hours

⑪ $\frac{1}{2}$ of a year = _____ weeks

⑫ $\frac{1}{4}$ of an hour = _____ minutes

Write a number sentence and solve these problems.

⑬ A class has 28 students. $\frac{2}{4}$ of them are girls. How many boys are there?

_____

⑭ A box contains 136 apples. $\frac{1}{4}$ of them were sold. How many were left?

_____

⑮ Out of 30 people, $\frac{1}{2}$ had blue eyes. $\frac{1}{5}$ had brown eyes. The rest had green eyes. How many had green eyes?

⑯ There are 300 students in a school. $\frac{1}{4}$ of them walk to school. The rest go by car. How many students travel to school by car?

_____

⑰ There are 125 books in a library. $\frac{1}{5}$ of them need to be repaired. How many books do not need repair?

_____

⑱ A boat is carrying 180 passengers. $\frac{1}{6}$ of them get off and no-one gets on. How many people are now on the boat?

_____

Score 2 points for each correct answer!   SCORE /36   0-16   18-30   32-36

Statistics & Probability

AC9M5ST02

Line graphs

This is a line graph. It shows how far a train travelled over time. It also shows how long the train stopped at different stations before continuing on.

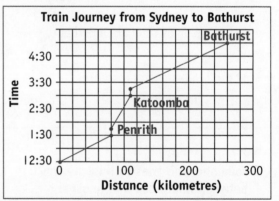

Train Journey from Sydney to Bathurst

Use the graph to answer the questions.

① What time did the train depart Sydney?

_____

② What time did it arrive in Penrith?

_____

③ The train stopped at Penrith before journeying on. How long did it stop for?

_____

④ At what time did the train depart Penrith?

_____

⑤ How far is Penrith from Sydney by train?

_____

⑥ How far is it from Penrith to Katoomba by train?

_____

⑦ Plot your own line graph using this temperature and time information:
12 pm – 25 °C, 1 pm – 28 °C, 2 pm – 30 °C, 3 pm – 34 °C, 4 pm – 35 °C, 5 pm – 31 °C, 6 pm – 25 °C, 7 pm – 22 °C.

For each time, put a dot on the graph at the correct temperature point. The first two points have been plotted for you.

When you have put in all the temperatures, use a ruler to join the dots with a line.

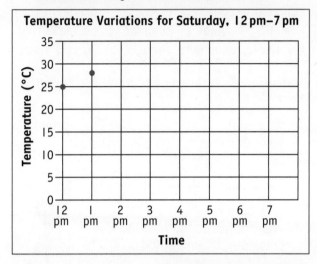

Temperature Variations for Saturday, 12 pm–7 pm

SCORE /14 0-4 6-10 12-14

Measurement & Space

AC9M5SP02

Coordinates

The grid below is a **coordinate grid**. To locate the point **D2** on this grid, read across the bottom to the letter D, the up the line to the number 2.

Use this grid to complete the following activity.

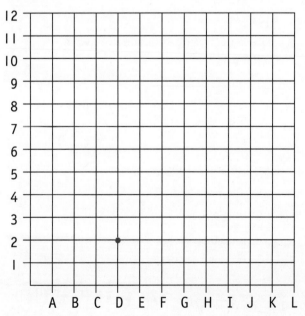

Mark these points on the grid. Use a ruler to join up the points in each group, in order.

① A5, D2, K2, K6, J6, J5, A5
② E5, E8, I8, I5
③ F8, F9, H9, H8
④ F6, F7, G7, G6, F6
⑤ J5, J6, K6, K5
⑥ G9, G11
⑦ G11, H10, G10

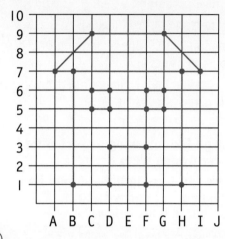

Write the coordinate grid points for this picture. List the points in groups, in the correct order, so the dots can be joined correctly.

⑧ _____
⑨ _____
⑩ _____
⑪ _____
⑫ _____

SCORE  /24 0-10 12-18 20-24

Problem Solving

AC9M5SP01

Top view

Colour the lines to show the top views for each of these 3D objects.

Example:

①   ②    ③

TERM 4 MATHS

Editing texts

A **paragraph** is a block of sentences built around a main idea. The first sentence in the paragraph often introduces the main idea. This is followed by sentences giving further details.

Begin a new paragraph when:
- a new person is introduced
- one person has stopped speaking and a new person starts speaking
- there is a change of place or setting
- time has passed.

Read through the following extract from *Teacher's Pet* **by Jan Weeks.**

Show where the 8 paragraphs should be by adding brackets [ ] and writing the first word on the numbered lines below.

①–⑧ A few days later we had to look up the meaning of some words in the dictionary and then use them in a sentence. The first word was 'revolting'. I wrote, Joel throws all his dirty socks under the bed and they smell revolting. "Is that true?" Miss Thompson asked. I nodded. "No-one can ever find anything in his room," I lied. "Mum reckons he's the untidiest person she knows. She's always picking up after him. She says when Joel gets married he'll be looking for a slave rather than a wife." "Don't you like your brother?" Miss Thompson asked, looking closely at me. "Yeah, I do," I answered. "He's my favourite person in the whole world." "Then how come you keep saying nasty things about him?" "I ... I don't," I stammered.

① _____   ⑤ _____
② _____   ⑥ _____
③ _____   ⑦ _____
④ _____   ⑧ _____

Prefixes con– and com–

Say each word in the word bank. The prefixes **con–** and **com–** loosely mean 'with' or 'together'.

Word Bank

concert	conceal	consider	contact
contribute	construct	convict	condemn
commit	combine	compare	compete
compile	comment	compliment	communicate

Choose words from the word bank to complete these sentences.

① We had to _____ a pottery bowl that was concave in shape.

② The gymnast tried to _____ a somersault with a backward flip.

③ It is easy to _____ your friends today with modern communication methods.

Change these verbs to nouns by adding either –ion or –ment. Write the new word.

④ conceal _____

⑤ commit _____

⑥ construct _____

⑦ combine _____

Match the words in the box with their definitions.

conceal	compliment	conspire	comply

⑧ to plan something together in secret:
_____

⑨ to act according to someone's wish or command:
_____

⑩ to say something to show you admire someone or something:
_____

⑪ to hide something:
_____

Score 2 points for each correct answer! **SCORE** **/16** (0-6) (8-12) (14-16)

Score 2 points for each correct answer! **SCORE** **/22** (0-8) (10-16) (18-22)

TERM 4 ENGLISH

AC9E5LY04, AC9E5LY05, AC9HS5K07

Persuasive text – Letter to the editor
Author – Merryn Whitfield

The Editor
Dunbeena Gazette
Locked Bag 040
Dunbeena NT 1010

Mr Crang Key
1A Mupset Street
Dunbeena NT 1010

14th February 2016

Dear Sir,

As a long-term resident of Dunbeena, I am frustrated and alarmed by the inability of the government to provide us with a consistent and reliable ambulance emergency service. I have been forced to realise that state ministers and public servants are unable to understand the plight of our little community. Don't they care about us?

For the past six long months, Dunbeena residents have been without 24-hour ambulance coverage. Instead, we have had to rely on the goodwill of the handful of community members with medical training to assist the sick and the elderly. That is simply not good enough!

What we need are strong leaders who are willing to make decisions to benefit all members of the local community. We need them to fund the ongoing rostering of ambulance officers, and we need them to commit to the building of a new and permanent ambulance station in the Dunbeena area. Anything else is frankly unacceptable!

Access to adequate emergency services is a right for all residents. You don't have to be Einstein to work out what should be done!

Yours faithfully

Mr Crang Key

Source: *Writing Centres: Persuasive Texts*, Upper Primary, Blake Education.

Write or circle the correct answers.

① **Who is the intended audience for the letter?**

_____

② **Why was the letter written?**

  a to inform b to protest c to complain

③ **What is the purpose of paragraph 3 in the text?**

  a to inform the editor that the community has been without an ambulance service for the past 6 months

  b to state that the community needs strong leaders who will act on the issue

  c to tell the editor that he has been a long-term resident of Dunbeena

④ **List two things that Mr Key demands should be done.**

_____

_____

⑤ **Which word in the text means 'acting in the same way over a period of time'?**

  a adequate

  b frustrated

  c consistent

⑥ **The letter is written using first person pronouns. List three examples of first person pronouns.**

_____

⑦ **Which is the odd word?**

  a intermittent

  b dependable

  c predictable

  d reliable

My Book Review

Title _____

Author _____

Rating ☆☆☆☆☆

Comment _____

_____

TERM 4 ENGLISH

Number & Algebra

AC9M5N02

Factors and multiples

Factors are numbers that can be divided into another number with no remainder.

The **multiple** of a number is a skip-counting number.

Example:

Factors of 10: 1, 2, 5 and 10

Multiples of 10 include: 10, 20, 30, 40, 50.

Are the numbers multiples of 5 as well as factors of 30? Write yes or no.

① 6 _____

② 10 _____

③ 15 _____

④ 23 _____

⑤ 25 _____

⑥ 30 _____

Are the numbers multiples of 10 as well as factors of 100? Write yes or no.

⑦ 10 _____

⑧ 15 _____

⑨ 20 _____

⑩ 25 _____

⑪ 30 _____

⑫ 50 _____

Are the numbers multiples of 8 as well as factors of 64? Write yes or no.

⑬ 8 _____

⑭ 16 _____

⑮ 24 _____

⑯ 40 _____

⑰ 48 _____

⑱ 64 _____

Are the numbers multiples of 9 as well as factors of 72? Write yes or no.

⑲ 3 _____

⑳ 9 _____

㉑ 27 _____

㉒ 36 _____

㉓ 63 _____

㉔ 72 _____

Prime numbers

A **prime number** is a number that is only divisible by 1 and itself. It has no other factors.

Prime numbers include 2, 3, 5, 19 and 131.

㉕–㉞ Write the numbers from the box that are prime numbers.

4	7	10	11	12
13	15	17	20	21
22	23	25	29	40
41	43	47	50	53

_____

_____

Write all the factors of these numbers.

㉟ 19 _____

㊱ 36 _____

㊲ 37 _____

㊳ 56 _____

㊴ 60 _____

㊵ 67 _____

㊶ 100 _____

Score 2 points for each correct answer!

SCORE /82 (0-38) (40-74) (76-80)

Statistics & Probability

There are no statistics & probability activities in this unit.

Measurement & Space

AC9M5M01

Metric and imperial measurements

Before 1974, Australia used **imperial** units of measurement, but now we use **metric** units.

Today, most countries in the world use the metric system. The United States of America is one of the countries that still uses imperial units.

Here are some approximate conversions of imperial and metric measurements:

Imperial	Metric
I inch	about 2.5 centimetres
I foot	about 30 centimetres
I yard	about I metre
I mile	about 1.6 kilometres
I ounce	about 30 grams
I pound	about half a kilogram
I stone	about 6.5 kilograms
I pint	just over half a litre
I gallon	about 4.5 litres

Circle the metric unit that is approximately equal to the imperial unit in bold.

① **10 yards**
- a 5 metres
- b 15 metres
- c 10 metres
- d 20 metres

② **4 pints**
- a I litre
- b 3 litres
- c 2 litres
- d 4 litres

③ **5 miles**
- a 5 kilometres
- b 7 kilometres
- c 6 kilometres
- d 8 kilometres

④ **6 inches**
- a 10 centimetres
- b 15 centimetres
- c 12 centimetres
- d 60 centimetres

⑤ **5 ounces**
- a 100 grams
- b 200 grams
- c 150 grams
- d 250 grams

⑥ **4 gallons**
- a 18 litres
- b 25 litres
- c 20 litres
- d 30 litres

⑦ **3 feet**
- a 30 centimetres
- b 90 centimetres
- c 60 centimetres
- d 13 centimetres

Use the metric ruler and imperial ruler below to answer the following questions.

⑧ Approximately how many inches equal 10 centimetres?

_____

⑨ 12 inches is approximately how many centimetres?

_____

⑩ 5 centimetres equals approximately how many inches?

_____

⑪ $7\frac{1}{2}$ inches is approximately equal to how many centimetres?

_____

⑫ 9 centimetres is approximately equal to how many inches?

_____

Score 2 points for each correct answer!   SCORE **/24** (0-10) (12-18) (20-24)

Problem Solving

AC9M5N10

What's the rule?

Work out the rule used for each group of numbers. Write the rules.

① Rule =	② Rule =	③ Rule =	④ Rule =
$1\frac{1}{2}$	5	7	65
3	20	11	57
$4\frac{1}{2}$	80	13	49
6	320	17	41
$7\frac{1}{2}$	1280	19	33
9	5120	23	25
$10\frac{1}{2}$	20 480	29	17
12	81 920	31	9

metric ruler: 1 2 3 4 5 6 7 8 9 10 11 12 13 14 15 16 17 18 19 20 21 22 23 24 25 26 27 28 29 30 cm

imperial ruler: INCH 1 2 3 4 5 6 7 8 9 10 11 12

TERM 4 MATHS

Grammar & Punctuation

Underline the adverbial clause.

① Though it was not his turn, Sam walked the dog.

Circle the correct form of the verb.

② The news (is   are) on every night at 6 pm.

③ *The Witches* (are   is) my favourite book by Roald Dahl.

Mark where the nine commas should go.

④–⑫ Yesterday Jack Sam and I went to the Melbourne Show. I really enjoyed looking at the farm animals. There were sheep goats pigs cattle horses chickens geese and alpacas. Personally I liked the goats best but Jack preferred the pigs.

Add the missing apostrophes.

⑬ Dont put your finger too close to the knifes sharp edge!

Underline the object that is being personified. Circle what they are doing that makes it personification.

⑭ Lightning danced across the dark sky.

Circle the correct text type to match the sentence beginning.

⑮ Once upon a time ...

   a biography   **b** fairytale   **c** narrative

Underline the idiom. Write what it actually means.

⑯ The spelling test was a piece of cake.
   Meaning = _____

   _____

Show where the paragraphs should be by adding brackets [   ].

⑰–⑲ Ben pulled out of his driveway without looking. "Hey, you nearly ran me over!" shouted an angry man on his bicycle. "Sorry mate, I wasn't concentrating. Are you OK?"

Write the correct form of the plural possessive noun.

⑳ the paintings of the students

   _____

Phonic Knowledge & Spelling

Write words opposite in meaning. Choose to add either the prefix mis– or dis–.

① judge   _____

② honest   _____

Change these verbs to nouns by adding –ion. Write the new words.

③ operate   _____

④ decorate   _____

Add in– or im– to these base words to make them opposite in meaning. Write the new words.

⑤ capable   _____

⑥ mobile   _____

Add –sion to the words to make nouns. Write the new words.

⑦ explode   _____

⑧ divide   _____

Match the words that are antonyms.

lightness   unfairness   unselfishness

⑨ selfishness _____

⑩ darkness _____

⑪ fairness _____

Circle the words that have the same 'our' sound as four.

⑫ colour   your   flour   court

Write the antonyms of these words by adding the prefix in–, im–, ir–, il–, un– or dis–.

⑬ movable   _____

⑭ pleased   _____

⑮ regular   _____

⑯ credible   _____

⑰ legal   _____

⑱ pleasant   _____

Add the suffixes –ing and –ion to these words. Write the new words. Remember your spelling rules.

   add –ing   **add –ion**

⑲ reflect _____   _____

Change these verbs to nouns by adding either –ion or –ment. Write the new word.

⑳ commit   _____

㉑ construct   _____

What a Find!

Imaginative text – Narrative
Author – Lisa Thompson
Illustrator – Brenda Cantell

Flynn ran towards the digging site, dodging everyone and everything in his way. He couldn't wait to show Uncle Earl and his best friend, Mia, what was in his hand. It was so amazing he could hardly believe it.

"And to think I thought this trip to Crete was going to be all hard work!" Flynn thought. "Ha! I've got the find of the century and I didn't even have to lift a spade!"

He could see his Uncle Earl's team up ahead sorting through an endless pile of rock and rubble, checking and rechecking everything. Uncle Earl, the world-renowned expert in archaeology, was in his element. Discovering the remains of a palace on the Greek island had been big news. Mia was loving the dig too. She had been given the painstaking job of cataloguing all the finds. Just the thought of this task gave Flynn an instant headache.

Source: *Saving Atlantis*, Treasure Trackers, Blake Education.

Write or circle the correct answers.

① **Where was Flynn?**
   a in America
   b in Crete
   c on another planet

② **What does 'the find of the century' mean?**
   a a new and very rare discovery
   b something very old
   c an archaeological find

③ **What does painstaking mean?**
   a a painful experience
   b something that causes pain
   c exacting and thorough

④ **What were the archaeologists digging?**

_____

⑤ **Which word in the text means 'making a systematic list'?**

   c_____

⑥ **What does in his element mean?**
   a thoroughly enjoying something
   b hating something
   c doing something scientific

⑦ **Which is the odd word out?**
   a instantaneous
   b instant
   c immediate
   d delayed

⑧ **Do you think Flynn had looked forward to his time at the dig?**
   a Yes, he enjoyed archaeology.
   b No, he thought it would be too much hard work.
   c We cannot tell from the text.

⑨ **Which phrase in the text tells you that Uncle Earl was an authority in archaeology?**

_____

Score 2 points for each correct answer!

SCORE /18   0-6   8-14   16-18

Number & Algebra

Write these numbers.

① 5 thousands + 8 hundreds + 3 tens + 5 ones + 8 tenths = _____

② 65 thousands + 8 tens + 48 hundredths = _____

Circle the decimal number that is between the two given numbers.

③ 556.78 and 557.03

   a 556.58   c 556.04

   b 557.13   d 557.02

④ 578 431.008 and 578 431.125

   a 578 431.1   c 578 431

   b 578 431.146   d 578 431.5

Are these numbers divisible by 9? Write yes or no.

⑤ 54 _____   ⑧ 2511 _____

⑥ 328 _____   ⑨ 34 561 _____

⑦ 5461 _____   ⑩ 56 322 _____

Solve these fraction additions and subtractions.

⑪ $\frac{5}{8} + \frac{2}{8}$ = _____   ⑭ $\frac{8}{12} - \frac{6}{12}$ = _____

⑫ $2\frac{1}{2} + 1\frac{1}{2}$ = _____   ⑮ $1 - \frac{4}{10}$ = _____

⑬ $\frac{9}{10} + \frac{6}{10}$ = _____   ⑯ $2\frac{4}{5} - 1\frac{1}{5}$ = _____

Use the commutative law to show the easiest way to add these numbers. Write the answers.

⑰ 25   17   25

_____

⑱ 17   98   2

_____

Use the vertical method to multiply.

⑲
```
      46
  ×    5
  
  +  ____

     ____
```

⑳
```
     684
  ×    6
  
  +  ____

     ____
```

Solve by dividing.

㉑ $\frac{1}{5}$ of 250

_____

_____

㉒ $\frac{1}{8}$ of 320

_____

_____

㉓ **Write a number sentence and solve this problem.**

There are 150 marbles in a bag. $\frac{2}{5}$ of them are red, the others are blue. How many blue marbles are in the bag?

_____

Are the numbers multiples of 6 as well as factors of 60? Write yes or no.

㉔ 5 _____   ㉘ 15 _____

㉕ 6 _____   ㉙ 20 _____

㉖ 10 _____   ㉚ 30 _____

㉗ 12 _____   ㉛ 60 _____

Score 2 points for each correct answer!

SCORE /62 (0-28) (30-56) (58-62)

Statistics & Probability

Write the numbers 1 to 6 above the correct arrows to show the probability of each of the following events.

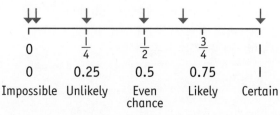

0	$\frac{1}{4}$	$\frac{1}{2}$	$\frac{3}{4}$	1
0	0.25	0.5	0.75	1
Impossible	Unlikely	Even chance	Likely	Certain

① Everyone in the world will win the lottery this week.

② You will have a drink today.

③ You roll a dice and get a 2, 3, 4 or 5.

④ You will become an astronaut.

⑤ You toss a coin and get a head.

⑥ You will pull a club out of a deck of cards.

What types of questions are these?
Write O for open-ended, M for multiple choice or Y/N for yes or no questions.

⑦ Where do you prefer to go on holiday? ___

⑧ Do you like cycling? ___

⑨ How often do you exercise? ___
once a day, once a week, sometimes, never

The line graph on the next page shows visitor numbers to Tiny Town's museum last week. Use the graph to answer the questions.

⑩ On which day did the museum have the most visitors? _____

⑪ What is the difference in visitor numbers between the busiest and quietest days?

_____

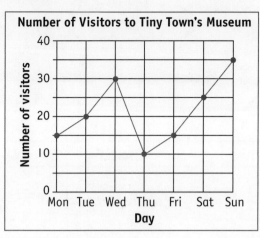

Number of Visitors to Tiny Town's Museum

(12) Which weekday do you think is most likely to be half-price entry fee day?

_____

(13) How many visitors did the museum have for the whole week? _____

Score 2 points for each correct answer! **SCORE** **/26** (0-10) (12-20) (22-26)

Measurement & Space

(1) Read and record the size of the angle.

_____

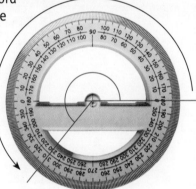

Use these jugs to answer the following questions.

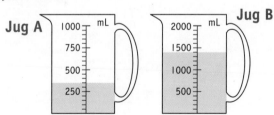

Jug A   Jug B

How much water is in:

(2) jug A? _____

(3) jug B? _____

A large cup holds 250 mL of water and a small cup holds 50 mL. How many large and small cups full are needed to make up the amount of water in each jug?

(4) jug A: _____ large cups, _____ small cups

(5) jug B: _____ large cups, _____ small cups

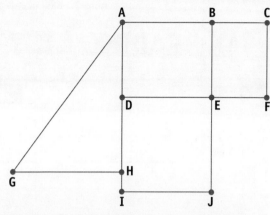

Use the diagram above to calculate the following. You will need to use a ruler. Measure to the nearest half centimetre.

(6) What is the length of line DI? _____

(7) What is the length of line GAB? _____

(8) What is the perimeter of rectangle BCEF?

_____

(9) What is the area of rectangle ABJI?

_____

(10) **What order of rotational symmetry does this shape have?**

_____

Use this grid to answer the questions.

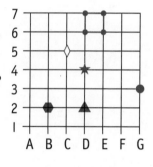

(11) What shape is at C5?

_____

(12) What shape is at D4?

_____

(13) What are the coordinates for the hexagon? _____

(14) Write the coordinates of the four points that make up a square. _____

(15) Draw a ☺ shape at A1.

Complete the following.

(16) If 1 inch is approximately equal to 2.5 centimetres, about how many centimetres is 10 inches? _____

(17) If 1 ounce is approximately equal to 30 grams, about how many grams is 5 ounces? _____

(18) If 1 gallon is approximately equal to 4.5 litres, about how many litres is 8 gallons? _____

Score 2 points for each correct answer! **SCORE** **/36** (0-16) (18-30) (32-36)

MY READING LIST

Name: _____

_____

	Title	Author	Rating	Date
1			☆☆☆☆☆	
2			☆☆☆☆☆	
3			☆☆☆☆☆	
4			☆☆☆☆☆	
5			☆☆☆☆☆	
6			☆☆☆☆☆	
7			☆☆☆☆☆	
8			☆☆☆☆☆	
9			☆☆☆☆☆	
10			☆☆☆☆☆	
11			☆☆☆☆☆	
12			☆☆☆☆☆	
13			☆☆☆☆☆	
14			☆☆☆☆☆	
15			☆☆☆☆☆	
16			☆☆☆☆☆	
17			☆☆☆☆☆	
18			☆☆☆☆☆	
19			☆☆☆☆☆	
20			☆☆☆☆☆	
21			☆☆☆☆☆	
22			☆☆☆☆☆	
23			☆☆☆☆☆	
24			☆☆☆☆☆	
25			☆☆☆☆☆	
26			☆☆☆☆☆	
27			☆☆☆☆☆	
28			☆☆☆☆☆	
29			☆☆☆☆☆	
30			☆☆☆☆☆	
31			☆☆☆☆☆	
32			☆☆☆☆☆	

TARGETING HOMEWORK 5 © PASCAL PRESS ISBN 9781925726473

Unit 1 ENGLISH: Grammar & Punctuation

1–16 The continent of North[1] America[2] is made up of 23 countries and 9 dependent territories. The largest country is Canada[3] and the second largest is the United[4] States[5] of America[6] (USA). Other countries in North[7] America[8] include: Mexico[9], Cuba[10], Panama[11] and Barbados[12]. The Atlantic[13] Ocean[14] is on the east side of the continent and the Pacific[15] Ocean[16] is on the west side.

17 C	18 P	19 C	20 P	21 C	22 C

Unit 1 ENGLISH: Phonic Knowledge & Spelling

1 model
2 pumpkin
3 commit, connect
4 object, inject
5 admitted, admitting
6 collected, collecting
7 permitted, permitting
8 committed, committing
9 relented, relenting
8 signalled, signalling

Unit 1 ENGLISH: Reading & Comprehension

1 b. informative
2 reduce
3 photosynthesis
4 dormant
5 drought
6 succulents
7 produce
8 a. animals or insects that transfer pollen from one plant to another
9 Any three from the following: the leaves can be used to store water; some plants have small leaves or no leaves — this means less water loss during photosynthesis; some leaves have hairs on them — this helps to shade the plant; some plants have leaves that can turn away from the sun; some leaves have a waxy coating to reduce water loss
10 a. in their green stem
11 Slow growth uses less energy so the plants do not have to make as much food and this reduces the amount of water needed.

Unit 1 MATHS: Number & Algebra

1 c. 2
2 c. 4
3 c. 8
4 a. 10
5 c. 5
6 b. 1
7 1, 2, 3, 4, 6, 12
8 1, 2, 3, 4, 6, 8, 12, 24
9 20, 25, 30, 35
10 24, 30, 36, 42
11 300, 400, 500, 600
12 3, 6, 9, 15, 18
13 2000, 3000, 5000, 6000

Unit 1 MATHS: Statistics & Probability

1 e. All colours have an equal chance.
2 b. 1 out of 4
3 d. 3
4 b. 6
5 $\frac{1}{3}$
6 $\frac{2}{5}$
7 $\frac{4}{8}$
8 $\frac{1}{1000}$
9 b. $\frac{1}{8}$
10 a. $\frac{2}{8}$
11 c. $\frac{3}{8}$
12 a. $\frac{1}{8}$
13 c. $\frac{1}{8}$

Unit 1 MATHS: Measurement & Space

1 centimetres
2 millimetres
3 metres
4 kilometres
5 millimetres
6 centimetres
7 measuring tape
8 odometer
9 trundle wheel
10 65 mm
11 58 mm
12 113 mm

Unit 1 MATHS: Problem Solving

Possible answers include:

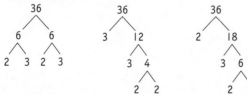

Unit 2 ENGLISH: Grammar & Punctuation

1 villages
2 eyelashes
3 princesses
4 viruses
5 beaches
6 prefixes
7 women
8 teeth
9 fishermen
10 geese

Unit 2 ENGLISH: Phonic Knowledge & Spelling

1 pantry
2 trolley
3 victim
4 symbolise
5 shimmering
6 shuddering
7 vandalise
8 legalise
9 advertise
10 terrorise
11 capitalise

Unit 2 ENGLISH: Reading & Comprehension

1 a. Everyone in the school quickly told others about the race.
2 b. qualified
3 b. simile
4 c. a street closed at one end
5 Jah doesn't want people to cheat or hurt others in order to win.
6 contraptions
7 neighbourhood
8 scouring
9 gouging
10 … the air was buzzing with excitement.

Unit 2 MATHS: Number & Algebra

1 10	5 90	9 120	13 720
2 70	6 50	10 660	14 460
3 30	7 90	11 550	15 380
4 40	8 70	12 810	16 270

17 $60 + 30 = 90$
18 $80 + 10 = 90$
19 $50 + 50 = 100$
20 $40 + 30 = 70$
21 $130 + 60 = 190$
22 $570 + 10 = 580$
23 $360 + 130 = 490$
24 $750 + 230 = 980$

25 200	29 700	33 4600	37 24 600
26 600	30 400	34 5300	38 67 500
27 600	31 600	35 2300	39 134 500
28 600	32 400	36 7900	40 786 700

Unit 2 MATHS: Measurement & Space

1 07:00	9 00:30	17 11:50 pm	25 05:00
2 05:30	10 20:59	18 9.30 pm	26 22:42
3 04:20	11 1:25 pm	19 4:12 pm	27 true
4 06:42	12 3:30 pm	20 10:05 pm	28 true
5 12:00	13 12:15 pm	21 14:00	29 true
6 14:00	14 7:20 am	22 23:30	30 false
7 19:30	15 6:45 am	23 11:38	31 false
8 18:45	16 7:10 pm	24 19:05	

Unit 2 MATHS: Problem Solving

1 1 hour 35 minutes
2 1 hour 30 minutes
3 18:15
4 15:30

Unit 3 ENGLISH: Grammar & Punctuation

1 The **bauble** had sparkly crystals and iridescent gems.
2 His bright yellow **jacket** made him stand out.
3 The snarling, ferocious **tiger** rushed out of hiding.
4 the abandoned house
5 every pair of red shoes
6 Tina's mobile
7 our new car
8 Sam and Su played for hours in the old, haunted house.
9 Each new player received a warm, blue hoodie.

Unit 3 ENGLISH: Phonic Knowledge & Spelling

1 arrange
2 arrive
3 amaze/amuse
4 adore
5 adoring
6 arrangement
7 appraisal
8 amused
9 achievement
10 arrival
11 assurance
12 acquiring

Unit 3 ENGLISH: Reading & Comprehension

1 b. The author wants Antarctica to be protected.
2 b. We must be vigilant and not allow any sort of tourism in this environmentally sensitive region.
3 c. keeping careful watch
4 a. a place that strongly maintains its special natural environment
5 crevasses
6 fjords
7 ardent
8 sanction ecotourism in Antarctica
9 allow the fragile natural environment to be disturbed further
10 put profits first

ANSWERS

Unit 3 MATHS: Number & Algebra

1. $13 \times 43 = 559$
2. $23 \times 12 = 276$
3. $14 \times 34 = 476$
4. $42 \times 53 = 2226$
5. $28 \times 15 = 420$
6. $37 \times 61 = 2257$

Unit 3 MATHS: Statistics & Probability

1. a. How often did you go to the cinema last year?
   • never • 1-3 times • once a month • every week
2. b. Car racing is a dangerous sport.
   • agree • neither agree nor disagree • disagree
3. a. Which languages do you speak? List them.
4. b. Which of these is your favourite fast food?
   • burgers • fish & chips • kebabs • other _____

Unit 3 MATHS: Measurement & Space

1. Perimeter = 24 cm
2. Area = 20 cm^2
3. Perimeter = 24 cm
4. Area = 32 cm^2
5. Perimeter = 16 mm
6. Area = 12 mm^2
7. Perimeter = 18 cm
8. Area = 20 cm^2
9. Perimeter = 22 m
10. Area = 18 m^2

Unit 3 MATHS: Problem Solving

1. Perimeter = 18 m
2. Area = 20 m^2
3. Cost of gripper = $18 \times \$2 = \$36$
4. Cost of carpet = $20 \times 40 = \$800$

Unit 4 ENGLISH: Grammar & Punctuation

1. thick, juicy hamburgers
2. three red robins
3. a delightful concert
4. a magnificent, weather-beaten house
5. The new house was enormous and had ten bedrooms.
6. The players were eager to start the game.
7. The frightened rat scurried past the watchful cat.
8. The Dalmatian dog was covered in black spots.
9. I prefer rap music to rock music.
10. The steam train pulled into the rickety, old station.

Unit 4 ENGLISH: Phonic Knowledge & Spelling

1. sofa
2. trophy
3. fluent
4. mobile
5. motorhome
6. motorboat
7. motorcycle
8. motorcyclist
9. motivation (4)
10. majority (4)
11. soloist (3)
12. momentous (3)
13. mobility (4)

Unit 4 ENGLISH: Reading & Comprehension

1. b. to explain why Australia needed more migrants in the 1800s and how the British Government encouraged people to move to Australia
2. colony
3. convicts
4. climate
5. c. the Potato Famine
6. b. a person who moves from one place to another to find work or better living conditions
7. The Government paid some or all of the fares through the assisted passage scheme.

Unit 4 MATHS: Number & Algebra

1. 10×3
2. 6×7
3. 7×8
4. 9×5
5. 8×8
6. 3×9
7. 5×7
8. 8×9
9. 8×4
10. 9×9
11. $180 \div 4, 90 \div 2, 45 \div 1.$
    $180 \div 4 = 45$
12. $288 \div 8, 144 \div 4, 72 \div 2, 36 \div 1. 288 \div 8 = 36$
13. $384 \div 16, 192 \div 8, 96 \div 4, 48 \div 2, 24 \div 1.$
    $384 \div 16 = 24$
14. $328 \div 4, 164 \div 2, 82 \div 1.$
    $328 \div 4 = 82$
15. $424 \div 8, 212 \div 4, 106 \div 2, 53 \div 1. 424 \div 8 = 53$
16. $656 \div 16, 328 \div 8, 164 \div 4, 82 \div 2, 41 \div 1.$
    $656 \div 16 = 41$
17. $336 \div 6 = (300 + 36) \div 6$
    $= (300 \div 6) + (36 \div 6)$
    $= 50 + 6$
    $= 56$
18. $434 \div 7 = (420 + 14) \div 7$
    $= (420 \div 7) + (14 \div 7)$
    $= 60 + 2$
    $= 62$
19. $425 \div 5 = (400 + 25) \div 5$
    $= (400 \div 5) + (25 \div 5)$
    $= 80 + 5$
    $= 85$
20. $496 \div 8 = (480 + 16) \div 8$
    $= (480 \div 8) + (16 \div 8)$
    $= 60 + 2$
    $= 62$

21. $378 \div 7 = (350 + 28) \div 7$
    $= (350 \div 7) + (28 \div 7)$
    $= 50 + 4$
    $= 54$
22. $657 \div 9 = (630 + 27) \div 9$
    $= (630 \div 9) + (27 \div 9)$
    $= 70 + 3$
    $= 73$

Unit 4 MATHS: Measurement & Space

1. grams
2. millilitres
3. centimetres
4. centimetres or metres
5. degrees Celsius
6. kilograms
7. degrees
8. centimetres or metres
9. seconds
10. litres
11. Answers will vary.
12. Answers will vary.
13. Answers will vary.
14. False
15. True
16. False
17. False
18. True

Unit 4 MATHS: Problem Solving

Two sides need to multiply to make 24.
The possibilities are:
• Side lengths: 1 cm and 24 cm. Perimeter: 50 cm
• Side lengths: 2 cm and 12 cm. Perimeter: 28 cm
• Side lengths: 3 cm and 8 cm. Perimeter: 22 cm
• Side lengths: 4 cm and 6 cm. Perimeter: 20 cm

Unit 5 ENGLISH: Grammar & Punctuation

1. The baby was as good as gold when I looked after her.
2. The thief was as bold as brass when he broke into the house.
3. My teacher has eyes like a hawk.
4. It was as clear as crystal what the man was trying to do.
5. I felt as wise as an owl when I got my test marks back.
6. I could sleep like a log after my long journey.
7. That girl can sing like an angel.
8. toddler's toy box
9. firecracker
10. house
11. lion
12. toast

Unit 5 ENGLISH: Phonic Knowledge & Spelling

1. scenic/historic/terrific
2. fabric
3. garlic
4. music
5. critical
6. tropical
7. historical
8. musical
9. –ick words: thick, flick, wick, chick
10. –ic words: traffic, automatic, fantastic, ethnic

Unit 5 ENGLISH: Reading & Comprehension

1. b. the sea
2. The sea is a hungry dog, Giant and grey.
3. Any 2 from: a new puppy as fat as butter; moves about like a clockwork toy; tripping around like an unfettered buoy; tongue like a sponge; runs in circles like a scalded cat; eyes like coal
4. b. clashing; c. rumbling; e. flop; f. snuffs; h. howls
5. shaggy
6. scarcely
7. unfettered
8. scalded
9. thatch
10. mayhem
11. He says the dog bounds to his feet, making snuffing and sniffing noises, shaking water all over the cliffs and howling — just like the sea actually behaves on stormy days.

Unit 5 MATHS: Number & Algebra

10. a. $\frac{1}{2}$
11. c. $\frac{1}{10}$
12. $\frac{1}{10}, \frac{1}{9}, \frac{1}{8}, \frac{1}{7}, \frac{1}{6}, \frac{1}{5}, \frac{1}{4}, \frac{1}{3}, \frac{1}{1}$
13. true
14. true
15. false
16. true
17. false

18–22

Unit 5 MATHS: Statistics & Probability

1. $\frac{1}{20}$
2. $\frac{1}{6}$
3. $\frac{1}{2}$
4. $\frac{1}{3}$
5. $\frac{1}{1000}$
6. $\frac{1}{1}$

TARGETING HOMEWORK 5 © PASCAL PRESS ISBN 9781925726473

7 $\frac{1}{10}, \frac{1}{5}, \frac{1}{2}, \frac{2}{3}, \frac{4}{5},$
$\frac{2}{2}$

8 true
9 false
10 true

11 false
12 true
13 true

Unit 5 MATHS: Measurement & Space
1 2 L
2 4 L
3 200 mL
4 1.7 L
5 10 L
6 2 mL
7 250 mL
8 1000 mL

Unit 5 MATHS: Problem Solving
They left home at 1:10 pm.
4:15 pm take away 45 minutes = 3:30 pm
3:30 pm take away 10 minutes = 3:20 pm
3:20 pm take away 40 minutes = 2:40 pm
2:40 pm take away one hour = 1:40 pm
1:40 pm take away 30 minutes = 1:10 pm

Unit 6 ENGLISH: Grammar & Punctuation
1 <u>Jasmine</u> **cycled** all the way to her cousin's house.
2 <u>Tracy and Tamsin</u> **play** netball every Saturday.
3 <u>The eastern pygmy possum of Australia</u> **can hibernate** for a long time.
4 <u>Lee's father</u> **owns** the local bakery.
5 The race horses crossed <u>the finish line</u> together.
6 The policeman rescued <u>the elderly lady</u> from her crashed car.
7 We found <u>fifteen broken bottles and five empty cans</u> in the park.
8 The cheetah tried to capture <u>a young wildebeest</u>.

Unit 6 ENGLISH: Phonic Knowledge & Spelling
1 citrus
2 gymnast
3 cyclone
4 bicycle
5 tricycle
6 unicycle
7 recycle
8 monocycle
9 hemicycle
10 circulation
11 circle
12 circulate
13 circular
14 circuit

Unit 6 ENGLISH: Reading & Comprehension
1 c. narrative
2 Any 3 from: satchel, Bates's General Store, Elvis Presley, milk bar, jukebox
3 b. a machine that plays music after a coin has been inserted
4 a. occasional
5 a. a house made from fibrous cement sheeting

Unit 6 MATHS: Number & Algebra
1 8000 + 400 + 30 + 9
2 6000 + 200 + 10 + 5
3 10 000 + 4000 + 600 + 30 + 6
4 30 000 + 8000 + 0 + 50 + 1

5–10

M	H Th	T Th	Th	H	T	O
		1	6	4	8	3
	5	6	8	3	4	9
3	9	4	0	7	3	5
		2	7	0	9	9
	1	6	2	4	8	0
7	8	0	4	2	9	3

11 7000
12 7 000 000
13 700 000
14 700
15 27 401, 29 401
16 44 900, 46 900
17 38 439, 40 439
18 134 688, 136 688
19 898 651, 900 651
20 5 674 449, 5 676 449

Unit 6 MATHS: Measurement & Space
1 grams
2 tonnes
3 milligrams
4 kilograms
5 5500 g, 5.5 kg, 5 kg 500 g
6 1 kg 200 g, 1.2 kg, 1200 g
7 2 kg 300 g, 2300 g, 2.3 kg
8 5000 g
9 7000 g
10 12 000 g
11 25 000 g
12 2500 g
13 6400 g
14 4 kg
15 7 kg
16 15 kg
17 32 kg
18 4.5 kg
19 1.45 kg

Unit 6 MATHS: Problem Solving
1 Carriage 1: Max can only ride with Tamsin (50 kg + 25 kg = 75 kg)
Carriage 2: Su can only ride with Tim, as Tamsin is with Max, (48 kg + 26 kg = 74 kg)
Carriage 3: Mignonne and Kate (40 kg + 35 kg = 75 kg)
2 150 ÷ 6 = 25 g each

Unit 7 ENGLISH: Grammar & Punctuation
1 My dad <u>has been</u> to Switzerland.
2 The kittens <u>were sleeping</u> in the sun.
3 Jackie <u>is building</u> a model aeroplane.
4 I <u>turned **off**</u> the television in the living room.
5 Riley <u>tripped **over**</u> a rocky outcrop.
6 Harry <u>will give **away**</u> all of his unused toys!
7 I took **off** all my wet clothes and put **on** my robe.
8 We will look **after** our neighbour's dog while he is away.
9 The students are putting **away/down/aside** all their books.

Unit 7 ENGLISH: Phonic Knowledge & Spelling
1 cinema
2 vinegar
3 pasta
4 hanger
5 cellar
6 seller
7 hangar
8 spectacular
9 familiar
10 beggar
11 peculiar
12 lunar

Unit 7 ENGLISH: Reading & Comprehension
1 argument
2 to provide reasons for and against the development of a new supermarket
3 opinion
4 fact
5 opinion
6 opinion
7 b. someone representing the new supermarket
8 The area already has a supermarket.
They don't want to lose any more green spaces.
9 Any two from: best quality food and household wares; right on your doorstep; brand new shopping complex; free parking; adventure playground; free crèche; free hourly bus service; state-of-the-art complex is bigger, brighter and more convenient

Unit 7 MATHS: Number & Algebra
1 b. 2
2 c. 6
3 c. 9
4 a. 5
5 c. 8
6 $\frac{2}{10}$
7 50
8 $\frac{7}{10}$
9 $\frac{4}{1000}$
10 $\frac{5}{10000}$

11–15

Fraction	Decimal
$\frac{3}{10}$	0.3
$\frac{54}{100}$	0.54
$\frac{8}{1000}$	0.008
$\frac{458}{1000}$	0.458
$\frac{3457}{10000}$	0.3457

Unit 7 MATHS: Statistics & Probability
1
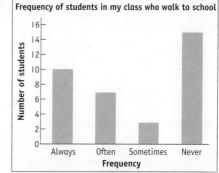

2

Hobbies	Tally	Frequency
Sport	ⅢⅢ ⅢⅢ ⅢⅢ	15
Computer games	ⅢⅢ ⅢⅢ	9
Reading	ⅠⅠ	2
Bike riding	ⅠⅠⅠ	3
Collecting	Ⅰ	1
Cooking/making	ⅢⅢ	5
Total		35

3 Frequency of favourite hobbies for students in my class
4 Number of students
5 Hobby
6 Collecting
7 Sport

Unit 7 MATHS: Measurement & Space

1. 40 °C
2. 36 °C
3. b. -30° C to 50 °C
4. 40 °C
5. 2 °C
6. 46 °C
7. -10°C

Unit 7 MATHS: Problem Solving

1. 25 – 14 = 11 °C
2. 31 – 8 = 23 °C
3. 180 – 162 = 18 °C
4. 25 – 13 = 12 °C

Unit 8 ENGLISH: Grammar & Punctuation

1. The dog's tail was wagging happily.
2. The girls' coats were hanging up in the hallway.
3. I put the books back in Tina's room.
4. Mum picked up Tim's bag and Helen's suitcase.
5. Tony and Sara's cat is a blue Persian.
6. Riley and Jack's mother came to collect them after school.
7. Mandy's and Cam's toys were sold at the fair.
8. Johnno loaned me his dad's camera.
9. Lisa and Tanya copied Anna's dance steps.
10. Galen played a game on his brother's phone.

Unit 8 ENGLISH: Phonic Knowledge & Spelling

1. dairy
2. fussy
3. sentry
4. steady, steadied, steadying, steadiest
5. dirty, dirtied, dirtying, dirtiest
6. tidy, tidied, tidying, tidiest

Unit 8 ENGLISH: Reading & Comprehension

1. b. explanation
2. reflect
3. minimum
4. transparent
5. pedestrian
6. go through it (transmit); bounce off (reflect); be stopped (absorbed)
7. The light enters the reflector, hits the prisms and is directed back out the front of the reflector in the direction it came from.
8. c. by means of
9. c. warns
10. Any two from: The reflector may be outside the beam of a car driver's headlights. It may be foggy. The reflector may be dirty.

Unit 8 MATHS: Number & Algebra

1. $\frac{3}{4}$
2. $\frac{7}{10}$
3. $\frac{1}{8}$
4. $\frac{5}{9}$
5. $\frac{3}{4}$
6. $\frac{4}{6}$
7. $\frac{7}{8}$
8. $\frac{9}{10}$
9. $\frac{4}{4}$ or 1
10. $\frac{4}{5}$
11. $\frac{4}{10}$
12. $\frac{6}{8}$
13. $\frac{2}{6}$
14. $\frac{1}{10}$
15. $\frac{2}{7}$
16. $\frac{6}{8}$

Unit 8 MATHS: Measurement & Space

1. nonagon
2. rectangle
3. square
4. triangle
5. pentagon
6. trapezium
7. b. reflection
8. a. slide
9. b. reflection
10. c. rotation
11. a. slide

Unit 8 MATHS: Problem Solving

TERM 1 REVIEW

Term 1 ENGLISH: Grammar & Punctuation

1. Melanie lives in Adelaide and her sister, Jackie, lives in London.
2. *The Sea* is a well-known poem written by James Reeves.
3. villages
4. eyelashes
5. viruses
6. trolleys
7. The clown wore a funny hat and enormous shoes.
8. his bright hat
9. those old shoes
10. thick, woolly jumpers
11. an exciting new movie
12. That boy can chatter like a monkey.
13. The firefighter rescued the cat from the tree.
14. Emma tripped over her own shoelaces.

15. We will get up really early tomorrow morning.
16. The horse's rein was hanging loose.
17. The boys' bikes were leaning up against the wall.
18. The Tasmanian Tiger once roamed the bushland of Tasmania.

Term 1 ENGLISH: Phonic Knowledge & Spelling

1. picnicked, picnicking
2. collected, collecting
3. vandalise
4. terrorise
5. adoring
6. arrangement
7. motivation (4)
8. soloist (3)
9. critical
10. historical
11. hangar
12. seller
13. wallabies
14. cities
15. lazier, laziest
16. emptier, emptiest
17. bicycle
18. monocycle

Term 1 ENGLISH: Reading & Comprehension

1. b. all the living things in an area
2. 30 per cent
3. tropical, temperate, boreal
4. South America
5. d. emit
6. conifers
7. stabilise
8. photosynthesis
9. erosion
10. boreal
11. c. by controlling water run-off after rain

Term 1 MATHS: Number & Algebra

1. 1, 2, 3, 5, 6, 10, 15, 30
2. 6, 12, 18, 24, 30, 36
3. 50
4. 240
5. 1490
6. 400
7. 1200
8. 13 800
9. 345
10. 525 ÷ 5 = (500 + 25) ÷ 5
    = (500 ÷ 5) + (25 ÷ 5)
    = 100 + 5
    = 105
11. 5000 + 400 + 80 + 2
12. 20 000 + 4000 + 500 + 90 + 1
13. 700 000 + 50 000 + 6000 + 200 + 40 + 8
14. c. $\frac{3}{10}$
15. b. 50
16. c. $\frac{7}{10}$
17. d. $\frac{4}{1000}$
18. c. 9000
19. 0.4
20. 0.05
21. 0.15
22. 0.367
23. $\frac{3}{5}$
24. $\frac{7}{7}$ or 1
25. $\frac{7}{10}$
26. $2\frac{3}{5}$

Term 1 MATHS: Statistics & Probability

1. d. $\frac{2}{8}$
2. c. $\frac{1}{8}$
3. a. $\frac{2}{8}$
4. b. How often did you go to a restaurant last month?
5. $\frac{1}{20}$
6. $\frac{1}{6}$
7. $\frac{1}{2}$
8. $\frac{1}{3}$

9–13

Animals	Tally	Frequency
Dog	## 1111	9
Dolphin	## 1	6
Cat	1111	4
Elephant	##	5
Snake	11	2
Tiger	1111	4
Whale	##	5
	Total	35

14. Favourite animals for students in my class
15. Number of students
16. Animal
17. Snake
18. Dog

Term 1 MATHS: Measurement & Space

1. 72 mm
2. 80 mm
3. 06:00
4. 02:30
5. 16:20
6. 22:42
7. 1:35 pm
8. 8:50 pm
9. 12:30 pm
10. 6:20 am
11. Perimeter = 20 cm
12. Area = 16 cm²
13. 75 cm + 125 cm + 75 cm + 125 cm = 400 cm
14. 1250 mL
15. 6000 g
16. 14 000 g
17. 3500 g
18. 17 800 g
19. 4 kg
20. 7.5 kg
21. 15 kg
22. 32.5 kg
23. 500 °C
24. 10 °C
25. 440 °C
26. 340 °C
27. c. rotation
28. a. slide

TARGETING HOMEWORK 5 © PASCAL PRESS ISBN 9781925726473

Unit 9 ENGLISH: Grammar & Punctuation

Answers will vary but the meaning of each word should reflect the following:

1 **mouse:** a small handheld device which is moved across a mat to move the cursor on a computer screen
2 **swipe:** to move fingers across a touchscreen
3 **surfing:** moving from site to site on the internet
4 **texts:** messages sent by mobile phone using SMS
5 **tablet:** a portable computer with a touchscreen panel

Unit 9 ENGLISH: Phonic Knowledge & Spelling

1 champion
2 chemist
3 chauffeur
4 **tch** sound: cheetah, chance, cherish
5 **k** sound: chrome, cholera, chaos
6 **sh** sound: chef, champagne, chateau
7 cherries
8 children
9 chimneys
10 chateaux
11 chaos
12 chateau
13 champagne

Unit 9 ENGLISH: Reading & Comprehension

1 b. report
2 a. electing politicians to govern the whole of Australia
3 candidate
4 constituency
5 independent
6 campaign
7 marginal
8 education, defence, security, health, the economy
9 a. hinder
10 Any 2 from: meetings, advertisements, rallies, door-to-door flyers
11 b. a survey to find out what voters think

Unit 9 MATHS: Number & Algebra

1 13 568
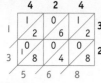

3 9476
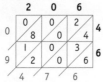

2 29 904

4 44 820
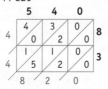

Unit 9 MATHS: Statistics & Probability

1 0
2 1
3 1
4 0
5 0
6 0.75
7 0.25
8 1
9 0.5
10 0.25
11 1
12 0

Unit 9 MATHS: Measurement & Space

Any two methods of the working out is acceptable.

1–2 12 + 2 + 12 + 2 = 28 cm
2 × (12 + 2) cm
= 2 × 14 cm
= 28 cm
(2 × 12) + (2 × 2) cm
= 24 + 4 cm
= 28 cm

5–6 10 + 5 + 10 + 5 = 30 cm
2 × (10 + 5) cm
= 2 × 15 cm
= 30 cm
(2 × 10) + (2 × 5) cm
= 20 + 10 cm
= 30 cm

3–4 4 + 8 + 4 + 8 = 24 cm
2 × (4 + 8) cm
= 2 × 12 cm
= 24 cm
(2 × 4) + (2 × 8) cm
= 8 + 16 cm
= 24 cm

Unit 9 MATHS: Problem Solving

The highest total is 158:

Unit 10 ENGLISH: Grammar & Punctuation

1 her or his
2 it
3 they
4 She is in the school choir.
5 Luke and I like to go fishing.
6 "Wait for me," said Tilly.
7 That book is **hers**, but she gave it to me. (that book)
8 This house is **ours** and that one is yours. (this house)

Unit 10 ENGLISH: Phonic Knowledge & Spelling

1 success
2 mattress
3 chess
4 press, access
5 classes
6 chalets
7 canvases
8 churches
9 compression, compressive
10 impression, impressive
11 succession, successive
12 expression, expressive

Unit 10 ENGLISH: Reading & Comprehension

1 c. narrative
2 He left the baby alone in his bedroom.
3 b. simile
4 Any one from: swooped, whipped
5 The baby was covered in purple paint which came off when the baby went into the water.
6 b. No, because he shouldn't have left the baby alone in the bath.

Unit 10 MATHS: Number & Algebra

1 c. 1.4   2 a. 1.7   3 a. 2.3

Ones		Tenths	Hundredths	Thousandths
1	.	2	3	4
1	.	3	4	0
1	.	4	0	0
1	.	7	0	0
0	.	7	0	0
1	.	5	6	8
2	.	3	0	0
1	.	3	5	9
2	.	2	4	0

4 0.002, 0.2, 1.02, 1.2
5 1.003, 1.03, 1.3, 1.32
6 1.5, 1.589, 2.001, 3.2
7 0.5, 0.516, 1.5, 5.0
8 =
9 <
10 =
11 <
12 >
13 >
14 >
15 <
16 <
17 1.5, 1.6, 1.7
18 0.9, 1.1, 1.3
19 9.5, 9.4, 9.3
20 5.2, 6.2, 7.2
21 10.6, 9.6, 8.6
22 8.0, 10.0, 12.0

Unit 10 MATHS: Measurement & Space

1 7
2 15
3 10
4 8
5 18
6 12
7 5
8 8
9 5
10 5
11 9
12 6
14 triangular prism
16 pentagonal prism
18 square-based pyramid

Unit 10 MATHS: Problem Solving

1 185.4 − 165.2 = 20.2 cm
2 20.0 − 7.5 = 12.5 bars
3 1.589 − 0.530 = 1.059 cm
4 0.4 + 0.3 + 0.2 = 0.9
0.9 or $\frac{9}{10}$ of the cake had been eaten.
0.1 or $\frac{1}{10}$ of the cake was left.

Unit 11 ENGLISH: Grammar & Punctuation

1 **She** often goes with **them** to the park. (3rd person)
2 **You** need to get up early tomorrow. (2nd person)
3 Yesterday, **I** ran in a competitive race. (first person)
4–12 When I[4] was very young, I[5] used to stay at my[6] Nan's house during the school holidays. I[7] was allowed to take all my[8] favourite toys, including my[9] bike. Nan was very kind to me[10]. We[11] used to bake lots of yummy cakes to take with us[12] on a picnic.
13 1st person

Unit 11 ENGLISH: Phonic Knowledge & Spelling

1 echidna   4 emit   7 erode
2 erupt   5 elect   8 evade: avoid
3 event   6 evade   9 eject: expel

Unit 11 ENGLISH: Reading & Comprehension

1 Richard Owen and Waterhouse Hawkins
2 anatomy
3 skeleton
4 emerge
5 a. curious
6 Greek
7 c. together
8 c. He used his knowledge of how animals' bodies are put together.

Unit 11 MATHS: Number & Algebra

1 $\frac{15}{100}$ 3 $\frac{26}{100}$ 5 $\frac{90}{100}$ 7 $\frac{34}{100}$
2 15%   4 26%   6 90%   8 34%

9   11   13

10 $\frac{3}{10} = \frac{30}{100} = 30\%$ 12 $\frac{5}{10} = \frac{50}{100} = 50\%$ 14 $\frac{8}{10} = \frac{80}{100} = 80\%$

Unit 11 MATHS: Statistics & Probability

1 22
2 4
3 8
4 10
5 1
6 4

7
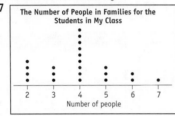

The Number of People in Families for the Students in My Class
Number of people

Unit 11 MATHS: Measurement & Space

1 lake   4 house   6 G3
2 garden   5 swimming pool   7 red
3 D4

Unit 11 MATHS: Problem Solving

3, 5 and 6

Unit 12 ENGLISH: Grammar & Punctuation

1 The trees <u>were swaying</u> **gently** in the breeze.
2 The children <u>yelled</u> **excitedly** and **quickly** <u>raced</u> out the door.
3 The man <u>spoke</u> **angrily** at the dogs who <u>were barking</u> **loudly**.
4 Ben <u>looked</u> **anxiously** at the waves that <u>were pounding</u> **relentlessly** on the boat.
5 **Tomorrow** Dad <u>will play</u> tennis. He **usually** <u>wins</u>.
6 We'<u>ll go</u> **now** and you <u>can join</u> us **later**.
7 **Sometimes** I <u>stay</u> at my friend's house.
8 We **eventually** <u>reached</u> the beach after a long trek.
9 The bee <u>flew</u> **here** and **there** following the scent of the flowers.
10 We <u>looked</u> **around** but <u>couldn't find</u> him **anywhere**.
11 The cat <u>was</u> **nowhere** to be seen but we knew she <u>was hiding</u> **somewhere**.
12 The mother <u>took</u> the baby **outside**.

Unit 12 ENGLISH: Phonic Knowledge & Spelling

1 alarm   4 advice   7 abrupt
2 afloat   5 advise   8 adjacent
3 alert   6 afloat   9 adventure

Unit 12 ENGLISH: Reading & Comprehension

1 sunglasses, jeans, bike, peace and quiet
2 milk, bread, bananas
3 Wants are things we would like to have. Needs are things we require to live.
4 out-of-date
5 exasperated
6 gizmo
7 b. Gran didn't have many things and she didn't want anything.

Unit 12 MATHS: Number & Algebra

1 $1\frac{2}{4}$ or $1\frac{1}{2}$
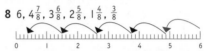

2 $2\frac{1}{6}$

3 $\frac{2}{10}$ or $\frac{1}{5}$

4 $\frac{7}{8}$

5 $1\frac{2}{4}$, 3, $4\frac{2}{4}$

6 $2\frac{1}{2}$, 5, $7\frac{1}{2}$

7 5, $3\frac{1}{2}$, 2, $\frac{1}{2}$

8 6, $4\frac{7}{8}$, $3\frac{6}{8}$, $2\frac{5}{8}$, $1\frac{4}{8}$, $\frac{3}{8}$

Unit 12 MATHS: Measurement & Space

The new drawings should look like the given illustrations, but larger.

Unit 12 MATHS: Problem Solving

1 $\frac{1}{2}$ 2 $\frac{3}{8}$ 3 1
4 $\frac{5}{8}$

Unit 13 ENGLISH: Grammar & Punctuation

1 faster   4 furthest   7 more   10 least
2 earlier   5 shorter   8 most
3 higher   6 more   9 less

Unit 13 ENGLISH: Phonic Knowledge & Spelling

1 pointless   4 helpful   7 hopeful   10 awfully
2 resourceful   5 harmless   8 usefully   11 fearfully
3 reckless   6 fruitless   9 painfully

Unit 13 ENGLISH: Reading & Comprehension

1 b. disaster   2 It melted.
3 The heat of the kitchen and the sun shining through the window caused the chocolate to melt.
4 b. It froze solid.
5 a. Lord Bingley was an impatient man and wouldn't wait for Johnson to answer.

Unit 13 MATHS: Number & Algebra

1 $5.00 + $2.00 + $8.50 = $15.50
2 $20.00 − $15.50 = $4.50
3 $4.50 × 12 = $54
4 $20 ÷ $4.50 = 4.4 months, round to 5 months
5 $5.40 + $3.50 + $2.50 + $1.00 = $12.40
6 $12.40 + $7.60 = $20
7 $20 × 10 = $200
8 $7.60 × 10 = $76

TARGETING HOMEWORK 5 © PASCAL PRESS ISBN 9781925726473

Unit 13 MATHS: Statistics & Probability

1 12

2–7

Outcome	Number	Fraction
purple	1	$\frac{1}{12}$
dark blue	2	$\frac{2}{12}$
light blue	1	$\frac{1}{12}$
yellow	2	$\frac{2}{12}$
pink	2	$\frac{2}{12}$
green	1	$\frac{1}{12}$

8 $\frac{12}{12}$ or 1
9 pink and dark blue
10 light blue and green
11 red
12 10
13 $\frac{1}{10}$
14 $\frac{9}{10}$
15 $\frac{4}{10}$
16 $\frac{2}{10}$
17 $\frac{3}{10}$

Unit 13 MATHS: Measurement & Space

1 less than
2 less than
3 greater than
4 greater than
5 equal to
6 greater than
7 less than
8 greater than

Unit 13 MATHS: Problem Solving

1 three-eighths of Sam's money = $36
   To work out one-eighth, divide 36 by 3 = $12
   eight-eighths = 8 × $12 = $96
2 $24
3 $36

Unit 14 ENGLISH: Grammar & Punctuation

1 safari
2 alphabet
3 bamboo
4 billabong
5 tsunami

Unit 14 ENGLISH: Phonic Knowledge & Spelling

1 exhibit
2 outfit
3 outskirts
4 to take something that is offered to you: accept
5 not including: except
6 to think that something will happen: expect
7 exhibition
8 expansion
9 extension
10 exemption

Unit 14 ENGLISH: Reading & Comprehension

1 b. a very intense and destructive fire
2 a. a domestic animal, such as a cat, that has gone wild
3 Any 4 from the following: kill off vegetation; cause soil erosion; kill animals; animals that survive have less food and shelter; destroy farms and houses; smoke can cause breathing difficulties
4 c. to grow from a seed
5 eradicate
6 reduce
7 Any 4 from the following: some plants need fire to germinate; the ash from a fire provides nutrients for the soil; fire removes old and dead plants; low-intensity fires reduce the amount of fuel in an area; fires eradicate plant diseases

Unit 14 MATHS: Number & Algebra

1 8
2 54
3 5
4 7
5 5
6 10
7 5
8 56
9 3
10 2
11 6
12 144
13 3
14 c. 3
15 b. 2
16 d. 9
17 a. 1000

Unit 14 MATHS: Measurement & Space

1 50°
2 130°
3 110°
4 175°
5 44°
6 87°

Unit 14 MATHS: Problem Solving

1 All 3 angles need to add up to 180°, so if one angle equals 75° then the other two must add up to 105°.
   Possible combinations:

100° and 5°	80° and 25°	60° and 45°
95° and 10°	75° and 30°	55° and 50°
90° and 15°	70° and 35°	
85° and 20°	65° and 40°	

2 360° − 170° = 190°

Unit 15 ENGLISH: Grammar & Punctuation

1 "Go away!" shouted the angry boy.
2 Terry asked, "Are you going to Tom's birthday?"
3 "On Saturday," announced Jake, "we will get up early."
4 "My mother," replied Anna, "is a superb cook."

Unit 15 ENGLISH: Phonic Knowledge & Spelling

1 channel
2 caramel
3 normal
4 vital
5 physically
6 orally
7 vocally
8 mentally
9 casually
10 formally

Unit 15 ENGLISH: Reading & Comprehension

1 c. Nepal
2 b. a person who has been forced to leave their country due to war or a disaster
3 China invaded Tibet and Dawa and her parents fled the country to live in Nepal.
4 Tibetan, Nepalese and English
5 pagoda
6 sherpa
7 yak

Unit 15 MATHS: Number & Algebra

1 no
2 yes
3 yes
4 no
5 yes
6 no
7 yes
8 yes
9 no
10 yes
11 yes
12 no
13 yes
14 yes
15 yes
16 no
17 no
18 yes
19 yes
20 no
21 yes
22 no
23 yes
24 no
25 no
26 yes
27 yes
28 no
29 yes
30 no
31 no
32 yes
33 no
34 yes

Unit 15 MATHS: Statistics & Probability

1

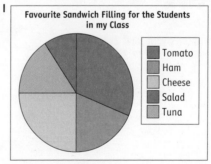

Favourite Sandwich Filling for the Students in my Class
Tomato
Ham
Cheese
Salad
Tuna

2 32
3 cheese
4 The exact number of students for each filling

Unit 15 MATHS: Measurement & Space

1 0 °C
2 10 °C
3 21 °C
4 49 °C
5 true
6 true
7 true
8 false
9 false
10 true
11 true

Unit 15 MATHS: Problem Solving

1 a. Yes. 3584 is an even number. It ends in 4 so it can be divided by 2.
2 b. No. The digits 3, 5, 8 and 4 add up to 20. 20 is not divisible by 3.
3 a. Yes. The last two digits, 84, are divisible by 4.
4 b. No. The last digit does not end in 0 or 5.
5 b. No. The number is divisible by 2 but not by 3 so it's not divisible by 6.

Unit 16 ENGLISH: Grammar & Punctuation

1 Tanya said that she was taking her first driving lesson today.
2 Michael offered to wash up.
3 "I'm going to be late," said the man.
4 "Do you want to go fishing tomorrow?" asked Dad.
5 "Will you look after my cat?" asked my neighbour.

Unit 16 ENGLISH: Phonic Knowledge & Spelling

1 cardboard	7 crossroads	13 lighthouse
2 fingernails	8 crossbones	14 flashlight
3 cupcake	9 crossover	15 birthday
4 headfirst	10 crossfire	16 motorcycle
5 crosswind	11 thunderstorm	17 seahorse
6 crossway	12 newspaper	18 grasshopper

Unit 16 ENGLISH: Reading & Comprehension

1 a. helping
2 Any one from: leaving some seeds behind when they collect them so new plants can grow; not hunting young animals or females carrying young; eating a variety of foods so no single food source runs out
3 b. fire-stick farming
4 law
5 shelter
6 savanna
7 b. a strip of bare land that helps to prevent the spread of fire
8 the combination of traditional Aboriginal ways and modern technology

Unit 16 MATHS: Number & Algebra

1 22.8	7 0 hundreds	17 9
2 36.15	6 tens	18 8
3 481.45	9 ones	19 4
4 2900.132	0 tenths	20 9
5 0 hundreds	8 hundredths	21 3
9 tens	0 thousandths	22 2
8 ones	8 5	23 3
4 tenths	9 9	24 7
5 hundredths	10 0	25 9
0 thousandths	11 9	26 3.126, 8.9, 55, 345
6 4 hundreds	12 5	27 123.6, 24.08, 6.359, 0.589
0 tens	13 1	
6 ones	14 5	
3 tenths	15 3	
4 hundredths	16 8	
9 thousandths		

Unit 16 MATHS: Measurement & Space

1 0.85	9 12.2 + 12.2 + 4.2 + 4.2 = 32.8 cm	14 25.6 mm
2 12.6		15 3 452 mm
3 3.15		16 240 mm
4 0.07	10 8.3 + 8.3 + 8.3 + 8.3 = 33.2 m	17 0.5 cm
5 4.25 m		18 3.8 cm
6 5.74 m		19 34.1 cm
7 10.08 m	11 150 mm	20 2.55 cm
8 0.62 m	12 16 mm	21 157.8 cm
	13 252 mm	22 347 cm

Unit 16 MATHS: Problem Solving

1 f	2 d	3 c	4 e	5 a	6 b

TERM 2 REVIEW

Term 2 ENGLISH: Grammar & Punctuation

1 That bicycle is **hers**, but she gave it to me. (bicycle)
2 **She** told **them** to sing louder. (3rd person)
3 Why are **you** upset? (2nd person)
4 **We'll go** <u>now</u> and they **can join** us <u>later</u>.
5 We <u>eventually</u> **reached** the motel after a long drive.
6 more
7 "**H**ave they arrived yet?" asked **T**im.
8 Dad offered to mow the lawns.
9 "I am going to be late," said Michael.
   or Michael said, "I am going to be late."
10 they
11 I

Term 2 ENGLISH: Phonic Knowledge & Spelling

1 cherries	9 advise	17 birthday
2 children	10 fearful	18 'tch' sound: chilli, children
3 chimneys	11 harmless	19 'k' sound: chord, chrome
4 chateaux	12 visually	20 'sh' sound: chef, chateau
5 oxen	13 physically	
6 mattresses	14 seahorse	
7 elect: vote	15 flashlight	
8 advice	16 toothache	

Term 2 ENGLISH: Reading & Comprehension

1 Edward Gibbon Wakefield	7 consort
2 It was a settlement without convicts.	8 king
3 1835	9 Colonel William Light
4 politician	10 Holdfast Bay
5 province	11 b. officially announced
6 ashore	

Term 2 MATHS: Number & Algebra

1 23 806

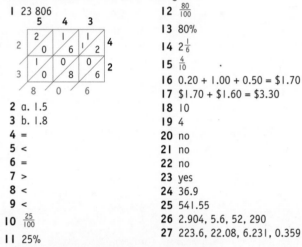

2 a. 1.5	12 $\frac{80}{100}$
3 b. 1.8	13 80%
4 =	14 $2\frac{1}{6}$
5 <	15 $\frac{4}{10}$
6 =	16 0.20 + 1.00 + 0.50 = $1.70
7 >	17 $1.70 + $1.60 = $3.30
8 <	18 10
9 <	19 4
10 $\frac{25}{100}$	20 no
11 25%	21 no
	22 no
	23 yes
	24 36.9
	25 541.55
	26 2.904, 5.6, 52, 290
	27 223.6, 22.08, 6.231, 0.359

Term 2 MATHS: Statistics & Probability

1 0	3 0.25	5 14	7 10	9 $\frac{8}{10}$
2 1	4 20	6 3	8 $\frac{2}{10}$	10 $\frac{6}{10}$

11

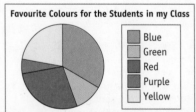

Favourite Colours for the Students in my Class
Blue / Green / Red / Purple / Yellow

Term 2 MATHS: Measurement & Space

1-2 Any two of the following is acceptable:
   14 cm + 2 cm + 14 cm + 2 cm = 32 cm
   2 × (14 + 2) cm
   = 2 × 16 cm
   = 32 cm
   (2 × 14) + (2 × 2) cm
   = 28 + 4 cm
   = 32 cm

3 triangular prism	10 10 °C
4 rectangular prism	11 180 mm
5 greater than	12 46 mm
6 less than	13 352 mm
7 45°	14 0.5 cm
8 150°	15 3.85 cm
9 0 °C	16 341.7 cm

Unit 17 ENGLISH: Grammar & Punctuation

1 P	6 The coach is explaining the rules to us.
2 A	
3 A	7 A goal was scored by Janine.
4 P	
5 Rocko wrote the letter.	8 The athletics are being watched by hundreds of spectators.

Unit 17 ENGLISH: Phonic Knowledge & Spelling

1 provide
2 reside
3 vivid
4 rigid
5 squalid
6 livid
7 rigidly
8 decided, deciding
9 confided, confiding, confident, confidence

Unit 17 ENGLISH: Reading & Comprehension

1 She was convicted of stealing and was sentenced to seven years' hard labour.
2 b. She had just spent many months at sea in squalid conditions.
3 c. a serious crime
4 makeshift
5 threadbare
6 guilty
7 illiterate
8 The reverend suggested that they could start a new life with a chance of freedom, land and independence.

Unit 17 MATHS: Number & Algebra

1 7000
2 4000
3 8000
4 1000
5 6000
6 5000
7 9000
8 5000
9 10 000
10 16 000
11 26 000
12 56 000
13 134 000
14 873 000
15 502 000
16 5 675 000
17 6 843 000
18 b. 6000
19 c. 9000
20 a. 35 000
21 b. 5000
22 b. 3000
23 c. 213 000

Unit 17 MATHS: Statistics & Probability

1 dog
2 5
3 27
4 32
5 a. yes
6 no
7 no
8 yes
9 no
10 no
11 yes
12 yes

Unit 17 MATHS: Measurement & Space

1 16:15
2 23:45
3 21:15
4 14:30
5 5 hours
6 6 hours 45 minutes
7 2½ hours
8 1 hour 15 min
9 no
10 KingAir
11 3 hours 55 min

Unit 17 MATHS: Problem Solving

1 Add 42 minutes to each clock.
2 17:19

Unit 18 ENGLISH: Grammar & Punctuation

1 but
2 or
3 and/but
4 so
5 The penguins waddled up the beach and they went into their burrows.
6 The dog can eat tinned food or it can eat dry food.

Unit 18 ENGLISH: Phonic Knowledge & Spelling

1 predict
2 respect
3 verdict
4 inject
5 afflicted
6 inflicted
7 afflicted
8 inflicted

Unit 18 ENGLISH: Reading & Comprehension

1 Any three from: clearing land, chopping down trees, making bricks, building roads, building government buildings
2 working as servants, doing laundry, cleaning barracks
3 b. an amount each person is allowed when there is a shortage
4 officials
5 institutions
6 barracks
7 pardoned
8 Any four from: flogged with a whip, put into stocks or leg irons, solitary confinement, sent to a penal colony, hanged
9 c. to be kept alone in a cell away from other convicts

Unit 18 MATHS: Number & Algebra

1

$$10 + 10 + 10 + 5 = 35$$

$$5 \overline{)175}$$
$$-50 \quad 10 \times 5 = 50$$
$$125$$
$$-50 \quad 10 \times 5 = 50$$
$$75$$
$$-50 \quad 10 \times 5 = 50$$
$$25$$
$$-25 \quad 5 \times 5 = 50$$
$$0$$

2

$$10 + 10 + 10 + 10 + 2 = 42$$

$$6 \overline{)252}$$
$$-60 \quad 10 \times 6 = 60$$
$$192$$
$$-60 \quad 10 \times 6 = 60$$
$$132$$
$$-60 \quad 10 \times 6 = 60$$
$$72$$
$$-60 \quad 10 \times 6 = 60$$
$$12$$
$$12 \quad 2 \times 6 = 12$$
$$0$$

3

$$10 + 10 + 10 + 6 = 36 \text{ r } 2$$

$$5 \overline{)182}$$
$$-50 \quad 10 \times 5 = 50$$
$$132$$
$$-50 \quad 10 \times 5 = 50$$
$$82$$
$$-50 \quad 10 \times 5 = 50$$
$$32$$
$$-30 \quad 6 \times 5 = 50$$
$$2 \quad \text{There is 2 left over.}$$

4

$$10 + 10 + 10 = 30 \text{ r } 5$$

$$7 \overline{)215}$$
$$-70 \quad 10 \times 7 = 70$$
$$145$$
$$-70 \quad 10 \times 7 = 70$$
$$75$$
$$-70 \quad 10 \times 7 = 70$$
$$5 \quad \text{There is 5 left over.}$$

Unit 18 MATHS: Measurement & Space

1 b. 45° anticlockwise
2 c. 90° clockwise
3 c. 90° clockwise
4 a. 180° clockwise
5 a. 180° clockwise
6 c. 45° clockwise

Unit 18 MATHS: Problem Solving

16	2	3	13
12	6	7	9
5	11	10	8
1	15	14	4

Unit 19 ENGLISH: Grammar & Punctuation

1 cut: slice, snip
2 think: contemplate, reflect
3 ask: question, inquire
4 run: dash, scurry
5 see: glimpse, observe
6 drink: guzzle, sip
7 eat: devour, munch
8 sliced
9 examined
10 exhausted

Unit 19 ENGLISH: Phonic Knowledge & Spelling

1 cottage/village
2 advantage
3 vintage
4 hostage
5 teenage
6 sewage
7 voltage
8 damage
9 packaged
10 managing

Unit 19 ENGLISH: Reading & Comprehension

1 c. narrative
2 c. adjective
3 a. a prankster
4 a. joked
5 lung horn
6 Her face went red.
7 smirked
8 almighty
9 rampage

Unit 19 MATHS: Number & Algebra

1 3
2 8
3 10
4 7.63
5 0.78
6 0.05
7 5
8 6
9 100
10 42.9
11 4.8
12 0.7
13 $5.80
14 $63.80
15 $36.50
16 $401.50
17 $12.55
18 $138.05
19 $145.63
20 $1601.93

Unit 19 MATHS: Statistics & Probability

1 $\frac{3}{6}$
2 $\frac{2}{6}$
3 $\frac{2}{10}$
4 $\frac{3}{10}$
5 $\frac{4}{10}$

6

7

8

ANSWERS

Unit 19 MATHS: Measurement & Space

1 d	3 c	5 e	7 g	9 f
2 e	4 b	6 a	8 h	

Unit 19 MATHS: Problem Solving

1 b   2 d   3 a   4 c

Unit 20 ENGLISH: Grammar & Punctuation

1 <u>Unless you have another idea</u>, **we will play basketball this afternoon.**
2 **I like to eat lunch outside** <u>when the sun is shining.</u>
3 **Nathan,** <u>who was born in Sydney</u>, **decided to move to Adelaide.**
4 <u>Since his car broke down</u>, **my uncle catches the bus to work.**
5 **The wicked witch,** <u>who lives in the forest</u>, **slowly opened the cottage door.**

6 c   7 e   8 d   9 b   10 a

Unit 20 ENGLISH: Phonic Knowledge & Spelling

1 actor	5 dancer	9 bakery
2 senator	6 narrator	10 editing
3 dressmaker	7 inventor	11 jogging
4 plumber	8 sailor	12 tutored

Unit 20 ENGLISH: Reading & Comprehension

1 c. adapting to a new climate and environment
2 They wanted to make the environment look like the one they left in Europe.
3 prickly pear
4 It spread rapidly and made the land useless for farming.
5 They released a moth whose caterpillars ate the prickly pear.
6 unique   8 devastating
7 import   9 infested

Unit 20 MATHS: Number & Algebra

1

	30	+	5	
20 + 4	20 × 30 = 600	20 × 5 = 100	600 + 100 =	700
	4 × 30 = 120	4 × 5 = 20	120 + 20 =	140
				840

2

	40	+	6	
30 + 7	30 × 40 = 1200	30 × 6 = 180	1200 + 180 =	1380
	7 × 40 = 280	7 × 6 = 42	280 + 42 =	322
				1702

3

	60	+	4	
40 + 8	40 × 60 = 2400	40 × 4 = 160	2400 + 160 =	2560
	8 × 60 = 480	8 × 4 = 32	480 + 32 =	512
				3072

4

	50	+	1	
70 + 7	70 × 50 = 3500	70 × 1 = 70	3500 + 70 =	3570
	7 × 50 = 350	7 × 1 = 7	350 + 7 =	357
				3927

5

	80	+	4	
20 + 9	20 × 80 = 1600	20 × 4 = 80	1600 + 80 =	1680
	9 × 80 = 720	9 × 4 = 36	720 + 36 =	756
				2436

Unit 20 MATHS: Measurement & Space

1 True	5 False
2 True	6 False
3 False	7 Triangle and pentagon
4 True	8 Square and octagon

Unit 20 MATHS: Problem Solving

1 No   2 Yes   3 Yes   4 No   5 Yes

Unit 21 ENGLISH: Grammar & Punctuation

1 **The purse** <u>that you found</u> belongs to my sister.
2 **Melbourne,** <u>which I love to visit,</u> is the capital of Victoria.
3 Kerry ate **all the grapes** <u>that were left in the fruit bowl.</u>
4 Libby is the girl who bakes the cakes. (no commas needed)
5 The car, which was blue, belonged to my neighbour.
6 Danielle, who lives in Adelaide, is a pharmacist.

Unit 21 ENGLISH: Phonic Knowledge & Spelling

1 genuinely/honestly/quietly/presently/privately

2 heavily	5 Fortunately	8 awkwardly
3 quietly	6 gently	
4 noisily	7 immediately	

Unit 21 ENGLISH: Reading & Comprehension

1 b. few trees	4 amber
2 creamy-fawn, sleek hide, amber eyes	5 lair
3 sleek	6 d. disinterested

7 Any two from: scraping back of chairs, click of dishes, footsteps coming to the back door
8 He ate the soft parts of his food very quickly.
9 He leaped to his feet and went to meet the dingo. (At the beginning of the text it says they faced each other in the paddock.)

Unit 21 MATHS: Number & Algebra

1 $\frac{9}{12}$	4 $\frac{4}{16}$	7 $\frac{4}{16}$	10 $\frac{4}{15}$
2 $\frac{10}{12}$	5 $\frac{8}{16}$	8 Luke	11 $\frac{11}{15}$
3 $\frac{11}{12}$	6 $\frac{4}{16}$	9 $\frac{3}{12}$	12 $\frac{7}{15}$

Unit 21 MATHS: Statistics & Probability

1 $\frac{1}{52}$	3 $\frac{13}{52}$	5 $\frac{48}{52}$	7 $\frac{26}{52}$	9 0
2 $\frac{4}{52}$	4 $\frac{16}{52}$	6 $\frac{12}{52}$	8 $\frac{20}{52}$	10 $\frac{40}{52}$

Unit 21 MATHS: Measurement & Space

1 Membrey Road
2 pool
3 Jedda Rd, Devon St, Cohen Rd, East St
4 left, right, Grand Avenue, Martha, Kendall, left
5 Green Road, Dely, left, Devon, Berry, Membrey Road
6 Adam turns right into Cohen Road and then right into Devon Street. At the end of this street, he turns left into Jedda Road, then right into Rey Street. He crosses Membrey Road and Yi Avenue to reach the golf course.

Unit 21 MATHS: Problem Solving

1 $\frac{1}{5}$ of 125 m = 25 m, so $\frac{3}{5}$ = 75 m
2 $\frac{1}{5}$ of 75 m = 15 m, so $\frac{3}{5}$ = 45 m (3rd bounce) and $\frac{3}{5}$ of 45 m = 27 m on the 4th bounce

Unit 22 ENGLISH: Grammar & Punctuation

1 Ask the teacher <u>if this is correct</u>.
2 I don't understand <u>why he did that</u>.
3 That office is <u>where my dad works</u>.
4 <u>That he should behave</u> like that is very unusual.
5 She said she was good at skating.
6 I didn't know he could play the piano.
7 Are you sure you want this puppy?
8 Ned said the movie was awful.

Unit 22 ENGLISH: Phonic Knowledge & Spelling

1 prepare	6 precede, preceded, preceding
2 presume	
3 prevent	7 prepared, preparing
4 perfect	8 preserved, preserving
5 proceed	9 prevented, preventing
	10 protested, protesting

TARGETING HOMEWORK 5 © PASCAL PRESS ISBN 9781925726473

Unit 22 ENGLISH: Reading & Comprehension

1. a. on a radio or television program
2. a. That's for sure, mate.
   c. Crikey! That must have been terrifying!
3. It was like being hit by a train from behind.
4. They dragged him into the dinghy and took him to hospital.

Unit 22 MATHS: Number & Algebra

1. 45, 65, 85, 105, 125
2. 110, 85, 60, 35, 10
3. 5.0, 5.5, 6.0, 6.5, 7.0
4. 7.5, 7.0, 6.5, 6.0, 5.5
5. $\frac{1}{3}, \frac{2}{3}, \frac{3}{3}$ (1), $1\frac{1}{3}, 1\frac{2}{3}$, 2
6. $1\frac{2}{8}, \frac{7}{8}, \frac{4}{8}, \frac{1}{8}$
7. 24.5, 26.0, 27.5, 29.0, 30.5
8. 80.0, 78.5, 77.0, 75.5, 74.0
9. 235.1, 239.4, 243.7, 248.0, 252.3
10. 564.5, 563.2, 561.9, 560.6, 559.3
11. – 100
12. + 2.5
13. + 10.25
14. – 0.25
15. – 2.6
16. b. incorrect
17. b. incorrect
18. a. correct
19. a. correct
20. a. correct

Unit 22 MATHS: Measurement & Space

1. a.   b.   c.
2. a. 1 hour
   b. 40 minutes
3. a. 12:05
   b. 3:25
   c. 4:30
4. 2 hours 50 minutes
5. 1 hour 35 minutes
6. 4 hours 55 minutes
7. Answers will vary. Sample answer:

Flight 4	18:00	19:30	19:50	20:30

Unit 22 MATHS: Problem Solving

1 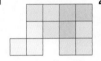 2   3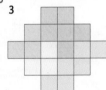

Unit 23 ENGLISH: Grammar & Punctuation

1. We put the jelly in the fridge to set. (d)
2. He is set in his ways. (e)
3. The alarm was set for 7 am. (f)
4. Ready! Set! Go! (b)
5. Jai set the table ready for dinner. (c)
6. The sailors set the sails. (a)
7. see
8. steer into place
9. be a candidate
10. helpful
11. move through the air
12. sway
13. penalty

Unit 23 ENGLISH: Phonic Knowledge & Spelling

1. quilt
2. quote
3. quay
4. quiz
5. quay
6. quarry
7. quote
8. quadrant
9. quest
10. quiver
11. quaver

Unit 23 ENGLISH: Reading & Comprehension

1. forests, water, soil, minerals, plants, animals, fossil fuels
2. b. fuels formed from animal and plant remains from millions of years ago
3. c. replanting forest that have been cut down
4. removing forests, burning fossil fuels
5. fact
6. opinion
7. opinion
8. renewable
9. atmosphere
10. endangered
11. sustainability

Unit 23 MATHS: Number & Algebra

1.

Rule: ÷ 10	
IN	OUT
50	5
200	20
80	8
1000	100
300	30

2.

Rule: × 10	
IN	OUT
7	70
8.5	85
24.5	245
62.5	625
75.2	752

3.

Rule: ÷ 8	
IN	OUT
64	8
80	10
640	80
800	100
160	20

4.

Rule: × 1000	
IN	OUT
2	2000
2.7	2700
40	40 000
41.2	41 200
13	13 000

5.

Rule: ÷ 1000	
IN	OUT
9000	9
5670	5.67
8000	8
678	0.678
12 000	12

6.

Rule: × 5	
IN	OUT
7	35
10	50
25	125
500	2500
5000	25 000

7. 20 × 5 = 1000 ÷ 10
8. 56 ÷ 7 = 64 ÷ 8
9. 500 ÷ 10 = 25 × 2
10. 20 × 3 = 6000 ÷ 100

Unit 23 MATHS: Statistics & Probability

1. 370
2. 369
3. 215
4. 485
5. 87
6. Australia
7–10. Australia, England, Pakistan, South Africa
11. 214
12. Bangladesh
13. England

Unit 23 MATHS: Measurement & Space

1. 500 ÷ 5 = 10; $2.00 ÷ 10 = $0.20
2. $3.00 ÷ 6 = $0.50
3. 1000 ÷ 50 = 20; $3.00 ÷ 20 = $0.15
4. 1000 ÷ 50 = 20; $3.00 ÷ 20 = $0.15
5. 300 ÷ 20 = 15; $2.25 ÷ 15 = $0.15
6. 300 ÷ 50 = 6; $3.00 ÷ 6 = $0.50
7. 200 ÷ 25 = 8; $1.60 ÷ 8 = $0.20
8. $3.10   9. b. $0.15   10. $0.20

Unit 23 MATHS: Problem Solving

Garment	Original price	10% off price	20% off price
T-shirt	$15.00	$13.50	$12.00
Dress	$25.00	$22.50	$20.00
Shorts	$12.50	$11.25	$10.00
Jeans	$79.00	$71.10	$63.20
Shirt	$35.50	$31.95	$28.40
Jumper	$65.00	$58.50	$52.00

Unit 24 ENGLISH: Grammar & Punctuation

1. Ted's pet shop claims that budgies make the best bird pets.
2. FlyNow Holidays guarantee this holiday is the cheapest.
3. Road Safety experts say this bicycle is the safest.
4–6. The school concert was held last night. It was a sellout with over 100 tickets sold. It was the best concert ever.[4] The school choir sang three songs, accompanied by Mr Jackson on the piano. The song choice was better than last year.[5] Nyall played the guitar and Max played the violin. The teachers did a funny play about Sinbad the Sailor. Supper was superb.[6]

Unit 24 ENGLISH: Phonic Knowledge & Spelling

1. listen
2. loosen
3. enlist
4. enjoy
5. encourage
6. endanger
7. enrich
8–11. In any order: ought, thought, brought, bought

Unit 24 ENGLISH: Reading & Comprehension

1. a. It helps the reader to relate more easily to Garth.
2. East Perth
3. b. weak and useless
4. c. a feeling that you haven't done enough with your life when you reach middle age

5 b. Garth is telling himself to be prepared for what will happen next.

6 As soon as I opened my mouth, he said, "Great. That's settled then. We'll take it."

Unit 24 MATHS: Number & Algebra

1 b. 2.3	**4** c. 156.5	**7** a. 2.35	**10** b. 156.21
2 c. 5.2	**5** b. 1.3	**8** b. 7.33	**11** c. 1.66
3 c. 24.2	**6** b. 5.1	**9** b. 12.76	**12** b. 5.92

Unit 24 MATHS: Measurement & Space

1 b. 75 minutes	**13** 115 minutes
2 c. 2 minutes	**14** 7 hours 50 minutes
3 a. 180 sec	**15** 4 hours 10 minutes
4 b. 300 minutes	**16** 3:45
5 2 hours	**17** 11:10
6 3 minutes	**18** 195 minutes
7 48 hours	**19** 4 hours 10 minutes
8 300 seconds	**20** 6 hours
9 300 minutes	**21** 2 hours 5 minutes
10 1440 minutes	**22** 2 hours 54 minutes
11 90 minutes	**23** 2 hours 12 minutes
12 285 minutes	**24** 5 hours 45 minutes

Unit 24 MATHS: Problem Solving

1 Answers may vary. Sample answers:
Share 1: 50, 200, 600, 125, 175
Share 2: 1000, 75, 75
Share 3: 550, 250, 60, 240, 50

2 Answers will vary.

3 Answers will vary.

4 No, because the total card value is 3450 which is not divisible by 4. Even if the total was divisible by four, the card values may not share equally.

TERM 3 REVIEW

Term 3 ENGLISH: Grammar & Punctuation

1 P	**2** A	**3** but	**4** or

5 The rabbits hopped across the grass and they disappeared into their burrows.

6 My mum decorated my birthday cake with lavish icing.

7 Will, **who plays for the Rosetown Tigers**, won the Player of the Year Award.

8 **Maxwell,** who lives next door, looked after our cat today.

9 The beach, which is near us, has been contaminated with oil.

10 Mum asked if I could help her.

11 The jelly soon set in the fridge. (firmed up)

12 a. That cake is the best.

Term 3 ENGLISH: Phonic Knowledge & Spelling

1 confide: confided, confiding, confident	**8** singer
2 inflicted	**9** editing
3 teenage	**10** easily
4 sewage	**11** fortunately
5 damage	**12** preserved, preserving
6 voltage	**13** ought, fought, bought
7 narrator	**14** quiver
	15 quarry

Term 3 ENGLISH: Reading & Comprehension

1 Darwin

2 Any two from: Her father played guitar and her mother sang. She sang with her sisters. She sang with her grandmother in the church choir.

3 a. to make people aware of something or someone

4 Any two from: "Saturday Night", "Inescapable", "Pop a Bottle (Fill Me Up)", "Never Be the Same", "Can I Get a Moment?", "Burn"

5 *The Sapphires*

6 c. unpopular

7 a. an agreement with a company that produces records and CDs

8 "Burn"

9 29

10 b. native to a particular place

Term 3 MATHS: Number & Algebra

1 6000	**2** 10 000	**3** 24 000	**4** 569 000

5
$$
\begin{array}{r}
10 + 10 + 7 = \mathbf{27} \\
5 \overline{) 135} \\
-50 \quad 10 \times 5 = 50 \\
\overline{85} \\
-50 \quad 10 \times 5 = 50 \\
\overline{35} \\
-35 \quad 7 \times 5 = 35 \\
\overline{0}
\end{array}
$$

6 2.02	**8** 20	**10** 84.3
7 5.40	**9** 7	**11** 100

12

	20	+	5
20	20 × 20 = 400		20 × 5 = 100
+			
4	4 × 20 = 80		4 × 5 = 20

400 + 100 = 500
80 + 20 = 100
600

13 $\frac{4}{12}$	**18** + 2.5
14 $\frac{8}{12}$	**19** 27.2
15 $\frac{4}{12}$	**20** 256.5
16 25, 45, 65, 85, 105	**21** 4.35
17 6.5, 6.0, 5.5, 5.0, 4.5	**22** 15.76

Term 3 MATHS: Statistics & Probability

1

	2 c. $\frac{1}{6}$	**6** Maya and Ellin
	3 b. $\frac{2}{6}$	**7** 25
	4 c. 0	**8** Date
	5 Max	

9 Cherry	
10 120	
11 14	
12 Yes	

Term 3 MATHS: Measurement & Space

1 d. 90° clockwise	**10** 3 minutes
2 c. 135° clockwise	**11** 72 hours
3 a	**12** 240 seconds
4 b	**13** b. almost ten minutes past one in the afternoon
5 b	**14** c. quarter to five pm
6 150 mm²	**15** 3 hours 36 minutes
7 100 mm²	**16** $0.75
8 Jug A	**17** $1.00
9 3 hours	

Unit 25 ENGLISH: Grammar & Punctuation

1 After I have walked the dog, I will read my book.

2 If Dad calls, tell him I am on my way.

3 Though it was not her chore, Elisa washed up.

4 We played on the beach until the sun set.

5 As it was wet outside, we all played indoors.

6 Because no-one was home, the thieves broke into the house.

7 After the match, we went to the pizza restaurant.

8 When she arrives, make sure to tell Alice the good news.

9 Will you vacuum the floor while I do the dishes?

10 If they win today, the Hammersmith Tigers will win the cup.

Unit 25 ENGLISH: Phonic Knowledge & Spelling

1 mistake	**6** discontinue	**11** disappear
2 discover	**7** disable	**12** misplace
3 dishonest	**8** misunderstand	**13** misprint
4 misbehave	**9** dismantle	
5 misfortune	**10** misinterpret	

Unit 25 ENGLISH: Reading & Comprehension

1 c. a star	**4** Pluto, Ceres, Eris, Makemake and Haumea
2 d. certain	**5** downgraded
3 hydrogen and helium	**6** Venus and Mars

Unit 25 MATHS: Number & Algebra

1 6546.4
2 12 824.502
3 78 050.008
4 345 902.48

5–10

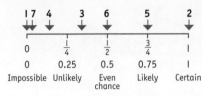

11 c. 337.03
12 a. 5024.08
13 c. 32 456.64
14 1.32, 1.3, 1.26, 1.11
15 0.10, 0.09, 0.04, 0.01
16 25.72, 25.7, 25.62, 25.06

Unit 25 MATHS: Statistics & Probability

17 4   3   6   5   2

0	$\frac{1}{4}$	$\frac{1}{2}$	$\frac{3}{4}$	1
0	0.25	0.5	0.75	1
Impossible	Unlikely	Even chance	Likely	Certain

8 1 in 6
9 5 in 6
10 5 in 5
11 0 in 5
12 5 in 7
13 2 in 7

Unit 25 MATHS: Measurement & Space

1 95°   2 120°   3 75°   4 30°   5 310°

Unit 25 MATHS: Problem Solving

1 180 − 75° − 60° = 45°
2 180 − 30° − 70° = 80°
3 180 − 25° − 20° = 135°
4 180 − 42° − 87° = 51°

Unit 26 ENGLISH: Grammar & Punctuation

1 has   3 has   5 were   7 is   9 was
2 is   4 have   6 are   8 is

Unit 26 ENGLISH: Phonic Knowledge & Spelling

1 cushion
2 auction
3 fashion
4 illustration
5 punctuation
6 decoration
7 irrigation
8 tense: tensile, tension, intense
9 view: vision, interview, preview
10 select: selective, selection, preselect

Unit 26 ENGLISH: Reading & Comprehension

1 Effects of industry
2 Controlling pollution
3 Capital resources
4 Human resources
5 Natural resources
6 H
7 N
8 C
9 c. at risk of becoming extinct

Unit 26 MATHS: Number & Algebra

1 b. no   6 a. yes   11 a. yes   16 b. no
2 a. yes   7 b. no   12 b. no   17 a. yes
3 b. no   8 a. yes   13 a. yes   18 a. yes
4 b. no   9 b. no   14 a. yes   19 b. no
5 a. yes   10 a. yes   15 a. yes

Unit 26 MATHS: Measurement & Space

1–10

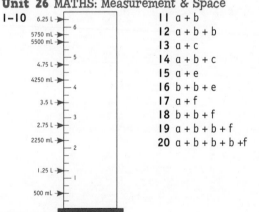

11 a + b
12 a + b + b
13 a + c
14 a + b + c
15 a + e
16 b + b + e
17 a + f
18 b + b + f
19 a + b + b + f
20 a + b + b + b + f

Unit 26 MATHS: Problem Solving

1 10 goldfish
2 30 goldfish
3 80 goldfish
4 241 goldfish

Unit 27 ENGLISH: Grammar & Punctuation

1 Wow, that new game/ is brilliant!
2 After school, Sam and her friends explored/the riverbank.
3 The activities you could try were sculpture, drawing, painting, collage and/ photography.
4 Doing homework, she thought, could sometimes/be interesting.
5 Finally, the endless journey through the desert/was almost over.
6–18 On Saturday,[6] Mum,[7] Dad and I went to the Ranelagh Show. I really enjoyed looking at the farm animals. There were sheep,[8] goats,[9] pigs,[10] cattle,[11] horses,[12] chickens,[13] geese and alpacas. Personally,[14] I liked the alpacas best but Mum preferred the goats. Dad,[15] on the other hand,[16] liked the horses,[17] especially the huge draught horses that were demonstrating how to pull a plough. After the show,[18] we went to Grandma's house for dinner. Then I fell asleep in the car on the way home.

Unit 27 ENGLISH: Phonic Knowledge & Spelling

1 improve
2 inform
3 include
4 inadequate
5 immobile
6 impossible
7 incapable
8 imagine
9 inflate
10 division
11 provision
12 implosion
13 erosion

Unit 27 ENGLISH: Reading & Comprehension

1 b. Food is essential to keep our bodies working.
2 F
3 O
4 F
5 Junk food is food with little nutritional value. Fast food is food that is prepared quickly.
6 low-sugar
7 rarely
8 essential
9 chemicals
10 Lollies; salty, deep-fried chips; fizzy drinks
11 c. rarely

Unit 27 MATHS: Number & Algebra

1 = 1
2 > 1
3 > 1
4 < 1
5 < 1
6 > 1
7 < 1
8 > 1
9 $1\frac{9}{10}$
10 $\frac{5}{5}$ or 1
11 3
12 $\frac{14}{10}$ or $1\frac{4}{10}$
13 $\frac{7}{10}$
14 $1\frac{5}{10}$
15 $2\frac{2}{5}$
16 $2\frac{4}{10}$

17 $1\frac{7}{10}$, $1\frac{3}{5}$, $\frac{10}{10}$, $\frac{1}{2}$, $\frac{1}{5}$

18 $\frac{1}{5}$, $\frac{1}{2}$, $\frac{3}{5}$, $1\frac{5}{10}$, $\frac{16}{10}$, $1\frac{7}{10}$

Unit 27 MATHS: Statistics & Probability

1 O   3 M   5 O   7 N   9 N   11 C
2 Y/N   4 M   6 Y/N   8 C   10 N

12–13 Answers will vary but must gather numerical data. Sample questions:
• How many times a week do you play sport?
• How many different types of sport do you play?
• How old were you when you first started playing your sport?
• How many wins did your team get last season?
• How many times a week do you practise for your sport?

14–15 Answers will vary but may include questions such as:
• Do you play a sport?
• On what days of the week do you play your sport?
• What is your favourite sport?
• Do you play your sport in a team?
• On what days of the week do you practise your sport?
• Who takes you to your sport?

Unit 27 MATHS: Measurement & Space

1 2 cm   3 14 cm   5 6 cm^2 7 2 cm   9 3.5 cm
2 7 cm   4 14 cm   6 10 cm^2 8 DF   10 7.5 cm

Unit 27 MATHS: Problem Solving

1 Two adults for 5 nights = 80 × 5 = $400
The total cost for the caravan park stay is $775, so take away the adult cost to leave $375. Divide $375 by 5 nights to get $75 per night for the children. There are 3 lots of 25 in 75 so there must be 3 children.
2 $100 × 5 = $500   3 $95 × 5 = $475
4 Total cost = $775 + $475 + $500 = $1750

Unit 28 ENGLISH: Grammar & Punctuation

1 Don't get too close to the cliff's edge!
2 Samantha's mother is selling her father's house.
3 I'd like to ride Tom's bike but it's a bit big for me.
4 The players' uniforms didn't arrive in time for the match.
5 The children's paintings are on the teacher's desk.
6 I wish they'd hurry up or we'll be late!
7 the chickens' eggs
8 the trees' leaves
9 the builders' tools
10 the mice's footprints
11 the girls' shoes
12 the spiders' webs

Unit 28 ENGLISH: Phonic Knowledge & Spelling

1 business
2 appointment
3 mismanagement
4 unselfishness
5 lightness
6 unfairness
7 government
8 agreement
9 sadness
10 weakness

Unit 28 ENGLISH: Reading & Comprehension

1 b. in the city
2 feeding the pigs
3 c. adverb
4 c. to urge a horse forward
5 a firm or hard tap

Unit 28 MATHS: Number & Algebra

1

2 + 1.5, + 1.0

3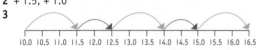

4 16.5

5 $-\frac{1}{2}, +\frac{1}{4}$

6

7 $3\frac{1}{4}$

8 + 6, + 8

9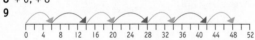

10 48

11 $+\frac{1}{2}, -\frac{1}{8}$

12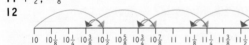

13 $11\frac{1}{2}$

Unit 28 MATHS: Measurement & Space

1 c. 4
2 a. 2
3 d. 5
4 c. 4
5 a. 3
6 b. 4

7 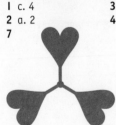   8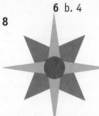

Unit 28 MATHS: Problem Solving

Diagram 1: 2 E, 3 S, 4 SW, 5 W
Diagram 2: 2 NE, 3 SE, 4 S, 5 W

Unit 29 ENGLISH: Grammar & Punctuation

1 The swimming pool **invited** me to jump in.
2 Rain gently **kissed** the earth for the first time in weeks.
3 The leaves **raced** each other across the lawn.
4 The candle flame **danced** in the breeze.

5–16 The March Wind

I come to work[5] as well as play[6],
I'll tell[7] you what I do,
I whistle[8] all the live-long day,
"Woo-oo-oo-oo-oo Woo-oo!"
I toss[9] the branches up and down,
And shake[10] them to and fro,
I whirl[11] the leaves in flocks of brown,
And send[12] them high and low.
I strew[13] the twigs upon the ground,
The frozen earth I sweep[14],
I blow[15] the children round and round,
And wake[16] the flowers from sleep.

Unit 29 ENGLISH: Phonic Knowledge & Spelling

1 famous/dangerous/adventurous
2 fabulous
3 flavour
4 court, pour, your
5 flour, hour, ourselves
6 dangerous
7 famous
8 outrageous
9 luxurious

Unit 29 ENGLISH: Reading & Comprehension

1 They only had 3 weeks to go before the Battle of The Bands so she was worried that they would not be able to get a new drummer in time.
2 c. very annoyed
3 She had climbed up the monkey bars to rescue her brother but she slipped halfway up and fell on her brother's bike.
4 Harriette, Matilda, Ruth and Becky
5 b. New Zealand (Waipatiki is in New Zealand)

Unit 29 MATHS: Number & Algebra

1 24 + 6 + 18 = 48
2 52 + 48 + 37 = 137
3 50 + 50 + 89 = 189
4 1000 + 4500 + 67 = 5567
5 5 × 2 × 48 = 480
6 4 × 25 × 52 = 5200
7 100 × 10 × 5 = 5000
8 50 × 2 × 73 = 7300
9 Answers will vary.
10 a
11 b

Unit 29 MATHS: Statistics & Probability

1 height 3.05 m, mass 5000 kg
2 84 km/h
3 3.06 m
4 213 000 kg
5 178 200 kg
6 15 km/h
7 5 tallest land animals
8 The scale should be numbered from 0 to 6 metres.

Unit 29 MATHS: Measurement & Space

1 a. yes   2 b. no   3 b. no   4 a. yes
5   6

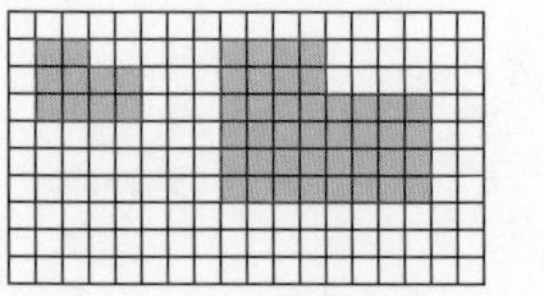

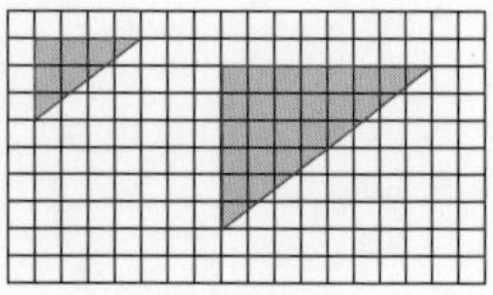

Unit 29 MATHS: Problem Solving

1 1 cm   2 2 m   3 2.5 m   4 3 cm

Unit 30 ENGLISH: Grammar & Punctuation

1 Should students wear school uniforms? (discussion)
2 Collect your ingredients. (instructions)
3 Yesterday, a funny thing happened. (anecdote)
4 James Mason was born in Canberra in 1965. (biography)
5 This book by JJ Ryle is the best I have ever read. (book review)
6 And they all lived happily ever after. (fairytale)
7 Thanks, Brad, for an amazing insight into your world. (interview)
8 Next time, I am going to go shopping with a friend! (anecdote)
9 I rate this movie 9 out of 10. (movie review)
10 To obtain your discount, please bring this coupon with you. (advertisement)

TARGETING HOMEWORK 5 © PASCAL PRESS ISBN 9781925726473

Unit 30 ENGLISH: Phonic Knowledge & Spelling

1. probable/possible
2. likeable/reliable/agreeable/flexible/sensible/responsible
3. changeable/miserable
4. comfortable
5. inaudible
6. immobile
7. irreplaceable
8. disadvantage
9. illegible
10. uncomfortable

Unit 30 ENGLISH: Reading & Comprehension

1. b. the substance in which something occurs such as water or air
2. c. It changes direction and speed.
3. c. thin
4. a. It splits into different colours.
5. red
6. A double rainbow forms when light is reflected twice inside each water droplet.

Unit 30 MATHS: Number & Algebra

1.
```
    36
  ×  3
 ────
    18
 +  90
 ────
   108
```

2.
```
    68
  ×  3
 ────
    24
 + 180
 ────
   204
```

3.
```
    47
  ×  6
 ────
    42
 + 240
 ────
   282
```

4.
```
    59
  ×  4
 ────
    36
 + 200
 ────
   236
```

5.
```
    92
  ×  5
 ────
    10
 + 450
 ────
   460
```

6.
```
    76
  ×  7
 ────
    42
 + 490
 ────
   532
```

7.
```
   543
  ×  6
 ────
    18
 + 240
 ────
  3000
  3258
```

8.
```
   362
  ×  5
 ────
    10
 + 300
 ────
  1500
  1810
```

9.
```
   479
  ×  4
 ────
    36
 + 280
 ────
  1600
  1916
```

10.
```
   172
  ×  9
 ────
    18
 + 630
 ────
   900
  1548
```

11.
```
   563
  ×  6
 ────
    18
 + 360
 ────
  3000
  3378
```

12.
```
   762
  ×  8
 ────
    16
 + 480
 ────
  5600
  6096
```

Unit 30 MATHS: Measurement & Space

1. none
2. c
3. d
4. a
5. b
6. none
7. e
8. none

Unit 30 MATHS: Problem Solving

1.
```
   573
  ×  8
 ────
    24
 + 560
 ────
  4000
  4584
```

2.
```
   168
  ×  9
 ────
    72
 + 540
 ────
   900
  1512
```

3.
```
   539
  ×  9
 ────
    81
 + 270
 ────
  4500
  4851
```

Unit 31 ENGLISH: Grammar & Punctuation

1. let your hair down
2. hit the road
3. last straw
4. on the ball
5. spill the beans
6. sitting on the fence
7. Last week it was raining cats and dogs. (meaning = raining heavily)
8. They were having a ball at the concert. (meaning = having fun)
9. The athlete was as fit as a fiddle. (meaning = very fit and healthy)

Unit 31 ENGLISH: Phonic Knowledge & Spelling

1. recycle
2. develop
3. reduce/decrease
4. recede
5. defy
6. resign
7. relating, relation
8. dehydrating, dehydration
9. reflecting, reflection

Unit 31 ENGLISH: Reading & Comprehension

1. Tasmania
2. c. someone who acts as a peacemaker between two groups of people
3. They abducted her sister and murdered her mother, fiancé and uncle.
4. Recherche Bay, Bruny Island, Flinders Island, Oyster Cove, Hobart
5. disease
6. a. abduction
7. a. someone who only has one race in their family history

Unit 31 MATHS: Number & Algebra

1. 39
2. 20
3. 60
4. 8
5. 50
6. 20
7. 30
8. 15
9. 25
10. 4
11. 26
12. 15
13. $28 ÷ 2 = 14$
14. $136 ÷ 4 × 3 = 102$
15. $30 - 15 - 6 = 9$
16. $300 - 75 = 225$
17. $125 - 25 = 100$
18. $180 - 30 = 150$

Unit 31 MATHS: Statistics & Probability

1. 12:30
2. 1:30
3. 15 minutes
4. 1:45
5. 80 kms
6. 30 kms

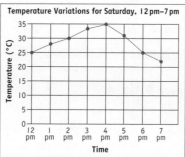
Temperature Variations for Saturday, 12 pm–7 pm

Unit 31 MATHS: Measurement & Space

1–7
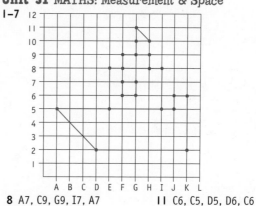

8. A7, C9, G9, I7, A7
9. B7, B1, H1, H7
10. D1, D3, F3, F1
11. C6, C5, D5, D6, C6
12. F6, G6, G5, F5, F6

Unit 31 MATHS: Problem Solving

Unit 32 ENGLISH: Grammar & Punctuation

1–8 [paragraph 1] A few days later we had to look up the meaning of some words in the dictionary and then use them in a sentence. The first word was 'revolting'.

[paragraph 2] I wrote, Joel throws all his dirty socks under the bed and they smell revolting.

[paragraph 3] "Is that true?" Miss Thompson asked.

[paragraph 4] I nodded. "No-one can ever find anything in his room," I lied. "Mum reckons he's the untidiest person she knows. She's always picking up after him. She says when Joel gets married he'll be looking for a slave rather than a wife."

[paragraph 5] "Don't you like your brother?" Miss Thompson asked, looking closely at me.

[paragraph 6] "Yeah, I do," I answered. "He's my favourite person in the whole world."

[paragraph 7] "Then how come you keep saying nasty things about him?"

[paragraph 8] "I...I don't," I stammered.

Unit 32 ENGLISH: Phonic Knowledge & Spelling

1 construct	5 commitment	9 comply
2 combine	6 construction	10 compliment
3 contact	7 combination	11 conceal
4 concealment	8 conspire	

Unit 32 ENGLISH: Reading & Comprehension

1 the readers of the Dunbeena Gazette
2 c. to complain
3 b. to state that the community needs strong leaders who will act on the issue
4 fund the ongoing rostering of ambulance officers; build a new and permanent ambulance station in the Dunbeena area

5 c. consistent   6 I, we, us   7 a. intermittent

Unit 32 MATHS: Number & Algebra

1 no	7 yes	13 yes	19 no
2 yes	8 no	14 yes	20 yes
3 yes	9 yes	15 no	21 yes
4 no	10 no	16 no	22 yes
5 no	11 no	17 no	23 no
6 yes	12 yes	18 yes	24 yes

25–34 7, 11, 13, 17, 23, 29, 41, 43, 47, 53
35 1, 19
36 1, 2, 3, 4, 6, 9, 12, 18, 36
37 1, 37
38 1, 2, 4, 7, 8, 14, 28, 56
39 1, 2, 3, 4, 5, 6, 10, 12, 15, 20, 30, 60
40 1, 67
41 1, 2, 4, 5, 10, 20, 25, 50, 100

Unit 32 MATHS: Measurement & Space

1 c. 10 metres	8 4
2 c. 2 litres	9 30
3 d. 8 kilometres	10 2
4 b. 15 centimetres	11 19
5 c. 150 grams	12 3.5
6 a. 18 litres	13 5
7 b. 90 centimetres	

Unit 32 MATHS: Problem Solving

1 + $1\frac{1}{2}$
2 × 4
3 consecutive prime numbers, from 7
4 – 8

TERM 4 REVIEW

Term 4 ENGLISH: Grammar & Punctuation

1 <u>Though it was not his turn</u>, Sam walked the dog.
2 The news is on every night at 6 pm.
3 *The Witches* is my favourite book by Roald Dahl.
4–12 Yesterday,[4] Jack,[5] Sam and I went to the Melbourne Show. I really enjoyed looking at the farm animals. There were sheep,[6] goats,[7] pigs,[8] cattle,[9] horses,[10] chickens,[11] geese and alpacas. Personally,[12] I liked the goats best but Jack preferred the pigs.

---

13 Don't put your finger too close to the knife's sharp edge!
14 <u>Lightning</u> **danced** across the dark sky.
15 fairytale
16 The spelling test was a piece of cake. (easy)
17–19 [paragraph 1] Ben pulled out of his driveway without looking.

[paragraph 2] "Hey, you nearly ran me over!" shouted an angry man on his bicycle.

[paragraph 3] "Sorry mate, I wasn't concentrating. Are you OK?"

20 the students' paintings

Term 4 ENGLISH: Phonic Knowledge & Spelling

1 misjudge	9 unselfishness	17 illegal
2 dishonest	10 lightness	18 unpleasant
3 operation	11 unfairness	19 reflecting, reflection
4 decoration	12 your, court	
5 incapable	13 immovable	20 commitment
6 immobile	14 displeased	21 construction
7 explosion	15 irregular	
8 division	16 incredible	

Term 4 ENGLISH: Reading & Comprehension

1 b. in Crete
2 a. a new and very rare discovery
3 c. exacting and thorough
4 the remains of a palace
5 cataloguing
6 a. thoroughly enjoying something
7 d. delayed
8 a. Yes, he enjoyed archaeology.
9 world-renowned expert

Term 4 MATHS: Number & Algebra

1 5 835.8	5 yes	10 yes	14 $\frac{2}{12}$
2 65 080.48	6 no	11 $\frac{7}{8}$	15 $\frac{6}{10}$
3 d. 557.02	7 no	12 4	16 $1\frac{3}{5}$
4 a. 578 431.1	8 yes	13 $\frac{15}{10}$ or $1\frac{5}{10}$	
	9 no		

17 25 + 25 + 17 = 67
18 98 + 2 + 17 = 117

19
```
     46
  ×   5
 ─────
     30
 + 200
 ─────
    230
```

20
```
    684
  ×   6
 ─────
     24
 + 480
  3600
 ─────
  4104
```

21 50	
22 40	
23 150 ÷ 5 × 3 = 90	
24 no	
25 yes	
26 no	
27 yes	
28 no	
29 no	
30 yes	
31 yes	

Term 4 MATHS: Statistics & Probability

1–6

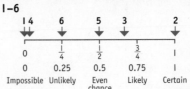

14	6	5	3	2
0	$\frac{1}{4}$	$\frac{1}{2}$	$\frac{3}{4}$	1
0	0.25	0.5	0.75	1
Impossible	Unlikely	Even chance	Likely	Certain

7 0
8 Y/N
9 M
10 Sunday
11 25 visitors
12 Wednesday as this day has the most visitors on a weekday.
13 150

Term 4 MATHS: Measurement & Space

1 230°	6 2.5 cm	13 B2
2 350 mL	7 7.5 cm	14 D7, E7, E6, D6
3 1400 mL	8 7 cm	16 25
4 1 large cup, 2 small cups	9 11.25 cm^2	17 150
5 5 large cups, 3 small cups	10 4	18 36
	11 diamond	
	12 star	

TARGETING HOMEWORK 5 © PASCAL PRESS ISBN 9781925726473